This Book belongs to
Norman W. Wil[illegible]

1-26-1977

TONGUE SPEAKING

TONGUE SPEAKING

AN EXPERIMENT IN SPIRITUAL EXPERIENCE

Morton T. Kelsey

Foreword by Upton Sinclair

WAYMARK BOOKS

DOUBLEDAY & COMPANY, INC.
GARDEN CITY, NEW YORK

Waymark Edition: 1968

FOREWORD BY UPTON SINCLAIR

This writer of too many books was confirmed in the Episcopal Church of the Holy Communion in New York City at the age of about thirteen. He was a very devout little boy and had made promises to his mother; the sips of communion wine which he took in that church were the only drops of alcoholic liquor that have passed his lips in eighty-five years. But the church did not hold him, because he saw, in all the world around him, cruel poverty in the midst of great riches, and he left the church to become an agitator of what he called "social justice." That went on for some seventy years; until, left alone, he wished to marry a lady who was a member of the Episcopal church. So it came about that he became acquainted with the rector of St. Luke's Episcopal Church in his home town of Monrovia, California.

A year or two passed, and this gentleman came to the author and reported that he had completed the writing of a full-length manuscript on the subject of the religious practice known as "speaking in tongues." The author had learned to shudder when authors approach him with such news; and this seemed the most unpromising case imaginable. But a short time later the gentleman came again, with the news that a leading publishing house had made an offer for the book—and what did the author think of their offer? The author thought very well of it; and presently the clergyman came again to say that the publishers would like to have the author read the manuscript and supply a preface for the book.

Now there could be no subject named in which this author would have expressed less interest than the practice known as "glossolalia," or speaking in tongues; and never before had he received a full-length manuscript with less expectation of pleasure. But he found that he was mistaken; he found himself reading a precise and careful study of a strange and fascinating subject, competently written and worthy of all praise. What it amounts to is an elaborate and detailed study of Christian ecstasy, from the days of St. Paul down to those of Dr. C. G. Jung of Switzerland and the Pentecostal churches all over America. The rich churches of America grow respectable; they cut out the ecstatics and the fanatics, and these go off and establish themselves as Pentecostals and other strange sects. You can read all about them in this book; and if you are interested to know how the Christian religion began and how it still works among the poor and lowly, you will thank me for telling you about this well-researched and well-written book; a work of scholarship and discernment.

AUTHOR'S PREFACE

It was never my intention to write a book about tongues. The subject interested me mainly as one of several neglected aspects of Christian experience. It interested me along with the dream, healing, the angelic and demonic, those other elements of the Christian tradition which are not talked about very much, and in that context I wrote a paper on tongues. The paper was received with such interest that it was suggested I expand its basic thesis into the present volume. The reader will find not only a discussion of the phenomenon of speaking in tongues, but also the sketch of a theological and psychological point of view in which this interesting experience, as well as these other neglected aspects of the New Testament, can be understood. The main reason that this experience has not been more widely appreciated is simply because most people have had no ground upon which to stand from where they could get a look at it.

The original paper would never have been written had not my interest been stimulated by the research of the Rev. Adams Lovekin when we were associated in the ministry of the same church. His excellent unpublished study was the foundation from which I built. It would be difficult for me to express adequately my appreciation to him for the permission to make use of his work, and for his interest and encouragement in this project. I am equally indebted to the Rev. Stuart G. Fitch with whom I have been associated for over five years. His interest and experience in tongue speaking and his sane and careful supervision of a group in which this experience has been meaningful have given me the opportunity to know the phenomenon at first hand. Without the materials which these two men have provided there would have been no book.

I am deeply grateful to those who wrote of their own experiences of tongues and gave me the permission to publish them. Two others have provided me with invaluable materials, Mrs. R. Jocelyn Crichton and the Rev. Francis Whiting. Through the courtesy of the Claremont Colleges the facilities of Honnold Library have been available and Mrs. Kenneth R. Jackman has given me help whenever it was needed.

The vestry and congregation of St. Luke's Church have been most understanding about having a rector who gets interested in such things and spends so much time in them. This year an extra six weeks of sabbatical leave was given me, which enabled me to complete this undertaking. The assistance and co-operation of the rest of the church staff has been invaluable in giving me the time to go on with this project, and I am deeply grateful for the help of Mrs. Clifford Speer, Mrs. Buryl Lottridge, Dr. Ollie Backus, and Miss Jean Carmichael.

A good friend and psychiatrist, Dr. Leo Froke, has provided a stimulating sounding board for most of these conclusions. Our discussions together have given me many of the ideas which have been incorporated into the text, and he has also provided me with some of the material crucial for the development of the thesis of the book. My understanding of Jung has come to me largely through friendship with three Jungian analysts, Max Zeller, Hilde Kirsch, and Dr. James Kirsch. I am deeply grateful to my friend the Rev. John A. Sanford for a careful reading of this manuscript and for his helpful suggestions.

I am also deeply grateful to Agnes Sanford, whose interest in healing stimulated my study of the gifts of the spirit. Much of the point of view expressed in these pages was worked out for presentation in the schools of Pastoral Care which she has inspired for many years.

The book would never have been completed in its present form without the able and dedicated help of Mrs. F. Harold

Roach, who has worked long and hard to turn my somewhat pedestrian phrases into more readable and interesting English. She has truly been the midwife of the present work. She has also searched high and low for materials when they were needed.

It is my wife and children, however, who have had most of the joy and suffering from the production of this manuscript. Not only have they been interested and co-operative, but my wife has helped with research, typing, and anything else that needed doing.

CONTENTS

Chapter I

A SPEAKING ACQUAINTANCE WITH TONGUES

During this century some two or three million, and perhaps a great many more, Americans have had a strange personal experience of religion known as speaking in tongues. Those who have tried fervently to explain its meaning to others have added terms like "spiritual baptism" or "Pentecost" which express the mystery inherent in the experience. But it has apparently been so difficult to explain to others that most people have been quite "in the dark" about what is being discussed.

The fact of glossolalia—the technical term for speaking in tongues—is not hard to set down. It is a spontaneous utterance of uncomprehended and seemingly random speech sounds. A casual hearer might think of pig Latin or of imitating a Chinese dialect as he listens to the speaking. Closer attention, however, reveals certain significant aspects of this speech. It occurs almost entirely among certain religious groups and seldom elsewhere; a religious practice similar to this is described in the New Testament. The speech itself rises in an effortless flow of usually complex structure, with the repetition and inflection characteristic of language. It is neither controlled nor directly understood by the speaker, but takes possession of his speech. While occasionally a listener can identify a foreign language known to him, but not to the speaker, the meaning is almost always spoken by an interpretation. It is given after the tongue-speech has ceased, either by a listener or by the tongue speaker himself. This interpretation is as spontaneous as the tongue-speech and apparently is given intuitively to the interpreter, who does not consciously understand the speech. Another significant aspect of glossolalia is its emotional value to the speaker, the fact that it is accompanied in nearly all cases by a sense of joy and a deep religious emotion. The experience can occur in quiet or private surroundings as well as in an atmosphere calling for display of emotion or even frenzy or trance states.

The accounts written by individuals who speak in tongues stress another, quite different facet, that of an experience which transforms lives, and this facet is best expressed in their own words. One description of an experience early in this century was written by an immigrant Scottish Jew, a highly educated, fluent linguist. Against his own religious conviction Myer Pearlman was drawn into a joyful mission meeting one night, and later described his reactions in an article in *The Pentecostal Evangel:*

> As I stood there, I felt some strange influence come over me, indescribable but delightful. I saw no one and heard no audible voice. But this was the turning point in my life. . . . As I knelt to pray one day not too long afterward, to my amazement I heard myself speaking words unfamiliar to me. It lifted me into a higher realm and gave me a sense of the nearness of God.

The writer of the following longer and more down-to-earth account is a clergyman in one of the major denominations, who entered his training for the ministry after a successful business career. He had had a wide educational background, four years in the army, and had already investigated numerous religious points of view. A mature attempt to make his life as effective as possible brought him into contact with psychotherapy, and the professional men with whom he worked were all impressed with the essential soundness of his personality. Speaking in tongues was a crucial experience of his life; following it, he found direction, purpose, and the ability to deal with the totality of his experience. This young man's unusual abilities also give unusual power and conviction to his words:

> You've heard about this "speaking in tongues" and the whole thing sounds quite odd to you. Yet, if you are a curious person, you want to see it for yourself. So, one night you go to a speaking-in-tongues prayer meeting. The people look unusually normal to you since you suspected that they would probably be quite queer. They begin to pray in English and then, they begin to speak in what seems to be a foreign language. It isn't gibberish, but a clear language. Then one of the group gets up and places his hands on your head and he is followed by others. They pray that you might receive the gift of tongues. They encourage you to begin to speak and let the Spirit guide your tongue. You feel self-conscious but something encourages you to try it. For a while nothing happens and then, you begin to speak in a tongue. At first this frightens you but with the encouragement of the others you continue. After a time it becomes fun and you want to talk on and on.
>
> As you drive home from the meeting you feel exhilarated. You speak in tongues to yourself. Then, as you drive on, you wonder what sense the whole thing makes. But you are happy and you don't really care.
>
> The next morning the whole evening seems like a dream. How could you, a sensible person, ever allow yourself to carry on like that? You're no different than you were before. The whole thing seems to you to be a hoax. Caught up in an emotional situation, that's what it was. Best to forget the whole thing and pretend that it never happened.
>
> The years pass and you still have your tongue. You've learned to live with it as a fact of your life. If you're a conservative person, you don't go to group meetings and display it. Yet it has earned an important place in your life. When a problem situation comes along, you find that you speak in the tongue to yourself. But that is not entirely true, because you feel that you are speaking to God at the same time. You are speaking to God with feeling rather than with reason. You aren't forming sentences and petitions, you are express-

ing your emotions. You sincerely feel that the Spirit is praying to the Father through you in a way which you could never express yourself. There is such a deep feeling that God in fact does understand your situation after you have expressed yourself, that you feel a real sense of release.

What is speaking in tongues? Is it a leaven that works in your life to bring about God's ends? Does it take a man who has left the Church and bring him not only back into the Church but into the priesthood? Does it transform a Churchman who for years has been going to church as a matter of habit and turn him into a person for whom Jesus Christ has become his all in all? In cases I have known, it has.

This is the first of seven descriptions, included in various contexts throughout the book, written by persons whom the author knows well, both through his function as a minister and also through psychological evaluation. All of these seven have found this experience one of the most valuable of their lives, and none of them have left their traditional churches.

There is, however, another quite different reaction to tongue speaking within the Christian church. Even though it is mentioned in the Bible and practiced regularly by a growing group of Christians, many Christians of the older churches look with suspicion on this phenomenon and believe that there is no place in the modern church for it. Looking at it from the outside, they conclude that tongue speaking is only what it appears on the outside, a meaningless gibberish, with no value or purpose. It is merely emotional indulgence in sheer irrationality in the name of religion, a return to a more primitive kind of religion. As these people see it, this practice has no place in the highly developed ethical religion of today. Glossolalia is looked on by them as either a harmless release of emotion or even as a practice which is dangerous both religiously and psychologically and to be avoided. They point to the conflict which has arisen in some churches where the practice has occurred. From this point of view tongue speakers have been called all sorts of names, and most of the traditional churches, when they have spoken out on the subject, have either discouraged the experience or forbidden it.

CONTROVERSY IN THE ESTABLISHED CHURCHES

At the present time we have around us some Christian groups which see the experience of tongues as the very essence of Christian experience and others which view it as a dangerous escape from the mature religious way. This division of opinion has generated a lively controversy both inside the church and outside it. While there was some interest in tongue-speech when it broke out early in the twentieth century, this practice was then confined to the Pentecostal churches, but now it has spread and is scattered throughout the most conservative and traditional churches of America. The interest and curiosity about tongue-speech increases daily. The minister of a large suburban Protestant church begins to speak in tongues, tells of it openly, and finally faces opposition which results in his resignation. The news of this hits not only the metropolitan press of the area, but makes the television circuit and even the national news periodicals. A well-known bishop addresses a pastoral letter to his clergy on the subject of speaking in tongues, and news of it is carried in the daily press throughout the country. This attention may indicate only an interest in the bizarre, or it may go deeper than this.

In fact, looking at the broad religious scene in what has scarcely been a period of doldrums for religion, one of the most interesting phenomena has been the tremendous growth of the churches which stress speaking in tongues, the Pentecostal churches. While the more conventional, established churches have barely kept pace with the population explosion in the United States, these fundamentalistic and enthusiastic groups have skyrocketed in membership to seventh place, and have sprung up in every city throughout the country. These Pentecostal groups emphasize a strict adherence to Biblical authority, an austere morality, and an enthusiastic faith. They believe that the same life and vitality which was found in the apostolic church can be experienced now, and that speaking in tongues is the outward and visible sign of this new life. Glossolalia is the evidence, indeed, that one has been given a new spiritual endowment, the gift of the Holy Spirit.

This sign, on which Pentecostal groups place so much stress, takes the form of the utterance we have described. It appears to be almost forced out of the speaker, indicating that God's power has taken direction of his life. And, in fact, there is a physical basis for this belief. It seems to be a physical impossibility to duplicate tongue-speech by deliberate imitation; when gibberish is produced by conscious effort, this also produces muscular tension which soon differentiates the sounds from the effortless flow of glossolalia. Thus these groups are sure in their belief that this speech is a sign which comes from beyond the speaker's own power to produce it.

It was possible to ignore or to dismiss tongue speaking as meaningless and of no consequence in the past, when the practice appeared to be confined strictly to the unlettered and the unsophisticated and arose largely in the atmosphere of revivalism and wild emotionalism. In recent years, however, speaking in tongues is found under far different circumstances. It is found in church groups which are anything but unsophisticated, among people who are far from unlettered, and amid surroundings which are anything but emotional in the ordinary sense. In addition to the Pentecostals, whose backgrounds are as varied culturally as those of the rest of us, this experience has been known among Baptists, Methodists, Presbyterians, Lutherans, and Episcopalians. Indeed, more than one church in the major denominations has been deeply divided by controversy over the practice, while many other congregations in various parts of the country have accepted it in their midst, although not as a part of the formal worship of the church.

In Eastern Orthodox churches, the practice seems to have

gone on with less notice, apparently because tongue speaking was never allowed to die out completely. The Patriarch of Constantinople, during a recent visit to this country, discussed the matter with at least one church leader who has kept informed on the present revival of spiritual phenomena. When asked if speaking in tongues was known among his people, the Patriarch replied that it has been a continuing experience among them through all the ages, although confined chiefly to the monasteries, and that there are provisions in their church to govern it.

It would seem unwise, then, to dismiss the whole matter of speaking in tongues and Pentecostal religion as meaningless without first investigating what this experience is and what the New Testament has to say about it. This is particularly true since depth psychology has expressed an interest in the experience of glossolalia, and certain psychologists feel that this experience is an expression of the deep (or collective) unconscious within the individual, and, thus, that it springs from a level of the human psyche which is more than personal and actually transcends space and time.

Those who know modern psychological thought will realize that I am describing the psychology of C. G. Jung and others who look to him as a mentor. After many years of close association with Freud, during which he accepted Freud's discovery that man is largely motivated by forces of which he is unconscious, Jung came to the conclusion that there are levels of the unconscious beyond the personal, the buried memories, and the primitive impulses of the id. He believed that man is in touch with an objective realm of psychic reality containing elements both inferior and superior to human consciousness. Through dreams, intuitions, extrasensory perception, and other, more or less unusual, psychic phenomena, these elements break through into consciousness. Jung's conclusions were based upon the empirical evidence which thousands of patients presented him in over fifty years of psychiatric practice. Speaking in tongues, Jung found, is one evidence of a breakthrough of this objective psyche or deep, collective level of the unconscious.[1]

THE AUTHOR'S POINT OF VIEW

I would like to make it clear that I myself approach glossolalia, as far as the actual practice is concerned, from the same side as most of us. I have not experienced it personally. I do, however, have many acquaintances who have experienced tongue-speech, some of whom are leaders in the movement among members of the traditional Protestant churches. I have also been present many times while individuals have spoken in tongues, and I have been closely associated with a number of these people as friend, spiritual director, and counselor. I have known them very well.

I also speak from a point of view beside that of the traditional Christian clergyman. For twelve years I have been deeply interested in analytical psychology, the depth psychology of the late Dr. C. G. Jung of Zürich. The insights of Dr. Jung and some of his followers have had a profound influence on me. So great has my interest been that in 1956 I spent my sabbatical leave in Zürich, for a semester of work at the C. G. Jung Institute there, and returned three years later, after some correspondence with Dr. Jung, for a stimulating interview with him. Returning to my own suburban parish, I met numbers of requests for religious and psychological counseling from our own parish and from surrounding communities, and this resulted in the formation of a clinical group associated with my church. During the past seven years I have had to be in constant contact with psychologists and psychiatrists who have worked with this group or have served it as consultants.

My study of Jung had another surprising effect upon my

1. C. G. Jung, *Collected Works*. New York, Pantheon Books, Inc., Vol. 9, Part I, p. 55; Vol. 11 pp. 162 f. and 284.

religious belief, including my interest in glossolalia. Having been brought up in an environment which was predominantly rationalistic and materialistic, I had doubted many of the experiences described in the New Testament. Then I discovered that this eminently successful psychiatrist had dealt with numerous similar experiences in his patients, and had made careful and empirical scientific studies of some of them. Reenforced with such reliable current knowledge, I began to reread the New Testament with a greater open-mindedness, and I was surprised by what I found. In addition, my parishioners began to come to me, tentatively and half afraid, telling me of similar experiences in their own lives. At about the same time a group of tongue speakers developed in my parish. Among the subjects in which Jung was interested was speaking in tongues. The psychological interest of this great medical man stimulated my religious interest in tongues.

It is with this background that I have examined the experiences of many people who have spoken in tongues. I speak, therefore, with some assurance in saying that, even apart from Biblical considerations, this phenomenon cannot be dismissed as just fraud or meaningless irrationality. Indeed the very experience of speaking in tongues occurred in certain of these people at the very time when their problems began to be resolved and maturity was growing. The experience of glossolalia certainly had meaning and significance to many of these people.

The best way to get into a study is to describe the subject in detail, and the description I offer now does just this. It came to me, through a series of fortuitous events, in the form of a letter, written in November 1962, from the Yale campus. The writer is an undergraduate from a conservative eastern background, both religious and cultural. In this first contact with the experience, he walked into a group in which tongue speaking took place, actually unaware that there were experiences of this kind, and with no previous bias. This is the best attempt at outer delineation I have yet run across.

A NECESSARY PART OF THE STORY

Any attempt to describe an experience as unique as this fails in some way, just as attempts to explain color to the congenitally blind end in inadequacy. The inner, psychic experience of either one refuses to be completely disclosed. The following letter tells a necessary part of the story, and, with the knowledge that it is only a part, we read the young man's words. The letter begins by quoting from the second chapter of Acts, and for two pages goes on to exhaust the New Testament references to tongues, as if in reassurance; then:

> This day have these words been fulfilled in my sight.
>
> Feeling a little bit guilty that I had been unable to get to church earlier on All Saints' Day, at 9:15 tonight, just an hour and twenty minutes ago (my exactness is only to convince myself of the accuracy and believability of what I say), I found myself entering a very small chapel at the base of Harkness Tower, with a company of fifteen or twenty of whom I knew maybe five by sight and three of them from conversation. I was attending what had been described to me earlier as a "quaker-type service." My curiosity observed the details closely—a small room twenty feet square with chairs facing a small altar with a cross on it. The ceiling was very disproportionately high for the size of the room, being perhaps four or five times higher than the length of one side. A chandelier of brass hung from the center. I sat down next to a divinity student and next to him was the Rev. . . . . There were only three seats on either side of the center aisle.
>
> After a period of silence we sang a hymn without accompaniment and it was strong and beautiful, a familiar tune with unfamiliar words. We read responsively, from side to side, Psalm 39. A senior explained the procedure. I was, I think the only new comer. It was simply to be a reading followed by a period in which we would each praise God in the way we felt called to, in silence or prayer or song, and then a similar period of intercession. He urged us to let ourselves go, that

the particular place had not been struck by the Holy Spirit yet, but one could never predict anything. I was a little puzzled as we all knelt or bowed our heads according to which of the traditions we sprang from.

I had not even opened my mind before I heard whispering from the row in front of me, then from behind and all sides. Suddenly a voice broke out loud and clear, a beautiful, smooth, flowing sound, somewhat like my English prof reading Chaucer. It was not gibberish but sounded articulated, though nothing resembling a familiar word could I hear. The first voice was joined by another from the other side of the chapel, sounding very similar, and suddenly the whole room was filled. The writer of Acts has done better than any description I could give. It was a sound of gentle waves, billowing back and forth across the room, unlike anything I have ever heard. It was melodious. A single voice in the midst began to sing and soon the entire chapel was filled with the most beautiful music I have ever experienced, with the accompaniment of words in a tongue of graceful strength without the harshness of English, and the strangeness of a foreign language.

As the sound died down after a period whose duration I can only guess, a voice in the front row offered a prayer of thanksgiving for the gift of the Spirit. The silence that followed was broken by a voice of prophecy: "You have received the gift of openness. To you a task has been given. Await and you will be shown what you are to do." The quotation marks should not be there, for what I have written is only the essence of what was said in a loud, clear, quick, and sure voice. The tone of authority in it was strong in my ears and I can only describe this as a prophecy. I could have seen the speaker well, though I was not looking in his direction.

The period of intercession was begun by the leader and as soon as he stopped talking, a voice in a language recognizably foreign and of men, not angels, began for a short time. There followed a number of spontaneous prayers of intercession in English. The leader closed the period and stood up and spoke briefly of the dangers of pride inherent in spiritual gifts and of the warnings of Paul about the need for the whole of the armor of Christ and that whatever our "hobby" we must remember that the base of all religious experience is God himself; he is the cake in which is found all of the frosting. (I am always re-impressed by the capacity the church and her members show for self-criticism.) Another hymn, and the service ended.

My own relation to all of the above was as observer and not as one gifted. All I could do was to ask for mercy and wonder why I was there and become very aware of my unworthiness.

As I walked out I became aware that this has been happening here . . . for the past month and perhaps springs from some of what has been happening on the West Coast, now called the Charismatic revival. A boy next to me said that he also had been a non-charismatic and could not intellectually believe what he had just heard.

I suppose this is what the Pentecostals are all about. It is a judgment on the quality of my faith and my imagination that I have been so astounded. After all, isn't this exactly what the words in the Bible said happened?

I stand speechless, but could not wait a moment to start this letter to share what is happening with you. . . . Struck dumb with awe I don't know what more to say, except, go well, C———.

The young man was writing to one of his preparatory school masters and a second letter eight days later clarifies the intellectual atmosphere in which the experience occurred. He speaks of a "service of tongues (a bad name!). . . ." This letter also makes clear the meaning of this experience, as expressed in the life of this particular individual. He writes:

Since then my awakening has become much more complete and my awareness of the mystery and the strength of what the Holy Spirit does. It has produced a change in me which I am still in the process of understanding the meaning of. For about a week following the first flow of wonder which you received on paper I was in the midst of a more complete self-examination than I'd ever known before. This process was in itself the work of the spirit I'm convinced; but it was painful and in the end cleansing. It continues to be a part of my life, but it has also released me for effective (in my eyes) action, aware a little better than before who and what I am.

[After describing the extra-curricular activity which especially interests him, he went on.] I am beginning to realize that if I am not able to find motivation a little higher than personal satisfaction I may have trouble accomplishing much. . . . However, I have learned something today, that is to make best use of the immediate situation to achieve what I am aiming for, rather than be hindered by preconceived notions of how things should go. . . .

[Sports and other matters take up the body of the letter, and then . . .] last Sunday night we went to a Pentecostal Negro service. . . . A——— said that it was the best service he had ever been to and in many ways I agreed with him. Because it was highly emotional, it responded to the needs of these people. I found that it did a lot for me. We all need to find a way to express the love and joy and thanks bottled up within us. . . . My best to all, C———.

The sensitivity of this description and of the boy's later reflections brings one fact out. Most of us who have never witnessed tongue speaking or happen to have seen it only in emotionally charged surroundings, hold to the general belief that an uncorked emotionalism is necessary to the experience. I can testify this is simply not true. Tongue speaking occurs just as readily in a quiet devotional atmosphere. This truth cannot be emphasized enough. One who has once spoken spontaneously in tongues can open himself to the experience at will and without any particular stimulus or emotional effect. Several groups in which tongue speaking occurs in this way are described in a later chapter.

It is also possible for tongue-speech to occur apart from any group. A few years ago a friend who had experienced tongues in her prayer alone, and only in this way, started to attend a prayer group in which tongues were spoken. She looked at me dumfounded after she discovered that she had been speaking in tongues. "It's incredible! I would have cut it off before it started if I had known," she told me candidly, and added, "How different the experience really is, and how much I'd have missed!"

At a recent conference a Baptist minister told me how he had received the ability to speak in tongues following a visionary experience at the age of twelve while he was alone in his own room. Since then he had never displayed his tongue-speech to anyone except his own family and, on this occasion, to me, and he did this only after he was sure that I would listen open-mindedly to him. He too spoke of the quiet joy of praying in tongues and of his long-felt desire to communicate with someone about this experience which was so meaningful to him.

With this introduction to glossolalia, let us turn to the New Testament and take up the passages in it relating to tongue-speech. Let us follow the history of tongue speaking from apostolic times up into our own, with particular emphasis upon the expression of this experience in the churches today. Then let us see what luck we have understanding the Biblical texts and the more recent phenomena, and to what philosophical, theological, and psychological points of view our understanding leads. With some of this rather unusual religious fare under our belts, which has been unusual and valuable for me as well, we shall be in a position to draw some conclusions then about both the dangers and the values of this practice.

Chapter II

THE BIBLICAL EVIDENCE

Our original and most important evidence about speaking in tongues comes from the New Testament. For those who look at the Bible as religiously authoritative, the discussions of tongues found in it are as significant today as ever. For those who look at the Bible as an interesting source book of religious experience, it will be significant to see how much emphasis it places on this experience.

Glossolalia was an integral part of the apostolic religious life. If one reads the New Testament narrative with objectivity, he finds that it tells stories about men who received not only ethics but a new life which was *given* from beyond their ordinary capacities. When this divine power was given to man, his character improved, his love and faith and patience increased, and he was also given greater wisdom and perception of spiritual things. Receiving this divine power was known as being filled with the Holy Spirit. And it was further believed that the Spirit could speak directly through the man whom it had indwelt, who had been filled. It could speak aloud, and in two ways, intelligibly or unintelligibly—"in the tongues of men or of angels."

The first of these ways was known by the early church as prophecy. This was the way of human speech, uttered through the power of the Holy Spirit, that is, by the Holy Spirit speaking through the individual in his own tongue. Jesus himself said: "But when you are arrested, do not worry about what you are to say; when the time comes, the words you need will be given you; for it is not you who will be speaking: it will be the Spirit of your Father speaking in you." (Matthew 10:19)[1] Most of the sermons of Acts are spoken thus in the Spirit. They were not the contrived or carefully developed message of the preacher, but the spontaneous outpouring of the Spirit through him.

The meaning of the word prophecy has become clouded by its being primarily attached to future events, to predicting or foretelling. In the time of the King James translation, however, the word carried mainly the sense of preaching, mediating, forth-telling.[2] Prophecy in the New Testament then is a supernatural gift of the Spirit, of God, by which His Spirit speaks in a man, telling forth the wisdom and power of God for the edification and upbuilding of God's people and the conversion of those who are not yet a part of the people of God. Sometimes a man in prophesying does foretell the future, but this is only an occasional accompaniment, one side effect of prophecy, as the Spirit seizes and uses human speech.

Along with prophecy and, the early church believed, related to it as another linguistic manifestation of the Spirit was glossolalia or speaking in tongues. Just how close this other experience was to prophecy, we shall try to show later. But about one thing there can be no question; the authors of the New Testament believed in the supra-personal origin of these experiences, and associated them with being possessed by the Spirit.

In prophecy there is always the inherent difficulty of distinguishing it from artistically contrived and emotionally mo-

1. Unless otherwise noted, the Biblical quotations that follow are taken from the New English Bible.

2. See the Oxford English Dictionary (*A New English Dictionary on Historical Principles,* Sir James A. H. Murray, ed. Oxford, The Clarendon Press, 1909), Vol. VII, Part II, pp. 1472 ff. Not until the seventeenth century was there a definite split in the Christian usage of the word "prophecy" or its related forms; before then scattered references to Merlin or the Sybil did place a primary emphasis on foretelling the future, but in the main, this was considered merely an incidence of the divine inspiration.

tivated speech. How can we be sure whether one speaking powerfully is motivated by ego promptings or is speaking from a deeper center? Actually, prophecy always remains open to doubt. But if there is any reality to glossolalia, there can be no doubt that something beyond the man himself takes hold of him. It can then be known for certain that something outside the human ego, beyond the human will, can and does take hold of certain men. Tongue speaking is, therefore, at least important for its evidential value, in addition to giving expression to the religious feelings of the speaker.

The Biblical passages which refer to speaking in tongues may be divided into two groups: the direct references to this gift, and passages which may well refer to it but do not call it by name. The direct references are found in seven passages in the New Testament. In addition there are eight descriptions in which it could well be that glossolalia was meant. Though the author did not use the precise words, each of these comes from a context suggesting strongly that he had speaking in tongues in mind.

THE DAY OF PENTECOST

The event in the New Testament which places the greatest importance on speaking in tongues is told in the second chapter of Acts. Here this gift is given at the time the Holy Spirit is first poured out upon the new church, as the prophet Joel had foretold, and it became the sign of the new life of the community. Jesus had told the group to wait in Jerusalem until they received the promise of the Father. They would be baptized not by water but by the Holy Spirit. So they waited without knowing what to expect. In the familiar words of the passage:

> While the Day of Pentecost was running its course they were all together in one place, when suddenly there came from the sky a noise like that of a strong driving wind, which filled

> the whole house where they were sitting. And there appeared to them tongues like flames of fire, dispersed among them and resting on each one. And they were all filled with the Holy Spirit and began to talk in other tongues, as the Spirit gave them power of utterance.
>
> Now there were living in Jerusalem devout Jews drawn from every nation under heaven; and at this sound the crowd gathered, all bewildered because each one heard the apostles talking in his own language. They were amazed and in their astonishment exclaimed, "Why, they are all Galileans, are they not, these men who are speaking? How is it then that we hear them, each of us in his own native language? Parthians, Medes, Elamites; inhabitants of Mesopotamia, of Judaea and Cappadocia, of Pontus and Asia, of Phrygia and Pamphylia, of Egypt and the districts of Libya around Cyrene; visitors from Rome, both Jews and proselytes, Cretans and Arabs, we hear them telling in our own tongues the great things God has done." And they were all amazed and perplexed, saying to one another, "What can this mean?" Others said contemptuously, "They have been drinking!"

And then, of course, follows Peter's classic remark about drinking before nine in the morning. Whatever else we may say about the apostles, they do not appear as alcoholics who needed the hair of the dog.

These men were Jews, Jews by race, geography, social and political necessity, and also religiously. Seldom do we realize the burden it was to be so chosen. As I write I find myself recalling vividly the tremor of shock at a Jewish friend's response some years ago to my own recital of a time of deep suffering: "Now you know what it is to be one of God's chosen people." The Jews indeed carried a burden, a crushing burden. Their task was to make God's righteousness manifest in their external lives. They carried it through suffering and exile; political subjection only intensified it. They yearned for some direct manifestation of God. While Jesus was with the group, he appeared to meet and satisfy their Jewish thirsting. But after the crucifixion and the ascension they were alone again. The only stability these men had was to sit still and wait as they had been told, both by Jesus and in a vision; being men who had known suffering and hope, they did just that. They stayed together and prayed, not knowing what might come. It was then that the experience of glossolalia first occurred. This experience was evidence to them that God's spirit was with them. It helped give them the conviction which sent them courageously into a hostile world.

PETER'S EXPERIENCES

A passage in which the same elements are present, and one of the most interesting because it ties together many of the irrational aspects of New Testament religion, is the tenth chapter of Acts, and the continuation in chapter eleven as Peter relates his experience with the gentiles to the leaders of the nascent church in Jerusalem. Not only do we find mention of speaking in tongues, but references also to Peter's dream or vision, to the appearance of the angel who gives clairvoyant knowledge to Cornelius, and finally to the preaching of Peter which resulted in the coming of the Holy Spirit and tongues upon the gentiles. I hope you can read these words as if you had never seen them before, and see how extraordinary they are:

> At Caesarea there was a man named Cornelius, a centurion in the Italian Cohort, as it was called. He was a religious man, and he and his whole family joined in the worship of God. He gave generously to help the Jewish people, and was regular in his prayers to God. One day about three in the afternoon he had a vision in which he clearly saw an angel of God, who came into his room and said, "Cornelius!" He stared at him in terror. "What is it, my lord?" he asked. The angel said, "Your prayers and acts of charity have gone up to heaven to speak for you before God. And now send to Joppa for a man named Simon, also called Peter: he is lodging with another Simon, a tanner, whose house is by the sea." So when the angel who was speaking to him had gone, he summoned

two of his servants and a military orderly who was a religious man, told them the whole story, and sent them to Joppa.

Next day, while they were still on their way and approaching the city, about noon Peter went up on the roof to pray. He grew hungry and wanted something to eat. While they were getting it ready, he fell into a trance. He saw a rift in the sky, and a thing coming down that looked like a great sheet of sail-cloth. It was slung by the four corners, and was being lowered to the ground. In it he saw creatures of every kind, whatever walks or crawls or flies. Then there was a voice which said to him, "Up, Peter, kill and eat." But Peter said, "No, Lord, no: I have never eaten anything profane or unclean." The voice came again a second time: "It is not for you to call profane what God counts clean." This happened three times; and then the thing was taken up again into the sky.

While Peter was still puzzling over the meaning of the vision he had seen, the messengers of Cornelius had been asking the way to Simon's house, and now arrived at the entrance. They called out and asked if Simon Peter was lodging there. But Peter was thinking over the vision, when the Spirit said to him, "Some men are here looking for you; make haste and go downstairs. You may go with them without any misgiving, for it was I who sent them." Peter came down to the men and said, "You are looking for me? Here I am. What brings you here?" "We are from the centurion Cornelius," they replied, "a good and religious man, acknowledged as such by the whole Jewish nation. He was directed by a holy angel to send for you to his house and to listen to what you have to say." So Peter asked them in and gave them a night's lodging. Next day he set out with them, accompanied by some members of the congregation at Joppa.

The day after that, he arrived at Caesarea. Cornelius was expecting them and had called together his relatives and close friends. When Peter arrived, Cornelius came to meet him, and bowed to the ground in deep reverence. But Peter raised him to his feet and said, "Stand up; I am a man like anyone else." Still talking with him he went in and found a large gathering. He said to them, "I need not tell you that a Jew is forbidden by his religion to visit or associate with a man of another race; yet God has shown me clearly that I must not call any man profane or unclean. That is why I came here without demur when you sent for me. May I ask what was your reason for sending?"

Cornelius said, "Four days ago, just about this time, I was in the house here saying the afternoon prayers, when suddenly a man in shining robes stood before me. He said: 'Cornelius, your prayer has been heard and your acts of charity remembered before God. Send to Joppa, then, to Simon Peter, and ask him to come. He is lodging in the house of Simon the tanner, by the sea.' So I sent to you there and then; it was kind of you to come. And now we are all met here before God, to hear all that the Lord has ordered you to say."

Peter began: "I now see how true it is that God has no favourites, but that in every nation the man who is god-fearing and does what is right is acceptable to him. He sent his word to the Israelites and gave the good news of peace through Jesus Christ, who is Lord of all. I need not tell you what happened lately all over the land of the Jews, starting from Galilee after the baptism proclaimed by John. You know about Jesus of Nazareth, how God anointed him with the Holy Spirit and with power. He went about doing good and healing all who were oppressed by the devil, for God was with him. And we can bear witness to all that he did in the Jewish country-side and in Jerusalem. He was put to death by hanging on a gibbet; But God raised him to life on the third day, and allowed him to appear, not to the whole people, but to witnesses whom God had chosen in advance—to us, who ate and drank with him after he rose from the dead. He commanded us to proclaim him to the people, and affirm that he is the one who has been designated by God as judge of the living and the dead. It is to him that all the prophets testify, declaring that everyone who trusts in him receives forgiveness of sins through his name."

Peter was still speaking when the Holy Spirit came upon all

who were listening to the message. The believers who had come with Peter, men of Jewish birth, were astonished that the gift of the Holy Spirit should have been poured out even on Gentiles. For they could hear them speaking in tongues of ecstasy and acclaiming the greatness of God. Then Peter spoke: "Is anyone prepared to withhold the water for baptism from these persons, who have received the Holy Spirit just as we did ourselves?" Then he ordered them to be baptized in the name of Jesus Christ. After that they asked him to stay on with them for a time.

News came to the apostles and the members of the church in Judaea that Gentiles too had accepted the word of God; and when Peter came up to Jerusalem those who were of Jewish birth raised the question with him. "You have been visiting men who are uncircumcised," they said, "and sitting at table with them!" Peter began by laying before them the facts as they had happened.

"I was in the city of Joppa," he said, "at prayer; and while in a trance I had a vision: a thing was coming down that looked like a great sheet of sail-cloth, slung by the four corners and lowered from the sky till it reached me. I looked intently to make out what was in it and I saw four-footed creatures of the earth, wild beasts, and things that crawl or fly. Then I heard a voice saying to me, 'Up, Peter, kill and eat.' But I said, 'No, Lord, no: nothing profane or unclean has ever entered my mouth.' A voice from heaven answered a second time, 'It is not for you to call profane what God counts clean.' This happened three times, and then they were all drawn up again into the sky. At that moment three men, who had been sent to me from Caesarea, arrived at the house where I was staying; and the Spirit told me to go with them. My six companions here came with me and we went into the man's house. He told us how he had seen an angel standing in his house who said, 'Send to Joppa for Simon also called Peter. He will speak words that will bring salvation to you and all your household.' Hardly had I begun speaking, when the Holy Spirit came upon them, just as upon us at the beginning. Then I recalled what the Lord had said: 'John baptized with water, but you will be baptized with the Holy Spirit.' God gave them no less a gift than he gave us when we put our trust in the Lord Jesus Christ; then how could I possibly stand in God's way?"

When they heard this their doubts were silenced. They gave praise to God and said, "This means that God has granted life-giving repentance to the Gentiles also." (Acts 10 and 11:1–18)

A record like this one deserves a closer look, and it is interesting that the first facts the writer put down are the acts of this stranger, Cornelius: that he gave generously and was regular in his prayers. Cornelius was one of those gentiles, then, who was looking for something more in life than he already had, and who had been attracted by the monotheism of the Jews. Apparently he expected a great deal. And his expectations were fulfilled. He had a vision in which an angel brought him important clairvoyant information which was to lead to fulfillment of his hopes and yearnings. Therefore, the experience of glossolalia was preceded by other unusual psychic occurrences, and it should be noted that Cornelius reacted to them with the only appropriate reaction to speaking with an angel. He was terrified. Still, it never occurred to Cornelius to question if the instructions he had received were real, or to wonder if he would be playing the fool before his servants. Instead, he sent them immediately to Joppa.

It is a little better recorded how Peter was also being prepared by the same heavenly wisdom. And it made an impression, for Peter was a little stuffy about having much to do with gentiles and his fences had to be knocked down if the message was to be brought to Cornelius. Thus in a dream-trance experience, it broke in upon him that his religious particularism was no longer adequate. When the men from Caesarea arrived shortly after, Peter's direct question was typical of the blundering fisherman. "You are looking for me? Here I am. What brings you here?" Peter had been softened by his experience of the afternoon, but he was still skeptical.

In addition he had no expectation of anything like this happening from preaching to the gentiles. He came because he was told to. The others with him were also amazed at what happened, but it was Peter, interrupted by the praises spoken in tongues, who knew where this evidence had come from and cut short his sermon to ask, "Is anyone prepared to withhold the water for baptism from these persons, who have received the Holy Spirit just as we did ourselves?"

When Peter returned to Jerusalem, it took the whole story, point by point, to clear the air, for there was actually a great conflict in the apostolic church. Could Jews associate with gentiles and eat with them, and was the new religion of Jesus for the gentiles as well as the Jews? What settled the immediate question is most instructive. God had come to Cornelius and his household, for the Holy Spirit had fallen upon them just as upon the apostles in the beginning. The new dispensation took precedence over the old. Tongues was important enough to displace even laws. This experience gave evidence which overturned Jewish particularism and opened the church to gentiles.

Later in Acts, when Paul comes to Ephesus, he finds a group of men who have been baptized only in the name of John; note the correlation with Peter's memory. As Paul rebaptizes them and lays his hands upon them, they receive the Holy Spirit and speak in tongues. This passage reads:

> While Apollos was at Corinth, Paul travelled through the inland regions till he came to Ephesus. There he found a number of converts, to whom he said, "Did you receive the Holy Spirit when you became believers?" "No," they replied, "we have not even heard that there is a Holy Spirit." He said, "Then what baptism were you given?" "John's baptism," they answered. Paul then said, "The baptism that John gave was a baptism in token of repentance, and he told the people to put their trust in one who was to come after him, that is, in Jesus." On hearing this they were baptized into the name of the Lord Jesus; and when Paul had laid his hands on them,

the Holy Spirit came upon them and they spoke in tongues of ecstasy and prophesied. Altogether they were about a dozen men. (Acts 19:1–7)

In the last paragraphs of Mark—which are thought by many to be later additions to dress up the text, since this rounded-out conclusion does not occur in the earliest manuscripts—this reference to speaking in tongues appears:

> Afterwards while the Eleven were at table he appeared to them and reproached them for their incredulity and dullness, because they had not believed those who had seen him risen from the dead. Then he said to them: "Go forth to every part of the world, and proclaim the Good News to the whole creation. Those who believe it and receive baptism will find salvation; those who do not believe will be condemned. Faith will bring with it these miracles: believers will cast out devils in my name and speak in strange tongues; if they handle snakes or drink any deadly poison, they will come to no harm; and the sick on whom they lay their hands will recover."

Though it may be doubtful that these were the direct words of Jesus, this passage certainly represents the experience and expectation of the early church. In fact, the very probability that it comes from the second century makes it all the more significant. It then becomes a primary indication that the practice of tongues was not confined to the first days of the church.

PAUL'S VIEW

The most comprehensive discussion of the phenomenon in any of the early church literature is Paul's discussion of tongues in I Corinthians 14, and there is good reason for quoting it in full. This is authentic Paul, according to essentially all the scholars, and Paul had something to say, something which was backed up by experience. In the new translation which brings it a little closer to the fresh vernacular in which it was written, Paul's discussion can be heard as first-hand evidence. He wrote:

> Put love first; but there are other gifts of the Spirit at which you should aim also, and above all prophecy. When a man is using the language of ecstasy he is talking with God, not with men, for no man understands him; he is no doubt inspired, but he speaks mysteries. On the other hand, when a man prophesies, he is talking to men, and his words have power to build; they stimulate and they encourage. The language of ecstasy is good for the speaker himself, but it is prophecy that builds up a Christian community. I should be pleased for you all to use the tongues of ecstasy, but better pleased for you to prophesy. The prophet is worth more than the man of ecstatic speech—unless indeed he can explain its meaning, and so help to build up the community. Suppose, my friends, that when I come to you I use ecstatic language: what good shall I do you, unless what I say contains something by way of revelation, or enlightenment, or prophecy, or instruction?
>
> Even with inanimate things that produce sounds—a flute, say, or a lyre—unless their notes mark definite intervals, how can you tell what tune is being played? Or again, if the trumpet-call is not clear, who will prepare for battle? In the same way if your ecstatic utterance yields no precise meaning, how can anyone tell what you are saying? You will be talking into the air. How many different kinds of sound there are, or may be, in the world! Nothing is altogether soundless. Well then, if I do not know the meaning of the sound the speaker makes, his words will be gibberish to me, and mine to him. You are, I know, eager for gifts of the Spirit; then aspire above all to excel in those which build up the church.
>
> I say, then, that the man who falls into ecstatic utterance should pray for the ability to interpret. If I use such language in my prayer, the Spirit in me prays, but my intellect lies fallow. What then? I will pray as I am inspired to pray, but I will also pray intelligently. I will sing hymns as I am inspired to sing, but I will sing intelligently too. Suppose you are

praising God in the language of inspiration: how will the plain man who is present be able to say "Amen" to your thanksgiving, when he does not know what you are saying? Your prayer of thanksgiving may be all that could be desired, but it is no help to the other man. Thank God, I am more gifted in ecstatic utterance than any of you, but in the congregation I would rather speak five intelligible words, for the benefit of others as well as myself, than thousands of words in the language of ecstasy.

Do not be childish, my friends. Be as innocent of evil as babes, but at least be grown-up in your thinking. We read in the Law: "I will speak to this nation through men of strange tongues, and by the lips of foreigners; and even so they will not heed me, says the Lord." Clearly then these "strange tongues" are not intended as a sign for believers, but for unbelievers, whereas prophecy is designed not for unbelievers but for those who hold the faith. So if the whole congregation is assembled and all are using the "strange tongues" of ecstasy, and some uninstructed persons or unbelievers should enter, will they not think you are mad? But if all are uttering prophecies, the visitor, when he enters, hears from everyone something that searches his conscience and brings conviction, and the secrets of his heart are laid bare. So he will fall down and worship God, crying, "God is certainly among you!"

To sum up, my friends: when you meet for worship, each of you contributes a hymn, some instruction, a revelation, an ecstatic utterance, or the interpretation of such an utterance. All of these must aim at one thing: to build up the church. If it is a matter of ecstatic utterance, only two should speak, or at most three, one at a time, and someone must interpret. If there is no interpreter, the speaker had better not address the meeting at all, but speak to himself and to God. Of the prophets, two or three may speak, while the rest exercise their judgement upon what is said. If someone else, sitting in his place, receives a revelation, let the first speaker stop. You can all prophesy, one at a time, so that the whole congregation may receive instruction and encouragement. It is for prophets to control prophetic inspiration, for the God who inspires them is not a God of disorder but of peace. . . .

Did the word of God originate with you? Or are you the only people to whom it came? If anyone claims to be inspired or a prophet, let him recognize that what I write has the Lord's authority. If he does not recognize this, he himself should not be recognized.

In short, my friends, be eager to prophesy; do not forbid ecstatic utterance; but let all be done decently and in order. (I Corinthians 14)

In the twelfth chapter Paul has twice referred almost casually to tongues and interpretation of tongues among other gifts of the Spirit. He first enumerates the gifts; after mentioning wisdom, knowledge, faith, healing, prophecy, and discerning of spirits, he says: ". . . yet another has the gift of ecstatic utterance of different kinds, and another the ability to interpret it." (I Corinthians 12:10) Then in concluding the chapter, to sharpen his point that God does not give everybody the same gift but, instead, distributes them, he adds glossolalia again to the listings. He says that God has appointed apostles, prophets, teachers, miracle-workers, healers, counselors, and those with "the gift of ecstatic utterance of various kinds." (I Corinthians 12:28) And again last, just before the suggestion that there is a higher gift, he uses the words: "Do all speak in tongues of ecstasy? Can all interpret them?" (I Corinthians 12:30)

The allusion to tongues in the next chapter also appears to be incidental, though it is more prominent and now closely linked to prophecy and knowledge. Paul's words introducing his masterpiece on love are so familiar that we usually overlook their meaning. "Tongues of men or of angels" (13:1) commences another list of spiritual gifts, in this case to point up their worthlessness in the absence of love. In his final exposition he says, "Love will never come to an end. Are there prophets? their work will be over. Are there tongues of ecstasy? they will cease. Is there knowledge? it will vanish away; for . . . the partial vanishes when wholeness comes." (13:8–10) But Paul does not conclude glossolalia or other gifts of the Spirit out of existence; he goes right on, as we have seen, with a command to pursue love and also to seek earnestly for the spiritual gifts, particularly prophecy but not excluding tongues. The thirteenth chapter, then, which seems to stand so well alone, actually stands as a bridge between two discussions, one on a specific point about the embodiment of the gifts of the Spirit, the other on the inner working of two specific gifts, prophecy and speaking in tongues. Perhaps it would be easier to make something more than just poetry of this discourse if we realized that what Paul is talking about here is, in a very real sense, a bridge, and one on which we do not stand alone.

PETER AND JOHN IN SAMARIA

The most telling of the indirect references to tongues is the story of Peter and John in Samaria, told in Acts 8:9–24. The two apostles have come to lay their hands on a number of people who have heard Philip and watched his miracles, have "accepted the word of God . . . [and] been baptized into the name of the Lord Jesus," but, in the words of Acts, "that and nothing more." That is, they have not received the Holy Spirit. And with the laying on of hands, they do receive the Holy Spirit. Watching all this is Simon the magician, who has had quite a following of Samaritans. He has been "carried away" by the healings and the general sense of joy following their baptism, but his pocketbook (where Simon apparently kept his feelings) is still intact. Now he *sees*[3] something worth money! And he wants to buy this gift for himself, which he sees as the ability to confer a *visible* sign

3. The word used here is θεάομαι, which was principally used in the sense of "seeing with wonder, awe," but could also be used for the more direct meaning of watching a theatrical spectacle. (See Liddell and Scott, *Greek-English Lexicon*. Oxford University Press, 1940, p. 786.)

with one's own hands. But Peter forces him to ask for their prayers instead, flatly calling him wicked to offer money for the gift of God. In view of the other passages from Acts the gift Simon wanted to be able to use was unquestionably glossolalia. It is an impressive experience to witness a spontaneous outpouring of tongues, and it is certainly one that would interest Simon, a magician who was trading on the supernatural.

When Peter and John were released from prison in Jerusalem (Acts 4:23–32), the place where the apostles were gathered together was shaken, and they were all filled with the Holy Spirit and spoke the word of God with boldness. The similarity to other occasions in Acts when tongues were spoken, a similarity both of circumstances and of the experience described, indicates that glossolalia was included.

Paul writes in his first letter to the Thessalonians (5:19–20), and we translate his words literally: "Do not quench the spirit; do not be contemptuous of prophecies." Again with reference to what we know of the church at Corinth, is this not a reference to tongues? It was characteristic of Paul's writing to compare in this way. In Colossians (3:16) Paul exhorts the people to speak in psalms and hymns and spiritual songs. He is describing the same sort of ecstatic worship which was occurring at Corinth and which he has spoken of in the suggestion that each contribute a hymn, a lesson, a revelation, a tongue, or an interpretation. He instructs the Ephesians (5:18–20) even more clearly not to be drunk with wine but to be filled with the Spirit, speaking to one another in psalms and hymns and spiritual songs. Paul obviously alludes here to an experience as deeply moving as that of speaking in tongues. The same spirit of exaltation which he describes by simile is experienced by modern tongue speaking groups who speak of it as *more* satisfying by far than the "lift" from drinking. Joyousness is one element of their experience which keeps them together and often worshipping into the night as Paul did.

In Galatians 4:6 Paul writes: "To prove that you are sons, God has sent into our hearts the Spirit of his Son, crying 'Abba! Father!'" He uses almost the same words in Romans 8:14–15 and then goes on later in the chapter: "In the same way the Spirit comes to the aid of our weakness. We do not even know how we ought to pray, but through our inarticulate groans the Spirit himself is pleading for us, and God who searches our inmost being knows what the Spirit means, because he pleads for God's own people in God's own way." (8:26–27) These words, again, are very likely descriptions of the more than human speech of glossolalia.

This, then, is the evidence of the New Testament in support of the spiritual reality of tongue speaking. It is not nearly as extensive as the references to healing, or to dreams and visions, or to the angelic and demonic realm, but it is certainly central to the apostolic narrative. Paul spends three whole chapters in developing the subject, and the most important day of the early church's life is marked by this experience.

But the experience described in these passages did not end there. It continued spasmodically from that time until this, and the history of these occurrences tells us much more about both the experience and its Biblical meaning.

Chapter III

A PECULIAR HISTORY

After the time of Paul there were occasional references to speaking in tongues by the writers of the early church. This evidence is of importance for the person who wishes to understand and assess the significance of tongue speaking. If the practice had been confined to Biblical times and had not occurred again, it would be far easier to dismiss the matter there. If, however, glossolalia continued among those who established the foundations of the church, amid the most adverse circumstances, it deserves our careful attention. No one denies the vitality of the early years of the church. During these creative and productive years Christianity spread all over the ancient world and even justified itself before the intelligentsia of the time. Many of the writings of those who sought to explain Christianity to a hostile world have come down to us. These authors, the church fathers as they are called, are little known to readers today, even the highly educated reader of today, but many of these men were just as perceptive and able as the most capable pagan writers of the first centuries of our era. It is significant that among these intellectually sophisticated writers glossolalia was known and accepted as one of the special gifts which are given to Christians.

The next few pages dealing with the church fathers may seem as dull as ditch water because so little is known about this exciting period of the church's life. One must read between the lines of the material which has come down to us.

But this is not our job in these pages. The reader who is not concerned with Christian beginnings will have to take my word for it that these writers were real men, with as many healthy prides and fears and lusty desires as the rest of us, as we take a brief, technical look at a concentrated dose of their theological writing. These writings are an essential part of the lively history of tongues.

THE CHURCH FATHERS

As we read through the pages of the fathers we find, however, that the most surprising things were most often what these writers did *not* say. Thus, we must first ask: Why was speaking in tongues so seldom mentioned? If it had not ceased to occur, just what was happening?

The basic fact is that the church was hard-pressed, first from without and then later from within, and the church fathers were writing to gain acceptance from a hostile gentile world. As Paul had pointed out, tongue speaking is not meant as a sales pitch for a resistant buyer, but for private worship and edification; when used in this way, it is a sign which can be seen. But since most people were already irrational enough about Christianity, describing glossolalia would have been to magnify this sign into wild rumor. These first writers had had a good dose of the hatred that came from such rumors, accusations that Christians ate new-born babies, or conjured up crop failures and floods and earthquakes. They were trying to be rational in the face of so much feeling. They had to show that Christianity was a reasonable faith and adaptable to the world. Talking about tongues would only have added fuel to the fire that flamed into irrational rejection of Christians as monsters or, at best, queer people.

Inside, too, there was fire. As it became clear that the destiny of the church did lead into the world, there was a sprouting of inspired groups opposing its authority. Foremost among these were the Montanists, followers of a second-century Christian of Phrygia, who claimed that the Holy Spirit, the Paraclete, dwelt in him and employed him as an instrument for guiding and purifying the Christian church. His followers believed that the gifts of the Spirit, especially prophecy and tongues, were restored to great importance; the Montanists also practiced an austere strictness of life in preparation for the physical return of the Lord. Modern Pentecostal religion exemplifies many of the characteristics of Montanism. In fact, there are current Pentecostal writers who look back to Montanus with some of the same historical reverence a Presbyterian offers up to Augustine.

In those critical days the church could not permit a movement of this character to take over. Because the Montanists would not accept the authority of the church as a whole, they were forced to split off as heretical. As their enthusiasm degenerated into arrogance, their asceticism into legalism, the movement died out, and it seems fair to infer that tongue-speech disappeared with it. This does not mean that the church negated glossolalia; it simply could not let the kind of enthusiasm exemplified by Montanism take over the whole group and remove it to a cloister to die ingrained or persecuted. Tongue-speech was, as it were, filed away.

Besides this, the language of the apostolic fathers—these were the men who had had direct contact with Paul or a disciple, of whose writings only a handful of fragments remains—indicates that glossolalia became lumped into a single category with prophecy. This clue comes from the later Irenaeus. Stuck off in Gaul in the last part of the second century, he produced the first systematic exposition of the church's belief. His familiarity with source material was obvious. Telling of Paul's visit to the household of Cornelius in Caesarea, he wrote: "Neither for a like reason, would he [Peter] have given them baptism so readily, had he not heard them prophesying when the Holy Ghost rested upon them.[1] Irenaeus has substituted the word "prophecy" for the glossolalia which in the Biblical story made Peter so quick to administer baptism.

Irenaeus knew what he was talking about, however. He was not looking back at just words describing a strange and unknown phenomenon. This is seen clearly in several passages from *Against Heresies* discussing the experience of speaking in tongues. In the first he described the day of Pentecost in his own words:

> This Spirit . . . also, as Luke says, descended at the day of Pentecost upon the disciples after the Lord's ascension, having power to admit all nations to the entrance of life, and to the opening of the new covenant: from whence also, with one accord in all languages, they uttered praise to God, the Spirit bringing distant tribes to unity, and offering to the Father the first-fruits of all nations.

Then he told what was actually happening in his time by giving a list of the miraculous gifts of the Spirit, but omitting specific mention of glossolalia, which he called prophecy:

> For some do certainly and truly drive out devils, so that those who have thus been cleansed from evil spirits frequently both believe [in Christ], and join themselves to the Church. Others have foreknowledge of things to come: they see visions, and utter prophetic expressions. Others still, heal the sick by laying their hands upon them, and they are made whole. Yea, moreover, as I have said, the dead even have been raised up and remained among us for many years. . . .

For the classic passage which puts these two together, from the Bible and in current experience, occurs later in the same work:

1. This and the following references and quotations from the church fathers are found in *The Ante-Nicene Fathers* and *The Nicene and Post-Nicene Fathers,* First and Second Series. Grand Rapids, Michigan, Wm. B. Eerdmans Publishing Co., 1952 and 1956. For a complete list of the references included, see the bibliography.

> For this reason does the apostle declare, "We speak wisdom among them that are perfect," terming those persons "perfect" who have received the Spirit of God, and who through the Spirit of God do speak in all languages, as he used Himself also to speak. In like manner we do also hear many brethren in the Church, who possess prophetic gifts, and who through the Spirit speak all kinds of languages, and bring to light for the general benefit the hidden things of men, and declare the mysteries of God . . .

Thus, because of his thorough knowledge of the Bible and numerous references, and because his work was for a time the most complete discussion of Christian belief available to the church, Irenaeus becomes a starting point to see what passages of the church fathers may refer to glossolalia. The following are a few such possible examples, and a complete study of the use of the word prophecy, which should be undertaken, would undoubtedly reveal many more.

Ignatius, a bishop of the early second century, wrote of an ability to understand heavenly things, apparently in the same spirit he saw in the prophets and the apostles; he was frank about having a special gift which he must "restrain with humility," and instead stick to less abstruse subjects. Both the authors of the *Didache* and the *Shepherd of Hermas* (two more second-century writings) recognized that the prophet speaks in the Spirit; the former was worried mostly about false prophecy, while Hermas was much less skeptical because he had been carried away by the Spirit himself when he saw his visions. The First Epistle of Clement to the Corinthians makes a point of reminding the congregation in Corinth that ". . . a full outpouring of the Holy Spirit was upon you all," and that ministers of the grace of God have spoken by the Spirit.

A letter from the church in Smyrna, called the Martyrdom of Polycarp and written to tell what happened to their beloved old bishop before he was burned in 155 A.D., suggests an experience of speaking in tongues. The police allowed Polycarp just an hour to pray, and "he stood and prayed, being full of the grace of God, so that he could not cease for two full hours, to the astonishment of them that heard him." Justin Martyr, the first Christian philosopher writing about the same time, had to answer the claim that no prophet had risen again among the followers of Christ. He did it with a clear explanation that the Spirit had had to rest with the coming of Christ, cease the gifts, and then return, giving them to those who believe in Christ, those whom he deems worthy. And Justin added, "Now it is possible to see amongst us women and men who possess gifts of the Spirit of God. . . ."

These men were well aware of Paul's list of the gifts of the Spirit and what it included. In no place do they suggest that any of them had dropped away.

TERTULLIAN, ST. CHRYSOSTOM, AND ST. AUGUSTINE

But it took a man like Tertullian, who had to reconcile the irreconcilables and had the penetrating wit to do it, to be specific about speaking in tongues. This able lawyer from North Africa, who wrote voluminously about 225, was the first Christian writer to use Latin. He successfully opposed many of the heretical views current at his time. Even though Tertullian's judgment may have been suspect because it was colored by a Montanist point of view (which he spent much of his mature life trying to integrate before finally adopting it as his last home), what he presented could not be questioned. He was considered the heir of Irenaeus and the underpinning of Cyprian, Augustine, and so of the whole Western doctrine. He was obviously speaking of fact when he said:

> Let Marcion then exhibit, as gifts of his God, some prophets, such as have not spoken by human sense, but with the Spirit of God, such as have both predicted things to come, and have made manifest the secrets of the heart (I Cor. 14:25); let

him produce a psalm, a vision, a prayer—only let it be by the Spirit, in an ecstasy, that is, in a rapture, whenever an interpretation of tongues has occurred to him; let him show to me also, that any woman of boastful tongue in his community has ever prophesied from amongst those specially holy sisters of his. Now all these signs [of spiritual gifts] are forthcoming from my side without any difficulty, and they agree, too, with the rules, and the dispensations, and the instructions of the Creator; therefore without doubt the Christ, and the Spirit, and the apostle, belong severally to my God. Here, then, is my frank avowal for any one who cares to require it.

This passage, along with the references Tertullian made to instruction by the Spirit in the early church, is about the last direct discussion of the experience by the Western fathers. One purely historical account, however, was recorded of tongues occurring during the fourth century, a hundred years or more after Tertullian. The Egyptian abbot, St. Pachomius, who died about 346, was reported to have spoken the language of angels; this was told by the fifth-century historian Sozomen, with a parallel account in the life written by Gennadius about the same time. Pachomius, who is also remembered for his friendship with the great Athanasius, apparently led an interesting life, with three thousand monks, two nunneries, and quarrels with his bishops to worry over. It may have been this last which gave rise to the story told of him in Butler's *Lives of the Saints,* where it was originally recorded that he was given the godsend of a sudden spurt of Greek and Latin, tongues he had never had time to study. Whatever the precise fact behind this account, a gift of tongues was recorded, and it was to be almost a thousand years before there would be another report like it.

At any rate, there were men up into the fourth century who knew what it meant to speak in tongues and acknowledged that it could happen. Then, about the same time that Montanism lost its enthusiastic character, prophetic utterance in tongues ceased to be mentioned as a current possibility.

There was never any particular criticism of the experience; as far as the Montanists were concerned, the fathers had enough matters of doctrine on which to hang them. Nothing in patristic literature particularly rejected tongues as a gift of the Spirit. Under the name of prophecy it seemed to have been accepted as respectable—accepted, and then neglected.

From the time of Origen, the brilliant Christian philosopher who taught and wrote in Alexandria in the middle of the third century, the fathers did not seem to recognize that tongue speaking had ever been a common practice. Indeed from then on most of the references to tongues are explanations as to why the phenomena which had occurred in Biblical times were no longer occurring.

Origen obviously had no first-hand acquaintance with genuine ecstatic prophecy, for he showed no discrimination at all in countering the practical pagan accusation that certain Christians tried to act like deified John the Baptists and added meaningless phrases when they ran out of rational prophecies. The best he could muster against the reporting of the pagan Celsus—undoubtedly part fact, part healthy pagan imagination—was a blanket denial that living Christians still uttered real prophecies, whether intelligible *or* beyond their ability to put into rational speech. Origen also seemed to feel that Paul's gift of tongues made him a debtor to the Greeks and barbarians for his ability to speak their languages, and it is said he proved this by translating I Corinthians 14:18 as: "I speak more with tongues of you all."[2]

In the fifth century the bishop of Constantinople was St. Chrysostom, who laid the foundations of the Eastern church; he was another who was quick to express his doubts that

2. Quoted by George Barton Cutten, *Speaking with Tongues: Historically and Psychologically Considered*. New Haven, Yale University Press, 1927, p. 21. Though his source is not given, it is certainly a plausible story by reverse English; the point is that it was someone's idea, whether picked up by a later writer from one of Origen's lost works or out of the air. And there is ample source for Origen's opinions about Paul's conscious ability to communicate.

men could speak in ecstasy what they did not know enough to say rationally. When he got to Paul's discussion in I Corinthians 12 and 14, he said flatly, "This whole place is very obscure; but the obscurity is produced by our ignorance of the facts referred to and by their cessation, being such as then used to occur but now no longer take place." This is candid honesty, to say the least, and worthy of Chrysostom.

At the same time Augustine, who set the mold of Western Christianity for seven hundred years, was writing, and he took this view a step farther. In the Epistle of St. John he wrote:

> In the earliest times, "the Holy Ghost fell upon them that believed: and they spake with tongues," which they had not learned, "as the Spirit gave them utterance." These were signs adapted to the time. For there behooved to be that betokening of the Holy Spirit in all tongues, to shew that the Gospel of God was to run through all tongues over the whole earth. That thing was done for a betokening, and it passed away.

Thus Augustine was quite ready to make up the church's mind and get the matter out of the way. Glossolalia was a special apostolic dispensation for evangelizing, and that was that. There was no point in discussing it further (especially if the writer had no further knowledge). When he came to discuss baptism in answer to the Donatists, he simply read tongues out of existence again with these words:

> For the Holy Spirit is not only given by the laying on of hands amid the testimony of temporal sensible miracles, as He was given in former days to be the credentials of a rudimentary faith, and for the extension of the first beginnings of the Church. For who expects in these days that those on whom hands are laid that they may receive the Holy Spirit should forthwith begin to speak with tongues?

Who indeed? There was no need for tongues as an expression of the Spirit in a man, as a way for the Spirit to speak through men. The church was turning to fixed forms of worship to express *its* life and spirit. This strange phenomenon simply dropped from consideration along with dreams and the healing ministry.

So little impact did the experience of tongue speaking make upon that world into which Christianity was spreading that only one of its philosophers even considered the matter of superhuman speech. Plotinus in the third century did propose something akin to tongues as another of his popular eclectic ideas. When he was considering the possibility of direct communication between souls, he made the point that celestials (daimones) and souls in air might have speech with one another; still he did not even hint that their speech could really take hold of a man and make him express what wanted saying.[3] For lack of interest, the subject seemed to be a closed book.

TONGUES IN EASTERN CHRISTIANITY

With the fall of the Western part of the Roman Empire in the fifth century the stream of Christian thought and life divided and separated. Two very different traditions of Christianity developed. The Greek or Orthodox tradition in the East and the Latin or Roman tradition in the West developed different attitudes towards the gifts of the Spirit in general and speaking in tongues in particular. We who stand in the Western tradition tend to forget that there is an approach to the Christian life other than our own. If we are to grasp the history of this subject of tongue speaking, we must look briefly at Greek Christianity, which continued the traditions of the fathers, before returning to the history of the more familiar Western customs. The best place to discuss a different development is at the point of separation.

In the West the government disintegrated under the barbarian invasions. The church remained as virtually the only organization of civilized life and was forced to take upon it

3. Plotinus, *The Six Enneads,* IX, 3, 19.

many of the functions of secular authority. Thus, of sheer necessity, it became intensely practical and this-worldly. The church had already been shaped in this direction by the practical this-worldliness of the Latin mind. And since monasticism did not develop in the West until relatively late, it could not permit itself the wild enthusiasm and individualism of Greek monasticism. The West of necessity developed a practical, authoritative, extroverted, Latin Christianity. In such a tradition individual experience of the gifts of the Spirit was soft-pedaled. Authority rather than individual religious expression was stressed. There was little place for tongues which had already caused Paul and the church fathers some real difficulty.

In the Eastern Roman Empire the church grew up under contrasting conditions. At Constantinople a strong central government provided the base for a brilliant and colorful civilization which never passed through the throes of the Dark Ages. Indeed its capital city remained secure against pagan invasion until 1451. Thus the church was never forced to take over the secular functions which were forced upon the Western church. The Greek church remained far more otherworldly and mystical. It continued the Greek bent of introspection and individuality. Greek monasticism, even though it came to play an important part in Byzantine politics, was never as organized or controlled as that which grew up in the West. There was a strain of wild enthusiasm and individualism in the Greek way which could make a saint of a man who sat for years on a solitary pillar. The East developed a mystical, individualistic, otherworldly, introverted Christianity. In this tradition the individual gifts of the Spirit flourished. The door was never closed to experiences like tongues.

In 691 the Eastern church codified its "One Hundred and Two Canons" of the sixth council. One of these was a law which controls teaching by laymen, forbidding them to teach unless they have received the grace of teaching. The canon then refers to I Corinthians 12:29 with the inference that tongues is actually only a special teaching ability.[4] The final authority for teaching does not rest upon external authority, but upon grace, the gift of God. This reference to Paul's list of gifts which includes tongues may well be the basis of the statement by the Patriarch of Constantinople, which we have already mentioned, that his church had always recognized and controlled the practice of tongues. While historical evidence of tongues within the Greek tradition has not been compiled, it is a fair inference that tongue speaking, being no more bizarre than other Eastern monastic practices, has simply continued within the tradition of Greek monasticism without attracting much notice.

Among some of the Orthodox clergy there is a sympathetic understanding of the practice of tongues, and I keep running across reports that it is known, and has been known through the centuries, in the monasteries. One of the priests with whom I have talked suggested that the deep mysticism of the church, which permeates all aspects of life, makes any particular emphasis on this one gift of the Spirit unnecessary. He remarked that if a special emphasis on tongues broke out in his church, he would wonder how he had failed in bringing his people into contact with vital spiritual reality so that they had to express the need in this way. Glossolalia apparently continued, but never became the central religious experience which it did among the Corinthians and is in Pentecostalism today.

In fact, two practices within this discipline undoubtedly offer an occasional experience of tongues. The first, told to me by a Russian priest who did not have references at hand, was found in the religious babblings of the "fools for Christ" who took Paul's injunction to be fools literally. And the other is the use of the Jesus prayer which was described in *The Way of a Pilgrim*. This simple record, discovered about 1880

4. *The Rudder* (*Pedalion*), trans. D. Cummings. Chicago, The Orthodox Christian Educational Society, 1957, p. 363. (The Holy and Ecumenical Quinisext, Canon LXIV.)

in the possession of a monk at Mount Athos, tells the experiences of an unknown Russian pilgrim who wandered the country learning the secret of prayer without ceasing. The little stories of the people he met and what happened to them and to him occurred in the years between the beginning of the Crimean War in 1853 and the liberation of the serfs in 1861. They have probably had more influence among Western readers than any other modern devotional literature from the Orthodox church.

The prayer of Jesus, with its constant repetition of the name of Jesus, often results in strange experiences and a sense of being prayed through, sometimes with unknown words coming to the tongue. Since this repetition of Jesus' name is one of the common ways of leading Western seekers into the experience of tongues, it would be hard to believe that it did not also result in an occasional experience of tongue speech among the Orthodox who use the prayer. The Russian priest with whom I have talked confessed that his own use of the Jesus prayer sometimes resulted in strange experiences comparable to tongues.

The leading modern authorities on Eastern Orthodoxy bear witness to the charismatic quality of their church, a quality which lays a foundation for the practice of tongues. Let us listen to them in their own words. Sergius Bulkagov, dean of the Russian Orthodox Theological Academy in Paris from 1925 until his death in 1944, was one man who experienced a religious conversion which forced him to desert communism. As probably the leading Russian theologian of his time, Bulkagov wrote:

> Mystic experience has an objective character; it is founded on a departure from one's own narrow limitations and a resultant spiritual contact or encounter. . . . All the life of Orthodoxy is full of heavenly visions. This is what is essential in Orthodoxy, something which its travelling companions do not see, and thus they do not see its inner meaning, but only what seem to them its external "petrified" or "mummified" forms.

He goes on to say that the principal end of prayer is the acquisition of the Holy Spirit, and

> This "Spirit-bearing" baffles exact description, but it is instantly felt when one comes into the presence of such a person, as an "other" spiritual life within the human life. It is just this seal of the Spirit of God, this bearing of the Spirit, which the Orthodox soul seeks and desires above all and which it venerates most. This bearing of the Spirit, which corresponds to the ministry of the prophets of the Old Testament, is in Christianity connected with the prophetic ministry of Christ Who was annointed by the Holy Spirit. The "elders," the "spirituals" (pneumataphores) in Orthodoxy, all those infused by the Spirit, are in this sense Christian prophets or prophetesses (for this ministry does not, like the priestly office, belong only to the masculine sex).[5]

Nicolas Zernov, Spalding Lecturer in Eastern Orthodoxy at Oxford, in his more recent study of Eastern Christendom, makes the same point:

> The life of the Christian community has been greatly enriched by the monastic movement. It helped to accentuate those Charismatic gifts of the Holy Spirit, prophecy, healing, the knowledge of man's inner state, which the church offers to its members but which are often unexplored by Christians. The ascetics and mystics penetrated deeply into the mystery of communion between God and man and have made the path of its further discovery easier for others.[6]

Ernst Benz, too, makes this same point in his study of the value of icons in *The Eastern Orthodox Church: Its Thought and Life*. In his words, the icon is holy because the heavenly archetype has broken through in it.

5. Sergius Bulkagov, *The Orthodox Church*. London, The Centenary Press, no date, pp. 168 and 173. Used with the permission of A.R.E.O., 303 Broadway, Dobbs Ferry, N.Y.

6. Nicolas Zernov, *Eastern Christendom*. London, Weidenfeld & Nicolson, 1961, pp. 79 f. You will notice that there is no mention of tongues. The Orthodox live the irrational; they do not discuss it rationally except in its reflection.

Those who see the icon as a reflection of a heavenly archetype have no difficulty in expecting vocal chords as well to reproduce what heavenly forces have to tell. Since the Orthodox have also looked upon the monastic state as the state of the "angelic life," with the habit itself being known as the "angel's robe," they do not find it surprising that monks are also found speaking with tongues of angels.

TONGUES IN WESTERN CHRISTIANITY

Early in the development of the tradition of Western Christianity, tongue speaking came to be looked upon with grave suspicion. Evidently the experience occurred, but was linked in most cases with demon possession rather than angel possession. This has become the official position of the Roman church. This point of view is found expressed in the official Catholic book of public services, the *Rituale Romanum,* which came to a large extent to its present form around 1000 A.D. In the section on Exorcism of the Possessed, we find the priest who intends to perform an exorcism directed to learn "the signs by which a person possessed can be distinguished from one who is suffering from melancholy or some other illness. Signs of possession are the following: ability to speak with some facility in a strange tongue or to understand it when spoken by another; the faculty of divulging future and hidden events; display of powers which are beyond the subject's age and natural condition; and various other indications which, when taken together as a whole, pile up the evidence."[7]

Monsignor Ronald A. Knox, who has become known for his comprehensive study of Christian enthusiasm, expresses the same point of view when he comments: "I do not mean to deny the existence of glossolaly all through the period

[7] *The Roman Ritual,* The Rev. Philip T. Weller, trans. and ed. Milwaukee, The Bruce Publishing Company, 1952, Vol. II (Christian Burial, Exorcism, Reserved Blessings, etc.), p. 169.

under dispute. To speak with tongues you had never learned was, and is, a recognized symptom in cases of alleged diabolical possession. What does not appear is that it was ever claimed, at least on a large scale, as a symptom of divine inspiration, until the end of the seventeenth century."[8] With this point of view current it can certainly be understood why speaking in tongues was seldom mentioned in the West.

It is actually surprising that there were any instances recorded during this period. There are, however, occasional reports of the occurrence of tongues and several references to it by Western writers. Undoubtedly court records of the witchcraft trials, and also the particulars of exorcisms performed—although I know of no such accounts before the nineteenth century—would reveal other instances with a negative label. But it is not surprising that the rare individual cases which were identified with Biblical tongues involved the more acceptable gift of a foreign language, and that almost nothing is said about the religious emotions accompanying the utterance, or about ecstatic speech which could not be understood at all.

ST. HILDEGARD AND THOMAS AQUINAS

The first report in the Catholic church after that of Pachomius in the fourth century is found in the life of St. Hildegard, who lived through most of the twelfth century. She was a German abbess, brought up in the cloister but uneducated because she was sickly. Yet she was able not only to interpret Latin scriptures, but to speak and interpret an entirely unknown language. This was recorded, with an unknown alphabet of twenty-three letters, in a manuscript known as the *Lingua Ignota,* which was later printed.

St. Hildegard's first experience of this gift apparently came

8. Ronald A. Knox *Enthusiasm: A Chapter in the History of Religion.* Oxford, The Clarendon Press, 1950, p. 551.

as part of a strange and powerfully moving religious experience, and following a long series of visions which she had not discussed with anyone.

In the following century Thomas Aquinas was faced with the task of writing an exhaustive and complete Christian theology for a changing world. In the *Summa Theologica*, the book which he worked on until shortly before his death in 1274, Aquinas attempted to embrace every aspect of Christian experience, including of course glossolalia. When he came to this subject, he had only Augustine to fall back on; he concluded that tongue speaking had happened when God offered it, and it no longer happened. Reason could only confirm eight hundred years of belief: God came and gave for a purpose, and the purpose in tongues was to offer a miraculous gift of foreign languages, which could have been learned by study but probably less perfectly, and so they were needed as they were given. Since God is perfectly able to give supernaturally, to bypass "second causes" and still produce their effect, a natural ability to acquire other languages does not stand in the way (any more than the talents given the physician necessarily prevent some people from having perfect health without a physician). It does not seem to have occurred to Aquinas that the events in Acts had any relation to the experiences of the Corinthians; and just as well for Aquinas, for even he would have had trouble reconciling the church's point of view with this connection. So St. Thomas classified tongues as a supernatural gift, given to aid the development of the early church. And then he turned to the problem Paul raised of angelic speech.

And here the angelic doctor laid one of the cornerstones of his theological engineering. To understand where the history of tongues fits in here, we must see both sides of his thinking rather clearly. First, he was approaching an experience of which he could hardly have had first-hand knowledge, and therefore he had to accept a point of view about it. Tongues were once spoken in a particular way for a particular purpose which no longer existed. If someone claimed that God had given him this gift now, it was clearly an impossibility; and if he demonstrated a "gift," then there was only one place it could have come from, and the realm of demons was no place for an angelic doctor to be poking into. It is quite plausible that Aquinas had had no opportunity of even witnessing a current or demonic manifestation of tongues, and certainly he would have seen no similarity to the event of apostolic times.

And so, on the other hand, his thinking must proceed from the purely rational side, rather than from experience. Since angels are purely intellectual beings, *intelligentia intelligibilia*, their speech must be pure reason! When Paul is discussing angelic speech, therefore, he must be talking about pure reason. It appears that St. Thomas concluded that Paul, too, speaks in this way at times. By inference, he concludes that angelic speech can only be pure concept, pure intellectual communication. In the thousands of pages of the *Summa Theologica* Aquinas mentions nearly everything else, but tongues, along with most of the other gifts of the Spirit in Paul's list, are glaringly noticeable by their infrequent mention. As we shall show later, there was simply no place for such notations in the world view of Aristotle to which Aquinas was committed.

DANTE, LUTHER, AND FRANCIS BACON

In the beginning of the fourteenth century we next find a poet who felt the possibility of meaningful speech from beyond man's mind. Dante in *The Divine Comedy* heard speech which he could not understand, and he told in "Paradise" of the ineffable speech he hears (Canto XI), and later of one of the spirits who speaks to him in language which is too deep for him (Canto XV). In another of the experiences in "Paradise" (Canto VII), Dante again described speech which is beyond intelligibility, but which becomes intelligible as his understanding increases. Although these are facts only in the hereafter to which the author's imagination has taken him, each one points towards a certain facet of the meaning which tongue speakers say is found in their own experience.

Around 1350 there were again reports of the gift of tongues, this time concerning St. Vincent Ferrer, a native of Valencia, who supposedly spoke only Limousin, the local dialect. In view of his education, including a doctorate at Lerida, marvelous imagination is shown in parts of the story, but it also suggests some basis in fact. He reached and converted people all over western Europe, many in isolated areas. He was reported to have been understood in the Alpine regions and other parts of Switzerland, in Brittany and Flanders, in the Savoy and Lyons, by people who knew only the local tongue. While in Genoa he spoke to a group of men and women of mixed linguistic backgrounds, all of whom were said to have heard him in their own languages. He could also understand the Bretons in their own dialect. *The Catholic Encyclopedia* notes that many biographers of St. Vincent have held that he was endowed with the gift of tongues, remarking that it would be difficult to understand how he could make himself understood by the many nationalities he evangelized without such a gift. Indeed this is the closest parallel, in fact or imagination, to the experience of Acts 2 that we find recorded.

In the first half of the sixteenth century we find the same report about the two Catholic saints, St. Francis Xavier and St. Louis Bertrand. Both men were reported to have spoken foreign languages they did not know in the course of their missionary work. Cutten, whose work on glossolalia is considered the most thorough modern study of the subject, shows how the legends regarding this gift have grown over the centuries in the various accounts of St. Francis Xavier. He also notes that in the bulls of canonization of both saints the gift of tongues is mentioned. There appears to be no record, however, of any religious experience from which it arose. St.

Louis was said to have converted 300,000 Indians in South America from various tribes and dialects; undoubtedly there were historical facts which gave rise to this tradition.

In the nineteenth-century German work on Christian mysticism by Johann Joseph von Görres, nine other saints are described as having a similar gift of foreign tongues, among them St. Claire of Montefalco and the later St. Colette. The languages spoken varied from classical tongues to the Arabic which Jeanne of the Cross is said to have spoken out spontaneously, bringing those who heard to conversion, and the Greek, Turkish, and Armenian languages which St. Stephen used in his missions to those areas without having learned them. It is told that the Abbess Elizabeth received this gift in a religious experience similar to that of St. Hildegard. Others were Ange Clarénus, Martin Valentine, Jean of St. Francis, and the latest, Dominick of Neisse in Silesia, who died in 1650. The accounts given here do not appear to be substantiated by other authors, or have not been thought worth investigating.

Luther, who lived at the same time as St. Francis and St. Louis, is cited by one author as having spoken in tongues. In the third volume of his *History of the Christian Church,* Souer recorded that "Dr. Martin Luther was a prophet, evangelist, speaker in tongues and interpreter, in one person, endowed with all the gifts of the Holy Spirit." While some doubt has been expressed about the historian's conception of tongues, I would suggest that this is quite a plausible story. It relates closely to the other psychic experiences which broke in on Luther at intervals during the two years before he took final monastic vows, and which undoubtedly had much to do with the historical role of protest he later played out to the full.

The Renaissance also produced one philosopher who was attracted to an idea at least similar to tongues. Francis Bacon must have found real meaning in the thought of spiritual speech, since it turns up in two of his most important books.

In *The Advancement of Learning,* published in 1605, he concluded that speech between celestials and souls would not be contrary to any law of nature, but it must be against God's special law for man. But his most interesting thoughts on the subject are woven into *The New Atlantis,* a fantasy in which Bacon's imagination discovers the unknown island where his ideas have become reality. The inhabitants of Bacon's island were evangelized by the apostle St. Bartholomew, who gave them both a book and a letter written in a strange tongue which could be understood by anyone, native or foreign, who read it. In this fantasy, in which Bacon gave life to his own philosophical ideals, he recreated for everyone who peopled it a gift very much like the interpretation of tongues.

The historical record now skips nearly a century again to the sudden outbreak of a mass expression of speaking in tongues which occurred after the revocation of the Edict of Nantes by Louis XIV in 1685. The Huguenots, who had enjoyed a measure of religious liberty, now found themselves persecuted virulently. Many of these French Protestants fled to the New World, but among those who remained was a group in the Cevennes mountains of southern France who turned in contemplation to the New Testament and came to believe that they were called of God and were filled with the Holy Spirit. All the manifestations of great religious excitement were present. They saw visions and apparitions, heard music and strange sounds. These poor persecuted Cevennols believed that the angels were coming to their defense.

THE "LITTLE PROPHETS OF CEVENNES"

The first occurrence of tongues grew out of the prophetic utterance of a ten-year-old, Isabeau Vincent, who had fled from the mistreatment of her father and had seen the king's soldiers bayonet women and children worshipping together in their own church. In an ecstatic experience she called for repentance, speaking in the patois which was all the language she knew, to those around her. Then, her miraculous prophesying became known in other areas and people came to hear her. It was found that she spoke *to them* in perfect French, with good diction; and later she also recited parts of the Latin Mass (with which she had some familiarity because her father had forced her to attend) and then refuted what she had spoken. She showed no signs of unusual behavior or physical symptoms other than a periodic trance state.

Soon children all over the Cevennes were seized by the spirit and prophesied. Children as young as three were known to have exhorted the people in religious discourses. Adults, too, were seized by the spirit and found themselves speaking words of French they did not understand. ". . . a woman, considered almost idiotic, uttered discourses of so elevated a character, and in such good French, that her hearers said, 'This ass of Balaam has a mouth of gold!'" Over three hundred children were jailed and examined by the medical faculty from Montpellier, a university that was one of Europe's best. These men, with the free traditions from the days of supplying physicians and other services to the popes, could not stomach the word of the priests that the children were possessed by demons; instead they called them fanatics. And so a number of the young fanatics were sent to the galleys, many youths were impressed into the army, and a few were killed outright.

The messages these children spoke would not have been unusual from the pulpit, but the eloquent, well-chosen French was completely foreign to them; the inspiration was not at their command, for it apparently rose spontaneously from prayer. According to one author, those who received this prophetic inspiration were in many cases transformed morally and religiously. The experience was almost uniformly of tremendous religious significance for those who received it.

For just over ten years the "little prophets of Cevennes" spoke from every part of their province. Then, what had become a religious movement with prophetic and "tongue-like" experiences turned into a political and revolutionary one, and the little prophets became the "night-attackers" or Camisards. When their own prophecies told them to arm, they did it with a miraculous power like that of the Maccabees. For two years they withstood the armed power of the French government until an attempt at conciliation was tried. But after refusal of the leaders to accept terms, the movement lost strength and was finally defeated and punished. By 1711 the tongues, the prophecy, the revolution itself were over. On the eighth day of March 1715 by medals and a proclamation Louis XIV announced the entire extinction of heresy. (Seventy-four years later the main show was to start at the Bastille in Paris.)

The fame of the Cevennol courage and faith, however, was not over. Throughout Europe the Camisards and their prophetic utterances were discussed. The Earl of Shaftesbury commented on Cevennol enthusiasm in his *Characteristics of Men.* Benjamin Franklin described the "enthusiastic agitations" of his first employer, who had been one of the French prophets. When Conyers Middleton argued that no experience of tongues had been mentioned "in all history" since apostolic times, Wesley countered his denial with a description of the little prophets. And perhaps most interesting of all was the fact that "Sir Richard Bulkley, a wealthy English baronet, became a convert to the faith of some of the Cevennol refugees who came to London. He declares that he heard John Lacy, one of their leaders, repeat long sentences in Latin, and another refugee speak in Hebrew, neither one of whom could speak a single word in these languages when not in spiritual ecstasy!"[9]

There were strange reverberations of the Camisard movement. Among the French Catholics known as Jansenists similar religious experiences occurred in the year 1731. This

9. Cutten, op. cit., pp. 55 f.

group was a Catholic holiness sect whose doctrine was based on Augustine's thought. Since they were revolting against what was felt as coldness of spirit and lax morality among the prevailing Jesuits, it is not surprising that they showed characteristics of Montanism, including the manifestation of tongues. The movement was theologically sound, however, and had existed for nearly eighty years, attracting a brilliant man like Pascal to it, before they became the talk of Paris. Their fervent activity in St. Medard cemetery centered around the tomb of a singularly holy deacon who had defended the movement, and so their speaking in tongues was made a public display. To the ordinary citizens it seemed to be an absolutely meaningless torrent of syllables, but they maintained that their voices were possessed by angelic powers.

EARLY QUAKERS AND THE IRVINGITES

While the early Quakers have sometimes been referred to as tongue speakers, this has never been authenticated, nor was it apparently claimed by Fox or any of the early leaders. Cutten remarks that: "Probably nothing shows so clearly the good common sense of George Fox and the other early leaders as the lack of glossolalic expression." This attitude towards Fox and the early Quaker movement is somewhat idealistic. Many of the practices of the early movement were no less strange than glossolalia. Quite possibly manifestations of revival were confused with tongue speech in this instance, but one Quaker leader with whom I have talked told me of conservative Quaker groups who do practice tongue speaking and who believe that it originated with Fox himself. This statement is supported by a quotation, quoted several times over, from the work of one early Quaker, Burrough's *Preface to Great Mystery,* which stated that ". . . our tongues [were] loosed and our mouths opened, and we spake with new tongues as the Lord gave us utterance," and that this outpouring of the Spirit came often while they waited in silence.

Then, as suddenly as it began, this strange series of prophetic movements disappeared. There was no mention of the subject of glossolalia for almost another hundred years, until Edward Irving put his remarkable talents into the encouragement of enthusiasm in his church in London. Although this Scotch Presbyterian preacher never spoke in tongues himself, his interest in the phenomenon and his encouragement of it erupted into a new sect which took the name of the Catholic Apostolic Church. For three years, beginning in 1831, Irvingism was the *bête noir* of the religious world. The shock to conservatism of finding a personable man of the Spirit in its midst is shown by the strong reactions reported to Irving's "the Lord bless you!" or "Peace be to this house," in place of an ordinary greeting. Carlyle, who married the girl to whom Irving had been engaged, remained his close friend, and the Carlyle letters have been one of the best records of the changes which took place as this amazing young man permitted glossolalia to break out in his church. In 1830 he had written to John Carlyle that Edward Irving was a man "whose like, take him for all in all, I have not yet looked upon . . . with one such man I feel as if I could defy the earth."

The story begins in 1830 with an invalid Scotchwoman, Mary Campbell, whose illness the doctors called a "decline." Friends were praying with her one day when her weakness suddenly disappeared and she began to speak powerfully in an unknown tongue. Not long after that a James MacDonald, who lived in another city, was given the experience of tongues also. When he heard of Mary Campbell's illness and her experience, he wrote commanding her to get up from her sickbed. She did so immediately, and lived out a healthy life.

Irving heard of these experiences and found in them what he wanted for his church. Continuous prayer was offered by a group of his congregation, and before long tongue speaking occurred within the group. Irving had wanted it limited to the small devotional fellowship, but when tongues broke out four months later in his public service, he saw it as a sign from God which should not be restrained. As Carlyle wrote to a friend, his church service became pure bedlam. Irving himself was pushed to a constant state of spiritual excitement, and the opinions he expressed openly led to a charge of heresy. Excommunicated in London and deposed by the Church of Scotland, he left London for Wales. Although he was reinstated by his faithful followers in a new church, he finally retreated to Scotland where he died in 1834, worn out at the age of forty-two.

The Holy Catholic and Apostolic Church formed by Irvingites was described by Schaff in his *History of the Apostolic Church*, making it clear that tongue-speech continued among a limited group as late as 1879. The organization of the church was elaborate, headed by "Twelve Apostles" called from the laity, but no successors were called. In 1901 the last of the twelve died, and the membership and church property were dispersed among other churches.

SHAKERS AND MORMONS

Shortly after the Irvingite revival began, experiences of tongues broke forth in other countries. It was particularly noted in Sweden where there were widespread occurrences for a short time beginning in 1841. About the same time there were more prolonged experiences in two different spots in North America. Whether there was a causal connection between the practice in Mormonism and the occurrence in Shakerism I do not know, but the Shaker tradition of tongues was an old one which recurred as an intense revival about 1840 for a period of ten years. There was evidently a direct connection of the Shaker tradition with the prophets of Cevennes, and the enthusiastic characteristics of the Shaker group multiplied after they had migrated to this country. Along with tongues, there were predictions, songs written in unknown tongues, and a belief in the visits of departed spirits who spoke and acted through the members, as well as dancing and riotous rhythms.[10] Fortunately for the Shakers witches and demons had faded from the public imagination by the middle of the last century, and so they were not persecuted. Reading of these practices, one begins to understand the position of the *Rituale Romanum.*

The practice of tongue speaking was a part of Mormonism from the beginning. The official digest of Mormon doctrine by Joseph Smith established glossolalia with this statement:

> Art. 7. We believe in the gift of tongues, prophecy, revelation, visions, healing, interpretation of tongues . . .

During the early period of the church tongue-speech was generally understood among them as a completely unknown language requiring interpretation, and at the dedication of the Temple in Salt Lake City hundreds of elders spoke in tongues. Such practice was soon discouraged by the leaders, however, "because it has brought ridicule and disrespect from the ungodly."[11] Yet the same leaders were still firmly claiming their faith in tongues as a spiritual fact. The attitude of the Mormons in those times may well give a clue as to why the practice of tongues dropped from sight in the first centuries of church history.

Heber Grant, the seventh president of the church, was one who had experience with tongues. As a young church leader, with a young wife and a healthy burden of debt, he came home one evening to find that his wife had just spoken in tongues. Had she asked for an interpretation, he wanted to know. She had not, and so they immediately knelt together and prayed for the interpretation. She received it and spoke the reassuring message that he would live to be able to pay off all of their debts.[12]

10. Edward Deming Andrews, *The People Called Shakers* (New York, Oxford University Press, 1953), quotes descriptions by a former member of the colony, William Haskett, pp. 144 ff.; also, 153 f. and 237 f.

11. Cutten, op. cit., p. 76.

12. Carter Eldredge Grant, *The Kingdom of God Restored.* Salt Lake City, Deseret Book Co., 1955, pp. 206 and 259 f.

Later, as president of the church, Grant expressed their faith in tongues in these words: "Now, we have had many men who have had the gift of tongues, out in the world, preach this gospel in a language of which they had no knowledge. . . . Unless the gift of tongues and the interpretation thereof are enjoyed by the Saints in our day, then we are lacking one of the evidences of the true faith."[13]

Meantime there were reports of a great revival in Russia in 1855 with an outbreak of tongue speaking which carried over into Armenia. This was apparently a powerful movement among great numbers of the people, but a fleeting one except for a small group mainly in the Black Sea region who banded themselves together as Pentecostal Christians. A story of this sect and of the families who finally came to America is told later in this chapter.

At the same time in western Europe tongue speaking was occurring, but in association with demon possession rather than valid Christian experience. Leon Christiani, a French Catholic priest, has described the tongue-speech of those possessed at Lourdes in an epidemic of visions and trances which followed the original experience of Bernadette in 1858. Nearly all of those who had visions also spoke with strange tongues. This, in accordance with the *Rituale Romanum,* was one of the reasons for believing that their experiences were demonic. The case of two German boys is described, who spoke in various classic languages until they were released from the possession in 1869. The accounts, which include many similar cases in the late nineteenth century and on into the twentieth, are based on the original documents from the time of the occurrences.[14] There are also several instances cited by Cutten, including reports of the Lutheran Pastor Blumhardt's conversing with demons in foreign languages

13. Klaude Kendrick, *The Promise Fulfilled: A History of the Modern Pentecostal Movement*. Springfield, Missouri, The Gospel Publishing House, 1961, p. 24.

14. Leon Christiani, *Evidences of Satan in the Modern World.* New York, The Macmillan Company, 1962.

during some of the amazing exorcisms which took place in his famous sanitarium, Bad-Boll, in the Black Forest during the 1860s and 1870s.

And these are the experiences of tongues which have occurred in our culture up to our own century and have been described, often by observers with a variety of pungent reactions to them. They become increasingly well documented, except in those aspects which are entirely subjective. If this were the total extent of the practice, it would be an interesting study of an outgrown religious and psychological stage in our development from which we might learn something about our own place in history. But this is certainly not all. It is in our own time that speaking in tongues has become for some what our teen-age surfers would call "a ninth wave" ride to conversion, for others a quiet experience of religious meaning, and to many others a strange variety of meanings from complete contempt to deep understanding. In this century the history of glossolalia has suddenly become a living history.

The mainstream of the modern movement of tongue speaking began in this country, in the Middle West, against a background of individual experiences among revivalists from the 1870s on. One of the early experiences was described by the psychologist William James in these words:

> In the early seventies I was invited to see a young woman from the country, who had come up to Boston in the hope of finding some learned men in that city who might be able to determine the unknown language which her lips were irresistibly impelled to utter. I cannot now recall her account of the way in which this phenomenon in her had originated, but it was a curious thing to hear. When she gave herself permission, her vocal organs would articulate nonsense-syllables with the greatest volubility and animation of expression and with no apparent fatigue, and then again stop at the behest of her will. The young woman and the friends with whom

she stayed seemed sincere in their belief that this must be a religious miracle identical with the "speaking with tongues" so common among the earliest Christians. . . . I never heard of the later history of her case, and have never since met with this phenomenon of automatism until I became acquainted last year with. . . . the gentleman whose narrative follows . . .[15]

These were isolated occurrences, involving usually only a few persons in widely separated areas, from Rhode Island to Arkansas. They happened among members of several denominations, for instance in a Swedish Mission church in Minnesota, in a South Dakota Methodist church, and in a number of interdenominational revivals. Not much is known about either the people or their experiences of tongues. One minister in an eastern state remarked that those who spoke in tongues at his services were not accepted by people in the established churches. More often, it appears, the experiences of tongues were simply counted as one more reaction to the strenuous demands of revivalists for crisis experiences.

BIBLE COLLEGE IN TOPEKA

Then in 1900 a former Methodist minister, Charles F. Parham, opened a Bible college in Topeka, Kansas, with forty students housed in a converted Midwest mansion. These men and women, twelve of them ministers, had been asked to study informally the subject of baptism in the Holy Ghost while Parham was out of town preaching in December of that year. They did so, following his suggestion that they search the Biblical passages for some certain evidence of this baptism. On his return he was amazed to find that they had all reached the same conclusion: one evidence had come every time with the Holy Spirit in the Bible, and that was speaking

15. Albert Le Baron, "A Case of Psychic Automatism, Including 'Speaking with Tongues,'" introduction by William James, *Proceedings of the Society for Psychical Research,* Vol. XII, 1896–97, p. 277.

in other tongues. It was then that the group began to wait expectantly, praying and meditating, and the baptism of the Holy Spirit came upon them, first one and then upon several, and they spoke in tongues. This new religious phenomenon soon attracted attention, and newspapers in Kansas City and St. Louis reported what was happening at Bethel Bible College. Many people came to see for themselves, and Parham with several of the students enthusiastically planned a missionary tour of the country. It did not come off. After two weeks of meetings, which began as front page news, the group returned to Topeka.

For two years there was no wide acceptance of this experience; there were a few "Pentecostal baptisms" or conversions but not an immediate acceptance of the message that this was the same thing which had happened to the apostles originally, with presumably the same effects. The Parhams went on with the school in Kansas City after the Topeka mansion was sold, and then went to Lawrence, Kansas, where he held services. In the spring of 1903 one of his first converts there, a woman who was a Wesleyan minister, invited him to conduct services in her mission in Nevada, Missouri. Meetings at El Dorado Springs, Missouri, where people came for treatment at the medicinal springs, and then in Galen, Kansas, followed. There were many experiences of tongues, and many sick brought for healing. One healing was reported, and then another. The meetings were crowded, and at home the Parhams were besieged with requests for prayer for the sick. They went on to other small towns, with somewhat less success, but still attracting people from a wide area. Then early in 1905 an invitation came from Orchard, Texas, where a woman who had worked with Parham was trying to conduct her own mission. He preached there on Easter Sunday, and in two weeks almost an entire community had received his full gospel message.

The Parhams returned to Texas in the summer that year, and in Houston and a number of other cities the revival continued to grow. The experience of tongues was received by scores of people, and the healings and other amazing experiences continued to occur. In December he established a Bible school in Houston, similar to the Topeka college, and it was from here that Pentecostalism reached Los Angeles and really began to mushroom.

PENTECOSTAL BEGINNINGS IN LOS ANGELES

Los Angeles is now known as the mecca of strange religious groups, but in the early days of this century, it was considered the place where a revivalist would be least likely to succeed. Most of the Protestant churches had failed more than once before becoming established. Here, where oil fields and movies provided all that most people were looking for, the Pentecostal church took form. In 1906 a Negro woman, Neeley Terry, who had been visiting friends in Texas, brought back the story of receiving a baptism of the Spirit and the gift of tongues. The small mission church of which she was a member listened and promptly invited the evangelist William J. Seymour to come and preach. He came in April 1906.

But Seymour stirred up quite different responses in different hearers. He was one-eyed, unprepossessing in manner, and rather careless about his person. He was also positive about the message he had to bring, even though he had not spoken in tongues himself. He preached the first Sunday morning, April 1, talking about the second chapter of Acts and what should happen today, and then went home with one of the members for dinner. When they returned for the scheduled afternoon service, they found the mission locked. He was told that he could not preach such a doctrine from their pulpit again, and so, with no place to go, he went back home with the same family, none too welcome a guest. It was two or three nights later that he asked them to join him in prayer, and a different feeling about him began to grow. Several members of the church dropped by to find out what had happened to him. One of their friends was a Baptist minister who asked him to hold a prayer meeting in her home. And then people began to pray for this experience of which he spoke. A protracted prayer meeting began in the Baptist home. Meanwhile Seymour's host had a vision of the apostolic experience and he asked to receive it. In spite of Seymour's protest, "No, the Lord wants me to lay hands suddenly on no man,"[16] he continued to ask that evening, April 9. Finally, hands were laid on him and he fell to the floor as if unconscious, and spoke a few words in tongues. With Seymour he then went immediately to the Baptist home where a group were at prayer. As he walked in, he began to speak fluently in tongues. Suddenly there were seven voices, as those who were praying were "struck from their chairs," as one of them described it, and received the same experience.

For three days and nights the little house was filled with people praying and rejoicing, continuously and loudly. People came from all over until the streets around were crowded. The Negro group was soon joined by white people and outgrew the house in which they were assembling. (This is one way to accomplish integration.) It was then that an old livery stable on Azusa Street, which had been renovated as a church but not used for a long time, was found, and space was cleared to make a church in it again. For the next years this Azusa Mission was the center of Pentecostalism. People came from all over the country to receive baptism of the Spirit with the evidential sign of tongues. Pastors came from all over the country and carried back the news and also the experience in a chain reaction which has produced Pentecostal churches numbering nearly two million members in fifty years. Not only the Assemblies of God, the largest group, but the Foursquare church and a dozen others spring from this original prayer meeting in 1906. In all there are twenty-six church bodies which trace their experience with tongues and their

16. Frank J. Ewart, *The Phenomenon of Pentecost.* St. Louis, Missouri, Pentecostal Publishing House, 1947, p. 39.

Pentecostal doctrine of tongues to the events we have described.

Meanwhile across the sea in Wales there had arisen a mighty religious revival, and amid the magnificent Welsh singing, tongues broke forth there. It is interesting that, while the experience was observed and reported in 1904, there is at least one quite thorough account of the revival which makes no mention of speaking in tongues.[17] But the European press carried detailed accounts of the movement which began a little later in Norway and North Germany, and especially of a long Pentecostal revival held in Zürich in the fall of 1910. The occurrence was world-wide, part of a torrent of religious fervor. It was in the air, from India and Australia to Kansas, and instances could be multiplied to describe the gift with its characteristic unknown or occasionally recognizable languages, its sense of fulfillment and new life, its contagious vitality and joy. In many of the instances which occurred in this first twentieth-century revival there was also an emotional release with weeping, moaning and shaking, which was often thoroughly described and has since been so universally connected with tongues. One story in particular links together these far-flung occurrences with the stream which began to flow from Los Angeles.

VISIONS IN KARA KALA

It is told that in the year 1855, at the time the Pentecostal experiences we have mentioned in Russia were taking place, an eleven-year-old Russian boy in the village of Kara Kala in Armenia received a series of prophetic visions. During the period of a week in which he neither slept nor ate, this uneducated child produced a sheaf of intricate pictures, maps, and charts with a variety of written text, sometimes scrawled,

17. Mrs. Penn-Lewis, *The Awakening in Wales (1904–5)*. Leicester, England, Overcomer Book Room, 1922.

sometimes in beautiful handwriting. He foretold the end of peace and prophesied that the Turks would turn on the Christians and that those who were to go to a land across the ocean would be saved and blessed. The boy's visions were studied and pondered over, and he grew up in the village, respected as a prophet but with some wonder as the years passed and no great event took place. Then, about twenty-five years later, the experiences of the Holy Spirit which were similar to those in Russia began to take place in that area of Armenia. Many people spoke in tongues, and again as in Russia a small group, mainly Armenian Presbyterians with the prophet among them, banded together in Pentecostal worship.

Among this group was the Shakarian family in Kara Kala, whose name has become well known to Pentecostals across the United States and in many other places in the 1960s. These and the following events have been preserved and handed down in the records of this family, who were one of the first to receive the gift of tongues in Armenia in 1880. The father and head of the Shakarian family had not accepted the evidence of glossolalia either for himself or even as coming from God, though he attended and helped with their services of worship. It happened, however, that his son Demos spoke fluent Russian, and when the Russian Pentecostal community learned a few years later of the group similar to their own in Armenia, they began to make periodic visits, coming by covered wagon to share in worship and fellowship. It fell to Demos Shakarian to arrange homes for the visitors, provide their place of worship, and welcome them with a feast. Ritual required that he provide the best steer from his herd for this important occasion.

The story is told that this Armenian Presbyterian was notified one year that the Russian wagons were approaching and went out to find that his fattest steer had been blemished by the loss of an eye. Rather than break with his own ideas of providing the best, he quickly slaughtered it and hid the head in a sack under the wheat in his barn. After the visitors arrived, everything went as usual until a Russian elder was to bless the family and their offering of beef. The prophet had been standing by watching when suddenly he walked out of the room and the ritual halted. The elder began a hymn, not wanting to go on in his absence. In the midst of it the prophet returned with a sack in his hands which he opened in front of the kneeling family, telling how God had spoken to him in the moment before the blessing was to begin. Demos then confessed and was forgiven by the whole congregation, and two things happened. His father accepted completely the spiritual manifestations they had experienced as the work of God, and the entire community, both Russian and Armenian, determined to offer to God exactly what was required of them, no matter what their personal judgments might be.

And so in 1900, when the prophet began to speak warnings "out of a clear sky" that the time had come for the fulfillment of his original revelations, he had listeners, and the word was spread among both the Russian and Armenian groups. In the same year an exodus began. It continued until 1912, two years before Turkish destruction of the village, and by then the last of the Pentecostal families had left Kara Kala, taking with them the written prophecies, the family memories and stories, and their own knowledge of experiences through which God is known. The Shakarian family came to Los Angeles, where their home again became the place where Armenian and Russian Pentecostals gathered to worship.

One day in 1906 Demos Shakarian, his brother-in-law, and another Armenian friend were walking down San Pedro Street in Los Angeles not long after their arrival there, when they heard from a little side street sounds of worship that were familiar. They walked up to an old building on Azusa Street and to their amazement found people, other people right here in America, speaking in tongues. It appears, as these events have been related by Thomas R. Nickel in *The Amazing Shakarian Story,* that two streams of Pentecostal tradition had met in Los Angeles and that something was bound to happen.

It is in twentieth-century United States that speaking in tongues has come into its own and become a significant movement. In this country glossolalia is now found among three quite different groups. It is found among the Pentecostal churches, among certain fundamentalist churches, and in the past few years among the clergy and lay people of the large and well-known Protestant churches. Before we go on to describe the history and practice of each of these groups in which tongue speaking is found today, let us sketch the religious conditions in America which prepared the way for the development of the powerful tongues movement.

Chapter IV

THE PENTECOSTAL CHURCHES

The Pentecostal movement is more than an experience of tongues; it is a theory about tongues, a theology of tongues. Pentecostalism, in fact, did not begin as a movement until people had begun to think about the experience of tongues and see it as the keystone of a religious life. It is true, there had been experiences of tongues as early as 1875 among people in the United States, especially in the Holiness movement, and they were not experiences which had been sought just for "kicks." But the men and women who were involved in these revivals accepted whatever emotional reactions were given—and sometimes they were closer to a surfers' stomp than to prayer—without examining them very closely. Until the experience of tongue speaking was separated from these particular reactions and identified with events in the Bible, it was not especially valued.

W. Jethro Walthall, an early leader of the Pentecostal movement, has described what was happening. He had had an experience of tongues in 1879, but it was nearly thirty years before he saw its meaning. "At the time I was filled with the Spirit," he wrote, "I could not say what I did, but I was carried out of myself for the time being. Sometimes in the services and sometimes when alone in prayer, I would fall prostrate under God's mighty power. Once, under a great spiritual agitation, I spoke in tongues. I knew nothing of the Bible teaching about the Baptism or speaking in tongues, and thought nothing of what had happened in my experience."[1] The thought did not seem to occur even to the "gift people" that speaking in tongues might have a meaning in itself.

It is significant that when this thought did occur, it was in a Bible school, not in a revival meeting. Speaking in tongues simply had no chance to be valued, more or less, among the automatic responses to camp-meeting emotionalism. But when it occurred in the atmosphere of a Bible school, as it did in Topeka in 1901, it happened among people who had been thinking about the relationship of the experience to other events and trying to see its place theologically. When the outpouring of tongues did come, it was not only the overwhelming individual experience they were seeking; more than that, it was understood as a twentieth-century return to the experience at Pentecost which started the apostolic church. A group of students came to believe that tongues was the sign, the one sign, that the Holy Spirit had been given; it was the only indispensable evidence of an infilling of the Holy Spirit. With the development of this theology modern Pentecostalism was born.

THE HOLINESS MOVEMENT

If we are to understand Pentecostal practice, then, we shall have to know what they believe, and this theology has to be understood in terms of the soil from which it sprang—the nineteenth-century Holiness movement. This was a revival movement, almost exclusively Methodist in the beginning, which started immediately after the Civil War. No writer on the religious movements in this country has any trouble explaining this particular development.

The breakdown of authoritative, governmentally enforced orthodoxy, beginning in the late eighteenth century, had

1. Stanley H. Frodsham, *With Signs Following: The Story of the Pentecostal Revival in the Twentieth Century*. Springfield, Missouri, The Gospel Publishing House, 1941, pp. 11 f.

helped to make men more free; they were able to choose the religious way which pleased them. Many members of the major Protestant denominations, freed from the necessity of accepting traditional orthodoxy, began to propose religious ideas which were in keeping with the rising rationalism and materialism of that time. On the other hand, those who believed that the major churches were abandoning the true faith in accepting these ideas were also free to react by forming their own multiplicity of sects. The Holiness movement was a central part of this reaction. It denied three essential aspects of the growing Protestant liberalism.

Darwin's theories were published in the latter part of the nineteenth century and in the German universities where Darwin had his principal interpreter, Haeckel, the theologians were suddenly discovering the advantages of higher Biblical criticism. At the same time the textual critics were getting a new translation ready for the British and American public. The church, it seemed to many, was about to be left with a book on its hands that could no more be studied for literal truth than the novels of Charles Dickens. Against these ideas the Holiness movement affirmed vociferously the literal inspiration of the Bible.

It was about this time that Horace Bushnell's *Christian Nurture* became popular among Protestants, with its idea that man did not need an experience of conversion. This reaction to puritanical Calvinism, published in 1861, proposed in place of conversion that a child nurtured properly in the right Christian environment would simply grow into the full stature of Christian life, a rational, respectable, none-too-enthusiastic Christian life. Against this idea the Holiness movement proposed that Christian nurture was not enough, that man needed a personal and individual experience of salvation.

The social conditions in America following the Civil War fill the history books; the conditions of labor in contrast with growing wealth, the political corruption and individual vice and drunkenness, the big churches and their schools (with their cushioned pews and well-endowed budgets) all demanded a program on the part of the church. The major churches, following the basic philosophy of Bushnell, chose evolution over enthusiasm. The social gospel became the teaching of most churches, and it was widely accepted that the task of the church was to reform the world. The Holiness movement offered the alternative of transformation from within. It provided an enthusiastic religion to compensate for what it considered the worldliness and coldness of most of the churches. Holiness stressed the moral perfection of the individual; it saw the ability to give up alcohol, tobacco, and many similar interests as signs that the individual was achieving this state.

Since none of the major churches accepted these three Holiness ideas, the movement began to develop a separate life of its own. The major churches responded by condemning those who had separated from the older and better established church bodies. For instance, in 1870 the bishops of the Methodist Episcopal Church, South, were for a powerful revival of scriptural holiness to counteract the low spiritual state of the country, but twenty-four years later the same bishops practically denounced the "party with holiness as a watchword."

The first general camp meeting of the National Holiness Movement was held at Vineland, New Jersey, in 1867, with Methodist support. This group expressed a belief in literal interpretation of the Bible. It believed in striving for moral perfection, and it believed that man needed a second experience of grace known as the "second blessing." It also used the techniques of emotional revivalism which swept the movement across the United States and brought millions of men, women, and children flocking to the camp meetings. They found religious experience here, an expression of man's religious emotions, which was simply not provided for in most of the conventional churches. At first the movement remained interdenominational, but as the opposition to Holiness practice and doctrine increased among orthodox Protestants, groups of people who had found the Holiness movement more meaningful than their traditional churches banded together to form Holiness churches.[2]

The unique theology which these sects produced was to have another effect as well, that of opening the door for Pentecostalism. Gradually the belief developed among them that there was a third blessing to be had by Christians. The first blessing was conversion, in which one surrendered himself to God in Christ and was baptized. The second was the experience of sanctification, in which one was given the ability to live the morally perfect life. The third was the final experience, the "baptism of burning love," the baptism of fire, of the Holy Spirit, in which one was filled with a more than human spiritual life valuable in itself. The Christian who wanted fullness of life sought all three of these blessings. One description of this understanding of the nature of the Christian life was James H. McConkey's *The Three-Fold Secret of the Holy Spirit,* written in 1897, which sold hundreds of thousands of copies.

The Bible students in Parham's Topeka school in 1900 had been asked to study the means by which this "greater revelation of His power" was given, and they had each decided that it was the New Testament baptism of the Holy Spirit which described some evidence of tongues in every place. It was when they sought this baptism themselves that the experience of tongues hit like a thunderbolt among them. They had no previous experience or knowledge of what particular effect it would produce on them; what they did have was their understanding of the meaning of the experience in historical Christianity. These men and women received their experience of tongues as they expectantly desired a renewal and revitalization of their religious lives. The experience came to them, not

2. Elmer T. Clark, *The Small Sects in America.* New York, Abingdon-Cokesbury Press, 1937 (rev. ed.), pp. 73 ff. and 102 ff. lists sixty separate Holiness and Pentecostal groups, which came into existence between 1880 and 1930.

in an atmosphere of revivalism or emotionalism, but rather as they waited quietly, emptied themselves of other preoccupations, and opened themselves to whatever might occur. Then an inner experience struck them and they spoke in tongues.

It is this meaning of tongues, as a New Testament experience invariably accompanying baptism with the Holy Spirit, which has persisted in Pentecostalism. In the converted livery stable in Los Angeles the experience of speaking in tongues took hold and became an alternative to emotional revivalism. It attracted men and women all over the country who were interested in a renewal of spiritual life which conformed to New Testament practices. While a good bit of revivalism was still mixed with the experience in the Azusa Street Mission in 1906, yet it appears that many people who shied away from camp meetings were able to find a lasting fulfillment in the Pentecostal experience of tongues. It was obviously an expression which was genuine for them, seemed theologically sound, and also had a continuing religious value which the indiscriminate emotionalism of the camp meeting did not have.

THE CHRISTIAN AND MISSIONARY ALLIANCE

During the first years of the Pentecostal movement, another valuation of glossolalia developed which also accepts the experience as a genuine gift of the Spirit, but not by any means a necessary part of every infilling with the Holy Spirit. This view was given its classic statement by Dr. A. B. Simpson, leader of the Christian and Missionary Alliance, in 1907. This church, which is very active in a wide field today, had originated in 1887 as a non-denominational group which became one of the largest and most influential of the Holiness sects. In the early days of tongue speaking the experience was sought and received by a number of leaders within the Alliance as they opened themselves to the fullness of Christian experience. A problem in point of view arose when several

Alliance leaders who had experienced tongue speaking began to preach what was to become the confirmed Pentecostal doctrine, that speaking in tongues was essential to any true baptism with the Holy Spirit. Dr. Simpson's statement was written as a report defining the position of the Alliance when a sharp division arose over the value of the experience of tongues.

This report began by calling attention to the great interest in speaking in tongues at that time. Dr. Simpson was most concerned that the spirit of God be in no way limited or confined, and yet that the experience be carefully tested and weighed so that nothing counterfeit would be ascribed to God. He expressed the fear that the interest in tongues might lead to a greater concern for signs and wonders than for God himself, and then went on to note the divisions and controversies which interest in tongues had inspired. He also lamented that some of those who had received the gift had been treated with adulation. Tongues, he said, had seldom caused real trouble where wise pastoral leadership was given to a congregation and where tongues was not viewed as a necessary sign of being filled with God's grace. The presentation of Dr. Simpson's report in *The Alliance Witness* closes with these words:

> We believe the scriptural teaching to be that the gift of tongues is one of the gifts of the Spirit, and that it may be present in the normal Christian assembly as a sovereign bestowal of the Holy Spirit upon such as He wills. We do not believe that there is any scriptural evidence for the teaching that speaking in tongues is the sign of having been filled with the Holy Spirit, nor do we believe that it is the plan of God that all Christians should possess the gift of tongues. This gift is one of many gifts and is given to some for the benefit of all. The attitude toward the gift of tongues held by pastor and people should be "Seek not, forbid not." This we hold to be the part of wisdom for this hour.[3]

3. *The Alliance Witness*. Vol. 98, No. 9, May 1, 1963, p. 19.

This statement represents one of the two basic positive attitudes held by Christians today in regard to tongue speaking, and it is the belief of a large group of Christians. In 1963 when interest in tongues was rising again, the Christian and Missionary Alliance simply reprinted Dr. Simpson's statement, made to his council as president and general superintendent in 1907, in its official publication, *The Alliance Witness*. It was felt to be as clear and valid a statement as could be produced defining what is still the point of view of this church.

On this point, and on the basis of Dr. Simpson's definition of the relation of tongues and the Holy Spirit, those who believed in the Pentecostal experience as the necessary sign were forced to separate and form their own churches. Both groups have remained close to each other. When one prominent leader, F. F. Bosworth, found that he could no longer accept the basic Pentecostal belief, he was accepted back in the Christian and Missionary Alliance. Some Pentecostal churches accepted much from the Alliance in leadership and almost their entire doctrine. Hymns and books by Dr. Simpson and other Alliance leaders are in use in Pentecostal churches, and the largest and most influential of them, the Assemblies of God, has patterned its organization on that of the Alliance. In much the same way many of the Pentecostal churches have grown out of some Holiness sect.

THE PENTECOSTAL CHURCHES

Those who separated believed that their doctrine of tongues was a crucial one. They believed that without tongues there was no proof to one's self or his fellows that one had really received the Holy Spirit. And so some Christians whose greatest desire was to be filled with the Spirit have put primary emphasis on this doctrine which holds tongues to be *the* evidence. These men and women had been nurtured on the New Testament, in which the emphasis on being filled with the

Spirit is much more central than most modern Christians realize. Their one burning desire was to enter into the same supernatural experience which is described in the Book of Acts, and tongues became the door through which they entered this experience. They believed that they had been called by God to witness to a new Pentecost here in the first part of the twentieth century. Carl Brumback, the Assemblies of God historian, makes a point that the day on which tongues was first experienced among the students in Topeka, January 1, 1901, was actually the first day of the twentieth century. A new age had arrived which they had been called by God to usher in.

At first many of the groups called themselves the Church of the Latter Rain, pointing to the reference in James 5:7 to an early and latter rain. The early rain was believed to have been the first Pentecost which resulted in the early church, and the latter rain had now come in their Pentecostal experience. The sign of the new spiritual outpouring was the gift of tongues.

It is interesting that the Pentecostals were not alone in their speculations about the coming of a new age. At the same time Freud had waited for the turn of the century to publish his monumental *Interpretation of Dreams,* and later another psychologist, speculating on history, saw this time as the beginning of a new age. The idea was in the air.

Theologically the Pentecostals are fundamentalists with two distinctive beliefs. Their basic fundamentalism was settled in 1910 with the publication of the five beliefs on which this faith is founded: the inerrancy of the Scriptures, the virgin birth, the substitutionary atonement, the physical resurrection, and the imminent physical return of the Lord Jesus Christ. In addition Pentecostals add their own two articles of faith. They believe that tongues is the evidence of being filled with the Holy Spirit; even more important, they believe that this is the only experience a Christian needs in order to have the fullness of Christian life. The gift of tongues is not had by holiness in personal life, nor does it come on the heels of any gift of sanctification. Desiring the experience and waiting upon God (tarrying) for it are the real essentials. This experience of baptism in the Holy Spirit is known as the finished work, the beginning and end of Christian experience. Once received, the experience only has to be retained and applied to life. It becomes the foundation upon which the Christian life is built, the essential Christian experience. In this context of belief, it is not so hard to see why glossolalia has become such an important phenomenon in the lives of millions of people seeking for religious fulfillment.

From a strictly scriptural point of view the Pentecostal position is a little difficult to support, because more than one idea about tongues is expressed in the New Testament. The descriptions in the Book of Acts do tell of an evidential sign that the Holy Spirit has fallen on believing men and possessed them. But Paul's long analyses for the Corinthians describe tongues as a part of group, or private, devotional practice. Paul even asks the question, "Do all speak with tongues?" obviously expecting a negative answer. The Pentecostals simply keep these two passages straight and parallel. There are two kinds of tongues. First is the evidential sign in Acts which a Christian must have if he is really to be a Christian at all, and then there is one of several spiritual gifts which Paul discusses as a gift for the upbuilding and strengthening of the church. Everyone must have the first gift of tongues at his spiritual birth, but only a few chosen ones need continue its exercise after that; the Holy Spirit, it is apparently believed, manifests itself in two different experiences of tongues.

Underlining their doctrines about tongues is one more major Pentecostal belief. The Christian who receives spiritual baptism and speaks in tongues then enters into a charismatic life in which he is open to receive all of the other gifts of the Spirit. He will manifest the gifts of healing and discernment of spirits, of knowledge and wisdom, of faith and miraculous powers, of prophecy and also the continued use of tongues with a different significance. They believe that the fruits of love and compassion and brotherhood also flow from the Spirit as one receives it in an experience of tongues.

Then there are the lesser fruits. Although the publications do not often mention them in this connection, it appears to be a popular conviction among Pentecostals that possessing the Spirit will result in the ability to give up smoking, drinking, and other such habits. This ability gets a good deal of practical stress. The Holiness background of the Pentecostal churches is evident, and this may be one very good reason why the experience of tongues, in spite of the high value Pentecostals and even some non-Pentecostals put on it, was so long in reaching other Christians. While Pentecostals said they did not believe that Christian virtue was a prerequisite for an experience of tongues, they still stressed moral perfectionism as a result, much as in the older Holiness patterns, and very much like the early Christians who insisted on Jewish righteousness. Tongue speaking in the older denominations has had significance simply in showing that the experience can occur apart from either Holiness practice or fundamentalistic doctrine.

THE KEY TO PENTECOSTALISM

The key to Pentecostalism, however, is the belief that "the *full* New Testament baptism in the Spirit was made manifest by the *glossolalia,* and that it was the will of God to pour out His Spirit in this manner upon all flesh."[4] The importance of this belief is shown by the number of pamphlets and manuals providing instruction on how to prepare a candidate who wishes to receive the baptism of the Spirit with tongues. In my hand is the *Teacher's Manual on the Holy Spirit* by Frank M. Boyd, recent but undated, from the Assemblies of

4. Carl Brumback, *Suddenly . . . from Heaven.* Springfield, Missouri, The Gospel Publishing House, 1961, p. 92.

God official publications center, the Gospel Publishing House in Springfield, Missouri. This booklet outlines a theological background for tongues and then instructs on how to receive. There is no emotionalism suggested; instead the candidate is to read, to examine himself, prepare really to seek and possibly to wait, and to be consecrated and assured. The laying on of hands is described, but there are a good many more words warning the teacher not to use repetitious phrases or buzz with helpful instructions, or to believe that he does anything more than offer the atmosphere of his own praise.

Another booklet offers these seven instructions for dealing with the candidate:

1. Help the candidate see that the gift is already given and all that he has to do is to receive it.
2. Lead him to realize that anyone who is saved through baptism is prepared to receive the baptism of the Spirit.
3. Tell him that when hands are laid on him he is to receive the Holy Spirit.
4. Tell the candidate that he is to expect the Spirit to move on his vocal chords, but that he must cooperate with the experience as well.
5. Tell him to throw away all fear that this experience might be false.
6. Tell him to open his mouth wide and breathe as deeply as possible at the same time telling himself that he is receiving the Spirit now.
7. Don't crowd around and give all sorts of instructions. Keep an atmosphere of unity and devotion and quiet.[5]

Both of these manuals suggest very much the quiet atmosphere of a prayer group and an expectation of finding spiritual reality, rather than a need to force emotional release. They

5. J. E. Stiles, *The Gift of the Holy Spirit.* P.O. Box 3417, Burbank, California, undated, p. 104. This booklet, which is in use today, was written a number of years ago out of Stiles' many years of experience with the Assemblies of God. According to his widow, with whom we have talked, it represents his own contributions, including certain matters on which he could not agree wholeheartedly with Assemblies of God doctrine.

are both moderately good-humored about the human beings who are, of course, involved.

The actual accounts of Pentecostal experiences of speaking in tongues are legion; thousands have been published in *The Pentecostal Evangel* alone, each written in the belief that the individual was filled with the Holy Spirit. Carl Brumback gives many examples of experiences from the history of the movement, all of which follow a rather distinct pattern. Since the accounts are very similar to other descriptions we have included, we have chosen only one particularly interesting Pentecostal example to cite. The following account, which has been reproduced in the experience of Pentecostal believers literally thousands of times, seems particularly worth quoting since it was the *first experience* in the present Pentecostal revival of speaking in tongues. Agnes N. Ozman, later Mrs. LaBerge, wrote of her experience:

> I had been a Bible student for some years, and had attended T. C. Horton's Bible School at St. Paul, Minnesota, and A. B. Simpson's Bible School in New York City. . . . In the fall of 1900 I was in Kansas City and heard that a Bible School was to be opened at Topeka, Kansas. I had a desire to go to this school, and asked the Lord if it was His plan for me to go to provide the fare.
>
> We studied the Bible by day and did much work downtown at night. . . . Prayer was offered night and day continually in a special upper room set apart as a prayer tower. I had many blessed hours of prayer in this upper room during the night watches . . . Like some others, I thought that I had received the baptism of the Holy Ghost at a time of consecration, but when I learned that the Holy Spirit was yet to be poured out in greater fulness, my heart became hungry for the promised Comforter, and I began to cry out for an enduement of power from on high. At times, I longed more for the Holy Spirit to come than for my necessary food. At night I had a greater desire for Him than for sleep . . .
>
> During the first day of 1901, the presence of the Lord was

with us in a marked way, stilling hearts to wait upon Him for greater things. The spirit of prayer was upon us in the evening. It was nearly eleven o'clock when it came into my heart to ask that hands might be laid upon me that I might receive the gift of the Holy Ghost. As hands were laid upon my head, the Holy Spirit fell upon me, and I began to speak in tongues, glorifying God . . . It was as though rivers of living water were proceeding from my innermost being.[6]

YEARS OF RAPID GROWTH

The early days of Pentecostalism, from 1907 to 1940, were years of rapid growth. During this period the movement displayed many characteristics which repelled people who might otherwise have been interested, and brought criticism upon it which still clings to the movement in the minds of many. The modern spokesmen for the Pentecostal churches have acknowledged the failings and excesses of these early days and speak with regret about them.

At that time there was no central organization among these churches and some of them went off on doctrinal tangents and allowed practices which resulted in bedlam and confusion. Many of the churches were served by ministers who had no ordination except that of the Holy Spirit and speaking in tongues. They were often lacking in education, sometimes not even well versed in the Bible. The churches were anything but permanent and the ministers came and went. Since these leaders were concerned about little but enthusiasm in their services, they would use any device to achieve it. And the services frequently did approximate the stereotype which many people have of wild Pentecostal worship. The fear of cutting off the source of the Spirit if they stopped its flow resulted in a fanaticism about their church and their way of religion. Believing that they alone had the right way, they developed an exclusive attitude (these bodies are still not a

6. Brumback, *op. cit.*, pp. 23 f.

part of the large federations of Christians), which in turn led to proselyting among other Christian groups and did not enhance their acceptance as a Christian group. Another real problem was the fact that many of the leaders of the movement did come into serious moral difficulties. There were more than a few scandals involving the ministers of these churches. They were often men who had had little spiritual training before their religious experience, and they were not able to meet the difficult situations in which ministering to people places a person.

Pentecostals are often far more self-critical than most people realize. They are well aware of the difficulties inherent in their religious way, and those in the major Pentecostal bodies are trying to correct the abuses of other days. Indeed the editor of the English magazine *Pentecost* recently wrote an open letter to individuals in the historic churches who are being reached by the Pentecostal experience of tongues. Donald Gee, who has been a leader of the Assemblies of God in England for many years, warns these newcomers to the movement to avoid the excesses of some of the older pastors and evangelists which once kept the movement from being understood. He puts a good deal of mature thinking—wisdom, in fact, which has developed out of Pentecostal practice—into a few words. Since he demonstrates the attitude of the better established Pentecostal churches of today, we can do no better than to quote his six suggestions as representative of their thinking:

> May we be allowed, after long experience, to respectfully offer a few words of brotherly counsel? Do not allow the first rush of novelty where prophetic gifts are concerned to sweep you off your feet. It is all so wonderful, and is such a liberation of spirit, that it is easy to become unbalanced, with speedy disaster. Do not fail the purpose of God. Beware of making too much of "messages," whether through tongues and interpretation, or in any other way. The Spirit of God is not so prodigal with these things as we, in our folly, would have Him

to be. The Bible plainly teaches temperance in the use of inspirational gifts. . . . Above all, keep everything Christ-centered. A great illumination was in A. B. Simpson's hymn:

Once it was the blessing, Now it is the Lord:
Once it was the feeling, Now it is His word;
Once His gifts I wanted, Now the Giver own;
Once I sought for healing, Now Himself alone.

Never let your exercise of prophetic gifts cause your meetings to degenerate into what one writer caustically described as a "tongues club."

Be evangelistic above all. The baptism in the Holy Spirit is for power to witness to a Risen Christ who saves and keeps. Seek always to win souls. The greatest victories of the world-wide Pentecostal Revival have occurred where the Movement has been first and foremost an agency for fervent evangelism.

May we, with great humility of mind, offer another word of advice. Many of you are trained theologians with a good academic background. Do not, now you have tasted spiritual gifts, become fanatical in your repudiation of consecrated scholarship. Let the Spirit of truth set it all on fire and use it for the glory of God. Some of us in our early folly set a premium upon ignorance. Nothing could be a greater mistake when it comes to leadership. And leaders are needed.[7]

The distinctive doctrine and experience of the Pentecostals evidently have great value and meaning to many people. The movement has grown like the Sierra freshets in the spring. It has far outstripped the Holiness movement from which it sprang. From the Assemblies of God, with over half a million members in the United States alone, to the Pentecostal Fire-Baptized Holiness Church (573 at last count), there are twenty-six bodies which consider themselves a part of the Pentecostal movement today. They must be meeting a need which is not being met elsewhere in Christendom.

While it is impossible to give an account of all these groups, the Assemblies of God as the largest is a good representative

7. Editorial by Donald Gee in *Pentecost,* London, No. 58, December 1961 to February 1962. Reprinted in *Trinity,* Eastertide, 1962, Vol. 1, No. 3, pp. 51 f.

of the movement as a whole. Also, they have kept statistics since 1925. From 1925 to 1962 their membership rose from 50,386 to 514,317, the number of their ordained ministers from barely a thousand to nearly ten thousand, and the number of their churches at nearly the same rate. Their churches are found in every city of any size in the United States. They gave six million dollars to missions in 1960, had over twelve thousand missionaries in the field, and had made nearly a million converts in foreign lands. In Springfield, Missouri, the general staff runs a well-equipped modern headquarters, keeps in close touch with member churches, supervises the missionary work of the church, and operates a large publishing house. They maintain colleges and Bible schools in many places in the country. The tent has been given a new flat roof, and it is interesting to hear Pentecostals themselves admit that ". . . there is a general lessening of fervor and discipline in the Assemblies of God in America. This frank admission is not a wholly new sentiment, for down through the years in the pages of *The Pentecostal Evangel* and other periodicals correspondents have asked, 'Is Pentecost the revival it was in the beginning?' "[8]

Three other Pentecostal churches, together with the Assemblies of God, comprise the majority of Pentecostals in the United States. The United Pentecostal Church is similiar to the Assemblies of God in most matters of doctrine and practice. It was formed in 1931 by a merger of Pentecostal groups which had remained independent. This group stresses the "oneness" of God as against the more traditional Trinitarian position, seeing the members of the Trinity as mere aspects of the same God. It has grown rapidly to 175,000 members in the most recent census of churches. The other two large Pentecostal groups are Holiness Pentecostal churches. They disagree with the Assemblies of God belief that the experience of salvation is enough, but maintain that personal holiness is a necessary prerequisite for salvation.

8. Brumback, *Suddenly . . . from Heaven,* op. cit., pp. 349 f.

They have simply added another basic belief to the Holiness doctrine. In order to find salvation the individual must follow the way of Holiness *and* have the experience of baptism with the Holy Spirit in which he speaks in tongues.

One of these is the very large and loosely organized Church of God in Christ. This is primarily a Negro church, founded by C. H. Mason, who received his baptism of the Spirit at the Azusa Street Mission in 1906. The group lays little emphasis on formal education and has little control over the separate congregations. The older camp-meeting atmosphere is often found within these churches. This church as a whole has shown phenomenal growth, reporting over 400,000 members in 1963, while it claimed only 31,000 in 1936. It is the second largest Pentecostal group.

The oldest Pentecostal church in this country is third in size. It is the Church of God which was started in 1886. Early in this church's beginnings, in a revival held at Camp Creek, North Carolina, a number of people spoke in tongues, but apparently did not know what was happening to them, and the experience did not persist among them. The church took form as a typical Holiness body and remained so until their annual assembly in 1908 at which the principal speaker had come fresh from the revival at Azusa Street. After this time the experience of tongues became a part of the records of the church and this group became a Pentecostal church. Several other Churches of God have split off from this original body, and still this church records over 175,000 members in 1963. As in its sister Negro church, more enthusiastic practices and more emotionalism are to be found within this group than in the Assemblies of God.

THE FULL GOSPEL BUSINESS MEN'S FELLOWSHIP

In addition to the Pentecostal church groups there is a full-grown, or rather a growing, twelve-year-old lay organization of Pentecostal believers known as the Full Gospel Business

Men's Fellowship International. Its founder and international president is Demos Shakarian, grandson of the Demos Shakarian who came to this country from Armenia and whose story we have sketched. He has also related some interesting facts of his own surrounding the founding of this organization.

They start with his experiences after a childhood injury which left him almost deaf, and knowing he must pray. Three years later he was sitting at worship in church when the Holy Spirit filled him and for four hours he spoke in other tongues, unable to say a word in any of the three languages he actually knew. When he reached home after this experience, the thirteen-year-old boy was struck again. He tells of lying helpless on the floor while three times he heard the voice of God ask, "Demos, will you ever doubt my power?" Each time he answered that he would never doubt God's power, and from that time his hearing began to improve.

He also tells that in 1938, after he was married, he failed in business and desperate prayer led him to go out to a Los Angeles park and hold street meetings. What he says of this experience is that it was a hard one for the son of a successful business man, and was one that took the starch out of him. "From that time on I have never been afraid of man," he says. "Whether he is a ruler or a common laborer, I know he needs God; it is easy for me to talk to him about the Lord."[9] Shakarian began then to sponsor evangelistic and Pentecostal rallies, increasing in size as his business ventures became more successful. In 1951 he was in charge of location in Los Angeles for an Oral Roberts crusade and shared with the evangelist his dream of a full gospel group for business men. The encouragement he received was Roberts' offer to speak to a group; twenty-one men came to the first meeting.

His story tells of only obstacles for the next year, until

[9] William C. Armstrong, "A Decade of Divine Destiny," Full Gospel Business Men's *Voice*, October, 1963, Vol. XII, No. 10, p. 5.

one Friday night about midnight (the Los Angeles Fellowship meetings are held over breakfast at eight o'clock Saturday mornings) he announced to his wife that he intended to pray until he had an answer. Hours later he was still prostrate pouring out his troubles, when Mrs. Shakarian came into the room and sat down at their organ. As she played, she suddenly began to speak in tongues and then prophesy, "My son, I am with you . . . I am going to use you in a greater way . . . be not afraid . . ." Just then he saw a vision filling the room; the ceiling dissolved into a picture of millions of men, just men, arms folded as if they were dead. She went on, not knowing that he was possessed by a vision, ". . . the very thing that you see before you now, will come to pass." And he saw the dead men throw up their arms and begin to praise God. As he says, it was a picture of just what the business men do in Full Gospel Business Men's Fellowship meetings all over the country.

The next morning an offer for the publication of a magazine, the *Voice* (which now shows a distribution of around 250,000 copies), came from a man who had driven all night to be at the meeting. New members soon began to pour in with enthusiasm for starting new chapters and holding conventions. With incorporation and the establishment of a headquarters office in July 1953, and the first convention in October of that year, the Fellowship marks 1963 as the tenth anniversary year. While no membership statistics are published, the *Voice* speaks of "hundreds of chapters" all over the United States and as far away as Melbourne, Australia, Hong Kong, and Pretoria, South Africa. In the past months eight chapters have been started in Texas alone. Leaders at the 1963 convention, held in one of the larger New York City hotels, spoke of more than 100,000 members and millions of adherents.

Through the *Voice* there are told the stories of people from all over the country who have received an experience of the Holy Spirit with tongues, often in association with the

Fellowship. A number of the experiences described in the next chapter were originally published in this magazine, which includes the accounts of men and women, both lay and clergy, of many different faiths. Mr. Shakarian's own church, the Armenian Pentecostal Church in Los Angeles, he has described to us as an independent body, governed and ministered to by men chosen from among its lay members. He also tells us that during the 1940s he initiated meetings among the Pentecostal ministers in central and southern California which he feels helped these independent church bodies to form the Pentecostal organizations and assemblies which exist today.

Basically the Fellowship is a man's organization, headed exclusively by laymen, to provide association for those who have had the experience of being filled with the Holy Spirit and have spoken in tongues, and to gain new converts to "full gospel" religious experience. Many of the members are successful business men who have had the Pentecostal experience and seek fellowship with other men like themselves who are interested in the effect this experience has had in their daily lives. While the group originated among Pentecostals, the membership now represents many different churches, and ministers from several denominations have spoken at the conventions; the Rev. James Brown, a Presbyterian minister in Pennsylvania, and the Rev. Dennis Bennett, an Episcopal minister, have been frequent speakers. Regular meetings of the group are in many ways quite similar to the Pentecostal services we are about to describe, but more informal.

PENTECOSTAL WORSHIP SERVICES

And what *is* a Pentecostal service like today? I have attended several, each of them interesting and distinctive in some way, and five, three regular and two revival services, are included in the following general descriptions. For those who would like to know more about such services, I will wager that one can be found close by, where you would be received warmly and graciously.

My first impression was at a moderate-sized church where I drove into the parking lot a minute or two late and immediately thought I must be confused about the time. There were too many people coming and going. But like most suburban churches it was simply the station-wagon bunch and their children chatting after the earlier service. I went on in to a church auditorium so plain as to have almost a whitewashed look. It was the singing which took the place of stained glass; the service started and moved on gospel songs full of imagery, sung out full with once in a while a little clapping. Twice a hymn was stopped to repeat an especially meaningful verse.

During the service there were three prayer times, each different except that in group prayer there is *always* an undercurrent of individual praise and beseeching, and also clear expressions of agreement like "Hallelujah!" Standing separated by silence, one gets the feeling that well! some people are not frightened into whispers by finding themselves in a church. The first prayer was asked of a man in the congregation, who spoke a direct message and spoke well. Then, later, in the midst of a prayer from the pulpit, a voice from behind me broke forth in tongues, lyric syllables, well-consonanted and not loud. Immediately after, a voice across the aisle spoke an interpretation which evidently had meaning for many of the congregation, and then the minister went on with his prayer. At the beginning of a final prayer time, the people were asked to tell their special requests. The organist spoke about her brother who wanted to stop drinking, others named sick friends, and several asked for thanksgiving or the ability to put up with troubles; then those who did not want to speak out were asked to join in the prayer, and a murmur came from all over, affirmations of need and half-audible words, as the minister spoke for the need of all. I felt quite at home with other parts of the service, the comparative texts from the Bible, a straightforward Biblical sermon, announcements with a laugh or two. At the blessing those who wanted special prayers were asked to come forward. None did, and I got up to find the man behind me ready to shake hands and welcome a stranger.

Another service I attended was in a large church in a larger city; the auditorium was big enough for at least eight hundred people, and comfortably filled. There were families together, some older people and also quite a few teen-agers. Most of the people were actually dressed better than I, and I particularly noticed the excellent taste of the women (or would it be, of their men?). Here, in a richer but still clean-cut building, the baptistry was the center of attention and behind it a picture of river and mountains with great depth. On the platform below, a choir in formal vestments took their seats informally during the first hymn, and the service began with a camp-meeting favorite.

The leadership passed back and forth between the pastor, his assistant and another man, with first requests for prayer and then a prayer from the pulpit. Again they were accompanied by the same soft voices from all over the congregation, a hum of definite, sustained pitch. Later the sick of the parish were mentioned and prayer offered for them. The assistant himself spoke in tongues in the midst of the service and also went on to interpret. Announcements were a signal for a friendly period; the newcomers, whose cards had been collected, were introduced and asked to stand. A red rose on the pulpit told of the birth of a baby, and with the organ softly playing the wedding march, the announcement of a wedding was read. Then, before communion, a child was brought forward by her parents and grandparents for dedication.

The pastor's sermonette, in preparation for communion, was short and to the point. As he finished, a clear, high voice spoke in tongues, and then a man's voice, with almost overpowering strength that was like being grasped physically.

Each in turn was interpreted by another person. Communion was quiet and moving; with the reading of the account of the last supper from Mark and prayers of consecration, the elements were brought to the people by the deacons of the church.

The service had been long. And so the minister put his prepared sermon aside for another text, and gave his message in fifteen extemporaneous minutes. He spoke on the difficulty of becoming centered when one is satisfied with material things and thus prevented from seeking the spiritual. Then, he concluded, there is real need for supernatural blessing to have a truly full life. During the concluding hymn, those who wished left, and others came to the front of the church for special prayer and rededication. There was a sense of humility, a trust in something beyond themselves. There was a spirit of power present, and quiet tears in many eyes. The people got up one by one and left, until the church was empty.

The one midweek Pentecostal service is chiefly interesting because it was very different from these, very similar to the big city revival, and there was no tongue speaking. In fact the similarity here was striking in spite of the fact that one is a smaller church in a mixed neighborhood and the other a big city church on the edge of a fine business district. For one thing I felt the strength of a friendly, accepting atmosphere in both churches. Both services, however, were pushed by the beat of music, of clapping, of praying that mounted in volume; and there were no interstices. The sermons were both theatrical. In the small church a young man who had grown up among them came to the pulpit to preach; he was not much more than a boy who is preparing to be an evangelist, and he preached on a text about Saul. He preached good sense, but he told the story with his whole body, striding and jerking into postures, and in a voice that often got clear away from him and the words he was saying. In the revival the sermon was an interpretation of Revelation which caught interest but not fire. The hour of prayer at the end of the service seemed to bring people down to earth, many of them to their knees facing their own problems; it did not bring them to the experience of tongue speaking.

In the high mountains near Los Angeles, where the Assemblies of God have a magnificent campsite, I attended vesper services at another revival, indeed another kind of revival. This meeting *was* held in a tent, with a nationally known evangelist as leader. There was the same music, the same prayer with spontaneity, the same pitched hum. There were also a variety of talks in a very informal atmosphere. A missionary from the leper colony in New Hope Town, Liberia, told of their problems. The president of a Bible college spoke on the necessity of education along with the Pentecostal experience. The evangelist was a cultivated and eloquent speaker who used "Awake, O sleepers . . ." from Ephesians to point out the need for action, for total giving, and for an experience of salvation. Once while he was speaking tongues broke forth, more forceful and loud than is often the case, and with interpretation. There were other speakers who told of their own experiences of giving up, often of drinking or smoking, and there was discussion of the place of more enthusiastic experiences in Pentecostalism, such as the experience of "dancing before the Lord." Glossolalia was heard three times in all during the service and did not seem out of place with its basic dignity. One remarkable feature, however, was the ability of the leaders to show affection for each other. The men were free enough, as they said goodbye perhaps for years, to embrace, to demonstrate real Christian affection. Is it possible that Paul was right, and there is a religious experience which reduces, instead of increases, our need for taboos?

None of these services was comparable to the old camp meeting. There was friendly sociability and a warmth of prayer and fellowship. There was freedom and lack of structure. In the small church and the large city revival there were theatrical elements, and overplaying a part to arouse the enthusiasm of certain people, but I saw nothing that could be called emotionalism; if anything, these strictly Bible-structured sermons were causing people to consider, not let go. Where there was tongue speaking, the interpretations sometimes spoke of punishment for sins; more often they directed people to seek God in particular ways, or simply spoke of the nearness of the Lord, and sometimes of the second coming. There were surprises for people who have known worship only in one mold. It is a different form of worship, based on Paul's description of Christian worship in I Corinthians 14, and similar in many ways to the informal prayer groups among non-Pentecostal tongue speakers which are described in the next chapter.

Tongue speaking has returned to the Christian church. In the early days of the Pentecostal movement there were many abuses connected with it. Abuses still occur. Tongue speaking has been the cause of division and conflict, but this is by no means the rule. Tongue speaking also occurs where there is harmony, and even good spirits. Millions of people have found the central experience of the Pentecostal churches a revitalizing one. In spite of the prejudice and scorn with which the Pentecostals have often been viewed by the more traditional Protestant denominations, some members of these churches, seeking a more dynamic religious life, found the Pentecostal experience a valuable one. They discovered new life in the tongues experience and brought it into the traditional churches, where it has become far from uncommon. In the past five years more and more Protestant churches have become aware of glossolalia, and many of these churches have appointed commissions to study tongue speaking, and pronouncements have been made by church officials. We turn now to the last chapter of the history of speaking in tongues—its spread among Christians outside the Pentecostal churches.

Chapter V

TONGUES IN THE TRADITIONAL CHURCHES

It is common knowledge that speaking in tongues has spread in recent years into the traditional Protestant denominations. Accounts of this development are to be found in religious publications and also in the secular press. As long as the practice remained within the Holiness and Pentecostal churches, it could be ignored. But now both clergy whose excellence of training cannot be overlooked and sophisticated laity in the major denominations have spoken not only for the personal value of the experience, but of its theological significance. As tongue speaking has come to be practiced by Christians of the large Protestant churches, the subject has inevitably become more interesting both as news and as a matter for church discussion.

In recent years there has been a rising dissatisfaction with the impact that Protestantism has been making upon the lives of men. The liberal tradition of modern Christianity has failed to satisfy the religious needs of many men. Some of these Christians have turned back to a more serious study of the New Testament and the more orthodox theological ideas. Among these seeking Christians there is also found an open interest in the Pentecostal experience their fellow Christians are having. And among these Protestants are those who have sought the Pentecostal experience and found it. These Christians have no desire to become members of a new church. Rather they want to bring the vitality of the tongues experience back into their own churches.

As one minister who speaks in tongues has put it, "I was very happy being a Baptist; I still am; I wish you were all Baptists!" As for the Pentecostal groups, the gift of tongues has been freely shared, apparently with rejoicing, and the "orthodox" newcomers have not changed the character of the original movement. Thus there are two major movements today, one among the Pentecostals and another among members of the better known Protestant denominational churches. They are quite separate and distinct. The latter group has developed a theology of tongues more congenial to its own general doctrine and practice.

THE MOVEMENT AND THE EXPERIENCES

It is difficult to give a picture of the tongue speaker in the non-Pentecostal churches. The movement is so new that few records of its development are available. Furthermore, it has not been an organized movement; tongue speaking outside the Pentecostal churches has been largely a spontaneous, individual experience. And so there are no statistics and few scheduled services. There is the magazine *Trinity*, and there are Christian Advance meetings, like conventions, which have been held in various California cities, the first in 1962, in which clergy and lay people gather together for fellowship and inspirational talks.

There is no official organization of tongue speakers, however, as there is an Order of St. Luke for those who are interested in Christian healing. The Rev. David du Plessis, a Pentecostal minister and former secretary of the World Pentecostal Fellowship, has entered upon a ministry to tongue speakers outside the Pentecostal churches. He has compiled a list of clergy of various denominations who speak in tongues, and he has also written of his experiences among what he calls the "denominational churches." This story has been published as a booklet entitled *The Spirit Bade Me Go.*

Many tongue speakers among the more staid Protestant churches are loath to let it be known that they have had the experience, since it is looked upon with real suspicion by so many church leaders and members of their congregations. Indeed one must be on "the in" if he is to discover many of those among the older Protestant denominations who have spoken in tongues. Of necessity the fellowship of tongue speakers in non-Pentecostal Protestantism has some of the characteristics of a secret society. Otherwise they are likely to expose themselves to ridicule or censure. For example, one candidate for the ministry in 1960 was denied acceptance in one of the major denominations when it was learned that he spoke in tongues.

For these reasons the full extent of tongue speaking within Protestantism is difficult to assess. There has been a widespread interest in this movement which extends beyond those who have experienced tongues. The discussions of the experience in the religious periodicals become more frequent and are often a generator of much warmth today. They indicate a much broader concern with this phenomenon than official church publications have usually pictured. My own lectures on the subject, given in February of 1963, drew a larger attendance and stimulated more interest than any other of my talks in months.

The best picture of the movement can be found in the pages of the magazine *Trinity*. It is published by a small group independently of any organized church and speaks for the movement through both lay and clerical contributions. The articles discuss not only questions such as the theological and psychological meaning of tongues, but also give many excellent case histories and news about those who are active in this ministry in the older established churches. The meetings of those who are interested in the movement are also reported in *Trinity*.

BEGINNINGS IN VAN NUYS

It is not by chance that *Trinity* is published in Van Nuys, California, for it was from there that "orthodox" tongue speaking first broke into print in the national periodicals. The Rev. Dennis Bennett was the rector in 1960 of one of the largest Episcopal churches in the Diocese of Los Angeles, located in Van Nuys. He had originally come into the Episcopal church from the Congregational church, searching for a richer sacramental life. At Van Nuys he had accomplished a herculean task in building a magnificent church with a tremendous budget and requiring the work of three assistants. Still, he was looking for a deeper religious experience. This experience came to him through a friend, another Episcopal minister.

Father Bennett is also an acquaintance of mine. I was in close contact with him about the time that this experience came to him. The account which follows is his own account, drawn partly from what he told me at the time and partly from tape recordings of his talks which he has given me permission to use.

Father Bennett's friend talked with him about a couple who had been more regular in staying away than in attending his church; suddenly they began showing up every Sunday and made a pledge to tithe. This other minister was perplexed by their explanation of an experience of the Holy Spirit, but instead of finding that they had "gone off the deep end religiously" as he feared, he found that they were attracting a core group of a dozen or so who were equally enthusiastic about his church. The two priests, who at that time knew nothing of the history of the Holy Spirit revival, decided that this was worth investigating.

They met with the young couple in their home to talk, and then for several weeks as a regular study group; the Bible and other works were underlined and discussed. A few laymen from Father Bennett's church were invited to join the group from time to time, and others also came, both lay people and clergy, some of whom had spoken in tongues. Father Bennett came to the conclusion that these people had something, in fact an openness to God, which he wanted and needed. Essentially what they said, reverently although matter-of-factly, was that tongue speaking came "as a part of the package," and that it came as one prayed for the Holy Spirit and accepted that God would use one's voice in whatever way He saw fit. And so, when the group met one night, Father Bennett prayed together with them for a solid hour, and nothing happened. He went home thinking that perhaps it was not meant for him to have such an experience.

But his curiosity was much aroused, as was that of several of his fellow ministers, and one Saturday afternoon he went to the couple's home with another Episcopal priest. They sat talking in the living room; then as the couple instructed them, the four quietly prayed for twenty minutes or more, each speaking praise of God. Father Bennett describes that he then began to be able to form "words" and to speak and pray in "other words" which he did not recognize and which came out fully formed, not stammering or at all like baby-talk babble or gibberish. He spoke for several minutes and then stopped, because he was tired. His feeling was that he had had a rather strange experience, but he did not feel spiritually moved or filled by it. In fact, it was as if someone who did not know anything about music had picked up a violin for the first time and played a concerto. When the others began to praise God for the gift, he simply said, "Yes, it's quite amazing; I see it can happen, but what does it mean?" "You'll see," was the answer.

By now with his curiosity thoroughly aroused, he and still another minister went back to the home a few days later when a small prayer group was meeting. There were about eight persons, all of whom had received the gift of tongues, and Father Bennett was a little self-conscious. His young layman friend suggested that the two of them go back into the den. Again, sitting in comfortable chairs across the room from each other, they prayed and praised God as the others were doing, and after a few minutes the "strange words" began to form. Again, he spoke them and, with the layman's encouragement not to stop but to let the words flow, he continued to speak, sounding to himself very much as if he were speaking fluent Russian. And again there was no particular emotion, no lift or fullness. As he has remarked, if someone had come into the room just then, he would have greeted and asked them to sit down because he was busy, and then gone back to speaking in tongues.

Then suddenly, he says, "I realized what I was doing. It became clear, perfectly clear. I knew that God the Holy Spirit, whom I had never *directly* experienced in my life before, was putting these words on my lips. He was guiding, and I was letting Him. He was not taking over; I had to *let* the 'words' come and I could stop at any time. But I was letting God guide my voice, and these words were being formed in a language I had never heard, saying and expressing to God the Father, through Christ, all of the things that I had always wanted to say to God but had never been able to say. I had not known how to say them in my own language. Somehow this new language was more eloquent!" With this came the certainty that the words were being understood, and that his whole spiritual life, the same spirit and the same life, had suddenly moved over to a new position, into a new realm. He went back into the front room to exclaim, "Do you mean that a Christian can feel like this!" When he describes the experience, he is explicit about the beauty and moving quality of tongue-speech; to hear an individual speak in tongues is like hearing the high spots of an opera, and an interpretation in English has the same flowing beauty. But he is also explicit that the emotion it arouses in the individual comes from the meeting with God, not from the fact of speaking in tongues.

Then Father Bennett went home feeling wonderful and (in his own words) "also thinking to myself, 'You feel wonderful tonight, but you've felt wonderful before!' I figured by morning I'd probably be saying with Elisha, 'Where is the Lord God of Elijah!' or wishing I could call up *my* minister and say, 'Will you just give me that again over the phone, because I somehow lost the touch!' But the feeling did not go away." Instead, the following Sunday he seemed to feel for the first time the real beauty and meaning of the services of his own church. There was the same quality in daily experience, not of emotional release but of emotional collection, as if God had moved into daily life. He found that even in sleep something in him praised God as he slept. As Fénelon once said, "Those who have the Holy Spirit go forward even in sleep." More than this, he found that what had happened to him was being imparted to others. He continued to lay hands on the sick, as had been his practice, only now they began to recover, and quite frequently. And others in his parish also began to have an experience similar to his own.

In fact, it was contagious. A few had been in contact with the original small group; some received a language spontaneously when they were alone, others in much the same way that he had. Soon in his parish there were over fifty persons who had spoken in tongues, including many of the most substantial and well-known members of the church. They met together in prayer groups quite similar to those described in the leaflet he has entitled *Pentecost* from which we have quoted at length at the end of this chapter.

Unfortunately conflict and division arose within the Van Nuys church. The non-tongue speakers could not accept the practice and the tongue speakers were not always discreet. The clergy on the staff were split among themselves, while controversy raged among the laity. In an attempt to restore unity Father Bennett resigned, knowing that if he were called back over a resignation, he could carry on the practice with the support of his vestry. The vestry, however, accepted his resignation, and there followed several bleak months until he was appointed vicar of a small mission in the center of Seattle, where he is now located, and which has grown phenomenally under his ministry.

Father Bennett is a very dynamic and personable man, and through him a number of other ministers became interested in the tongues movement within the non-Pentecostal churches. Other Episcopal ministers became involved and also ministers in the Methodist, Reformed, Baptist, Lutheran, and Presbyterian churches. In Van Nuys the prayer groups in which tongue speaking had occurred continued under the name of Holy Spirit Fellowships after they were separated from the church, and these groups have spread from the Los Angeles area into northern California cities and several other communities in which there are ministers who have been in touch with this experience.

Father Bennett was not the first of the non-Pentecostals to receive the gift of tongues, but he is one of the best known because of the attention which was drawn to him by his frank and able presentation of his experience and by his resignation which attracted national notice. Many others had a similar experience without the dubious recognition which Father Bennett received. For many years members of the more conservative churches seeking a revitalization of their Christian experience have turned to Pentecostal ministers or laity to receive this experience, and have received it. Another example of the experience of an Episcopal clergyman is described in the following letter, which I received in June of 1963. The writer is a clergyman with a master's degree in theology as well as his four years of college and three years of seminary training which are necessary for entering the Episcopal ministry. He is a scholarly man with a quiet reserve, who has also had some experience with psychotherapy and is anything but psychologically naïve. Few people even know that he speaks in tongues although he values the experience highly. His own words tell the story:

I first had the experience of speaking in tongues in Denver, Colorado, over twelve years ago, the summer after my graduation from college. I had spent the summer working on a farm in Iowa, and I had driven West to Denver to meet my mother and younger brother, and to travel with them on to Tucson. The first evening that I arrived in Denver my mother and brother explained what had just happened to them in a prayer group meeting in the home of some Pentecostal friends. It all sounded rather strange to me, but I read a few chapters in Brother Stiles' book, *The Baptism of the Holy Spirit,* looking up the Scriptural references. As I think back on it now, if I had had more time to study the subject, I think that it would only have raised my defenses even higher, but there was only the morning meeting and then we were driving on to Tucson.

I went in the morning, to participate as best I could with the group. The speaking in tongues did seem rather bizarre to me, though it is hard to recollect all my feelings now. When the group laid their hands upon me, since there were many who were giving real freedom to their emotions, I was able to be released to cry quite freely. But mine were tears of joy. For I kept repeating over and over again, "Jesu, Joy," "Jesu, Joy," "Jesu, Joy," plus a few simple words in a tongue which I did not understand. I really felt quite an emotional release and afterward a real sense of exhaustion. Only later in group prayer did the full exercise of the ability to speak freely in a tongue come for me.

As I reflect back upon the experience, I am sure that I would not have been able to enter into it if it had not been for the confidence and trust which I had for both my mother and brother who had experienced it the day before and whose judgment I respected. If they could experience this phenomenon and consider it sane, not crazy, then I could also.

One of the more concrete results of this experience for me was the fact that the indwelling power of the Holy Spirit made me quite confident of my "call" to the ministry. I never had any doubts in my three years in seminary that I was called to the ministry as did many of my fellow seminarians. I was never plagued by these doubts, and I have always attributed this to the fact that I was possessed by the Holy Spirit and that I had his strengthening and confirming power within me during a period which frequently is a difficult one for many candidates for the ministry.

Through the healing movement the influence of a Pentecostal experience has also spread. Some have received the experience of infilling by the Holy Spirit accompanied by tongues during healing conferences held in various places throughout the country. Apparently, when people become interested in receiving one of the gifts of the Spirit, they open the door to a variety of such gifts. The account of an experience of tongues which occurred at a healing conference is described in this chapter beginning on page 131.

TONGUES AT YALE

Probably the most interesting tidbit of recent history in this movement is the account of what happened at Yale University in October of 1962.[1] As one of the students put it, the conservative Protestantism which is a backdrop for most college agnosticism, "though believing firmly in the supernatural action of God in Biblical times, tends to look with extreme scepticism and act with positive opposition to any claims of that same God's manifestation in the present day." During the summer of 1962, however, a number of Yale Christian Fellowship members had come into contact with the spiritual renewal in the historic churches, two or three of them with a healing mission in our Episcopal church led by Francis Whiting, who is a leader of the Baptist church in Michigan. One of the young men wrote of this: "I was stunned by this combination. I discovered that Baptist minister+Episcopal church+Healing=the Holy Spirit." Others

1. Most of the following story is found in the Rev. Harald Bredesen's "Discovery at Yale" and articles by five of the Yale students in *Trinity,* Vol. II, No. 2, Christmastide, 1962–63, pp. 3 ff.

had been led to groups in which they heard tongues and prophecy.

One Yale Christian Fellowship member carried back to the campus a copy of *Trinity* magazine given him by his rector. When the whole Fellowship, led by this small aware group, met early in the semester to pray that "the Holy Spirit would come in His own sovereign way," this student realized that what was described in *Trinity* answered their need for new religious life, as well as the need within himself. So, as president of the organization, he wrote to the editor of the magazine asking that someone be sent to them. She got in touch with the Rev. Harald Bredesen, pastor of a Reformed church in New York state, a man who knew the experience of tongues personally. This pastor came immediately onto the campus.

He met first with eight members in the president's top-story room, along with two of his youth workers and with two of the young women workers from his community praying in the commons room. As six of the young men spoke out in tongues, a Yale faculty member who had been listening outside the door looked in to investigate and was greeted warmly and almost hilariously. Even though he wondered, both rueful and wistful, whether "this is for me or not," he was among those who received the gift of tongues when Mr. Bredesen returned to the campus with ministers of the Maine Seacoast Mission and Mount Vernon's First Methodist Church a month or so later. Meanwhile, that first night at a Fellowship retreat seven others received the experience, and the crucial test of prejudice was met on the spot. One man who had spoken in tongues turned to those who had not with the remark that they must not feel unwanted, for "He just saw our greater need, and this experience makes us love you more than ever." This immediate evidence of the power that was moving was followed by others.

Within a month students from several denominations were being drawn to the movement, and a meeting between six students and their three chaplains had been held to ask for open services in the university chapels. The chaplains were a bit nonplused, but did not oppose the request. It may have been the remark of a man who had first spoken in tongues while listening to the pastor talk that did it; he told the chaplains that the Bible was now a living thing to him, that words seemed to jump off the pages and "this fellow Jesus suddenly became real and living." The letter quoted in the first chapter describes one of these evening prayer services.

The students themselves remarked that infilling with the Spirit with this flow of strange language did not prove to be the emotional cataclysm they had half expected, nor was this powerful outpouring of tongues "a weird, psychotic occurrence." It had results in their daily tasks, their plans, and also in colleges on the West Coast, from Stanford to the Church Divinity School of the Pacific. Nor was comment limited to the students. When the mother of one of those involved shared her concern with Dr. Kenneth Scott Latourette, the famous church historian, he is reported to have said: "This is quite evidently a work of the Spirit." Bishop Leslie Newbiggin expressed his agreement by coming to the Yale campus to confer and pray with these young witnesses to the Christian way.

There is one Episcopal diocese in which the phenomenon is widespread, the Diocese of Montana, whose bishop is sympathetic to the practice. One of the most delightful stories concerning the tongues movement occurred there.[2] An Episcopal priest had preached to the young people at a youth camp in Montana about the Holy Spirit, and certain of the young people came home from camp speaking in tongues. You can imagine the parental reaction. Episcopal parents at that. Willis Haskell, chairman of the Department of Christian Education for the Diocese, decided that it was his duty to discover what had gone on. The committee which started

2. What happened is told by the Chairman of the Department of Christian Education, Diocese of Montana, in "The Testimony of Willis Haskell," *Trinity*, Whitsuntide, 1962, Vol. I, No. 4, pp. 16 f.

out to question and criticize returned filled with the Holy Spirit themselves. Six of the seven members received the gift of tongues. Then one day Mr. Haskell was visiting in a strange town in the diocese on business. Suddenly and quite unexpectedly in the plans he had made for that day, he found himself at the door of a house into which he was welcomed. These people, it turned out, had heard of the baptism of the Holy Spirit and had been praying to have Willis Haskell come. He had come, and with him the Spirit and the gift they had been asking for. How similar to the story of Peter and Cornelius in Acts.

ANOTHER ACCOUNT

Another personal account, written by the tongue speaker himself, helps to make clear the effect of the experience. The writer is a young man who has had several years of college and had carried rather more than his share of problems. He is now in a position of authority, happy in his marriage. His own words tell of the revival of meaning and spirit. They also suggest that the experience may mean more than the denomination in which it occurs. This young man has tried through counseling to integrate the full significance of his experience into his life.

> Coming from a rather lobersided Methodist Church about five years ago, to what initially seemed to be a *more* unemotional, if not austere communion (the Episcopal Church), I would certainly have been unable to predict at that time that I would be speaking in an unknown tongue in a "Holy Spirit fellowship"! Prior to my experience of receiving an infilling of the power of the Holy Spirit, I had felt that the only respectable and/or dependable route to our Creator God was through the *rational* of the intellect, since the *irrational* could not be trusted.
>
> When by a stroke of luck, fate, leading of the Holy Spirit, call it what you will (I now feel certain it was indeed the

Holy Spirit of God); when by his leading, my wife and I came to our present church, I somehow asked the right questions and found myself intrigued and somehow curious when I heard that what had been called heresy in another church, was in full blooming existence right here! (And I might add with a lot less notoriety.) Up until this point I had definitely felt that the "evangelical" approach to God was NOT for me. This type of thing was strictly for the open air, saw-dust floored tent meetings of the "Pentecostal" sects, not for *me,* nor the stately Episcopal Church. I wanted my God remote, not too personal. This way I felt you were able to look at the subject much more objectively. I went to my first Holy Spirit Fellowship meeting in January of 1961. My first reactions were the following: 1) I was not frightened; there was a spirit of love (agape), friendliness that was really indescribable: 2) Although curious about the particular gift of "speaking in tongues," I was not shocked, upset, nor did I feel that it was strange or out of place in the prayerful, praiseful atmosphere: 3) And I also had a feeling of wanting whatever it was that these people had, not just the speaking in tongues, but whatever it was that had given them a new power, a new strength for living.

Although wanting whatever it was these people had, I still was hesitant to plunge in. There was still too much of the logical thinking, rational me that said "Wait just a minute here old boy, you had better take a long look at what you are getting into!" "After all, this means a changed you." "Do you really want to be transformed by the firey power of the Holy Spirit?" "Don't you kind of like yourself as you are?" "At least you can depend on yourself as you are now!" These questions may sound a little strange coming from a person who had only been to a few of these prayer group meetings; however, seeing is believing, and I did witness transformations, healings, prophecies, glossolalia and many truly changed lives.

When I overcame that part of me that said, "Wait!", I seated myself in a chair in the center of the room while others in the group laid their hands on me, praying that the Holy Spirit would come into my life, my soul, my very being; in a new and vibrant way. As John Wesley said, "My heart was *indeed* strangely warmed!" Although I did not at that time experience the manifestation of "speaking in tongues," I truly felt that something had happened. What had happened? I probably couldn't have told you. I know however that God through his Holy Spirit had come to dwell within me. This was enough! And then, while driving home from a prayer group meeting a few weeks later, I found myself singing some of the Gospel choruses that are sung at the meetings . . . As I found myself running out of words, I began to supply my own words, or what I initially *thought* were my own words. As I went on I suddenly realized that the words I was singing or saying were not English, neither were they quite like any of the words or language that I had heard some speak at the prayer group. As I continued I realized to my mounting joy and wonder that the more I opened my mouth and spoke, the more fluidly and easily the words came out. I easily realized that I was not jabbering, nor was I uttering repetitious garble-de-gook, I was speaking an unknown tongue that I could turn on or off at will, and that did not need reinforcement of emotionalism to be again called to use.

In the past two years I have been given other tongues or languages that are clearly distinguishable from one another. This particular gift of the Spirit has been most edifying for me. It would be an almost impossible task to describe in what way.

A minister of the Foursquare Church once asked me two questions about our prayer group. These questions can and should be asked by each individual of himself:

1. Has your life been truly changed or transformed?
2. If so, in what way?

Obviously, the second of the two questions is the more difficult to answer. To a Foursquare minister it might mean giving up smoking or going to the movies. And for some this type of discipline might be one of the ways. However, I feel that it often goes a bit deeper than that. Whether you call it coming into a new relationship with your anima, or becoming a more loving, understanding, patient, less back-biting type of person makes no difference. Another apostle once said, "And now abideth faith, hope, love, these three, but the greatest of these is love."

SOME PRESBYTERIAN EXPERIENCES

The experience of speaking in tongues has not been confined to Episcopalians, however, in this movement outside the Pentecostal churches. A few accounts of its dispersion into other Protestant churches gives an idea of the character of the movement and how it has grown. One of the most interesting I have run across was the recent story of a Pentecostal awakening told in the July 1963 issue of *Christian Life*. It is the story of young Louis Evans in his magnificent new Presbyterian church on a mountain top just above fashionable Bel Air in suburban Los Angeles, and it is a report of how the Holy Spirit has come to this church with all of the gifts of the Spirit—new faith, new love, healing, and even tongues. Mr. Evans describes in his own words that, "Like many other churches in the historic denominations of our day, we have seen the gift of tongues given to many who found communication with God and people difficult. This was disturbing at first, but the beneficial results it has brought to our people have overcome many objections we had. I have seen people desperately in need completely transformed as God the Holy Spirit demonstrated Himself to them through the ability to worship Him in another language. We also have people who have received the gift of prophecy in its various aspects."[3]

The experience of another Presbyterian minister, in Jamaica, New York, began with his wife's speaking in tongues, after they had come into contact with a Pentecostal group. The Rev. Paul Morris says that he then waited for two years, much of it a time of soul-searching and knee-bending because he realized how different a Holy Spirit ministry could be. Then one night in 1957 they were visiting with friends,

3. Robert Walker, "Church on the Mountaintop," *Christian Life*, Vol. 25, No. 3, July 1963, p. 31. Mr. Evans has since moved to another Southern California church.

two Lutherans and one an Independent missionary who wanted to pray for a sick friend. They felt they needed guidance, and someone suggested that it might come through the interpretation of tongues. But none of them had the gift. In prayer the woman who was a missionary saw Mrs. Morris being given another gift; so they laid hands on her and when one of them spoke in tongues, a message of healing flowed from her lips even though she had been afraid to speak out before people. Before he slept that night Paul Morris felt the Spirit come over him and a power well up within that he had to express by speaking a new language. His doubts were "blasted out of the window," and he spoke with such force that his wife woke up and began to interpret. His story goes on to his ministry today, with a new quality of love and compassion which is reaching a surprising number of people.

Like many others this minister has commented on the great numbers of his denomination who have found a similar outpouring of the Holy Spirit. The strength of this movement among Presbyterians is indicated by the report that in their largest church in this country, Hollywood First Presbyterian, there are today nearly six hundred persons who speak in tongues. The pastor of a Presbyterian church in San Diego, California, recently discussed the gift of tongues from the pulpit. While he acknowledged that there are dangers, and also that there is real opposition to the movement, he concluded that: "This wonderful experience of the Holy Spirit is far more than a matter of speaking in tongues. It can mean a new flood of Christian love in the heart of a man. It can mean a better stewardship, and a better disciplined Christian life. . . . There is good evidence that many lives have been transformed and blessed by it."

The pastor of the First Reformed Church of Mount Vernon, New York, the Rev. Harald Bredesen, who now heads the Blessed Trinity Society which publishes *Trinity* magazine, has written of his receiving the gift of tongues. At the time he was public relations secretary of the World

Council of Christian Education. And he had just been offered a bigger job. One evening as he was walking down the sidewalks of New York, worrying over his doubts about accepting it and listening to an inner voice, a man stepped up behind him with the words, "You are a Christian!" His face was glowing, and telling Bredesen that God had shown him a need to speak, he went on, "God will open a door for you that no man can open." Then for two hours they talked. And some three weeks later Pastor Bredesen, with expectation, attended a Pentecostal camp meeting in Green Lane, Pennsylvania. There he received the gift of tongues, and a new joyful ministry opened up to him, a ministry which later sparked the outbreak of tongues at Yale which we have described.

LUTHERAN AND BAPTIST REPORTS

Several Lutherans have written of their experiences of speaking in tongues. Probably the best known is the Rev. Larry Christenson, pastor of Trinity Lutheran Church in San Pedro, California. He first came into contact with the experience in a group which was meeting to develop more competence in pastoral care. He did not see much purpose to such a religious expression, but he was open to find out. Returning home, he went one evening to hear Mary Westberg speak in the Foursquare Church in San Pedro. There they prayed that he might receive this gift, and laid hands on him, and nothing happened. During that night, however, he awakened speaking in tongues. He continued the practice, introducing it to his congregation, continuing to discover its value. He has written not only of his experience, but of the place of tongues in theory and church practice; his statement of convictions has been supported by other clergymen who speak in tongues. In 1963 Larry Christenson traveled to Europe where he found fellowship among Lutherans there who had known the experience of this gift for some sixty years.

What happens to a congregation when enough members to

fill all the front pews begin to speak in tongues within just a week? Another Lutheran, Pastor K. G. Egertson of Anacortes, Washington, has recently described the experiences of his church in detail for me. He explained, first, that he is not himself a tongue speaker; and second, that the experiences originated out of a series of evangelistic meetings for which there had been many weeks of prayerful preparation. They came without the use of pressure or emotionalism. At the time, July 1962, he wrote:

> I never anticipated what was to transpire during the days of the meetings, nor did anyone else. But I felt that the Spirit was leading these people and seeing the blessings they received I could not see that I should hinder in any way a gift so clearly spoken of by Paul. I further felt that I would want to keep my role as their pastor as firm as possible by being present when any should receive this gift. My part was to have a prayer and the absolution, after which the evangelist prayed for them that they might be filled with the Spirit and have any of the various gifts spoken of in I Corinthians 12. He then asked them to thank God by faith, not by feelings, that He had filled them with the Spirit as He promised. If they wanted the gift of speaking in a tongue he encouraged and helped them.
>
> With many it was a most spontaneous thing that happened as they began to speak forth. One of our council members had such an experience. His hands immediately assumed poses of prayer and adoration. When he stopped he said he saw visions of the glory of Christ. A few moments later the evangelist spoke to another who had received that gift and inadvertently said something in his tongue. This councilman, who was still in the room, realized that he knew what was said. It was not until the next day that he revealed this to me. He had heard him say, in his tongue, "The Lord bless you. The Lord loves all his children." He has since listened to others speak in their tongue privately and has been able to tell them what they said. He has no explanation as to how this happens. It seems that this would be the gift of interpretation. This is a

man who has been regular in church and in his family devotions, and has always impressed me with his sincerity rather than any pious airs.

In January 1964, Pastor Egertson expressed in the following words what such occurrences had meant to his church:

> It is now over a year and a half since there was a definite outpouring of the Holy Spirit on many people of our parish, when several dozen of the finest people of our congregation experienced "tongues" with other manifestations of the Holy Spirit's power. Though the novelty of tongues has long since gone, many experience the edification of tongues, mainly in their private devotions, and this has seemingly opened the door to other gifts of the Spirit. There has followed a greater appreciation for all the things we had before in Jesus, a greater love for one another, and a greater zeal for the Lord's work.
>
> At first it was a startling experience. The expected reaction against such an un-Lutheran experience was there. However, people's minds soon came to rest. There was no disruption in the on-going program of the church. There was a deeper tone of reality, awe, and praise experienced by many in the worship services.
>
> The cause of divisiveness is either that those "for" or "against" become militant. We were spared both of these in our congregation. So many people had been blessed that whenever anyone questioned, criticized, or was disturbed there was some well respected person in the congregation who could give the assurance that it was a blessing of the Lord. On the other hand, people were cautioned against going around trying to talk someone into something. The Spirit has His own times.
>
> There is always need for Pastoral supervision and guidance so that the blessings of the Lord may be used for the upbuilding of the Church. There seemed to be no "holier-than-thou" spirit noticeable. A gift of the Holy Spirit is not a sign of having arrived, but a tool to be used in building up the church. People must be aware that a "gift" is not some-

thing of which to be proud, but something for which to give thanks. Those who have not received some particular gift must understand this as well as those who have. All must have the same right to acceptance in the fellowship of love in the congregation.

There is not space here to tell in detail what the fruits have been. But if my experience as a pastor has taught me anything, I would judge that the fruits I have seen are the fruits that our church has been yearning for. In a renewed love of the Scriptures people read them with new eagerness and blessing. A renewed love flows among the members enriching the fellowship. There is a new interest in the healing ministry of the church. There is a new appreciation for the church, the body of Christ, each one receiving a gift for the upbuilding of the whole body. There is increasing concern to witness that Jesus Christ is the answer.

Perhaps the simplest way of describing what this has meant to our congregation would be to say that it has increased "our expectancy" that the Lord can and will do great things through us to his glory. It has encouraged and renewed my ministry to see how the Holy Spirit will work through us if we let Him fill our lives. There is a new realization that God is "real," an assurance of the indwelling and presence of the Spirit, a renewed sense of the presence of God in our lives. If He could and would do *this* in our midst He can and will do *other things* He has promised in His word. The Holy Spirit *will* work through us if we let Him fill our lives.

The leadership of the congregation must be left in the hands of the Spirit. He is able to unite us in the love of Christ so that all profit by His gifts. The Spirit must deal with us as individuals giving us gifts as He will. Jesus describes the Spirit's work as of greatest importance. We try to let the Scriptures say what they will and not interpret them through our criticisms of any other church. As His place is understood through the Scriptures, the prayer of the church will be heard. And as people thirst, ask, and receive, they will be filled and empowered to witness for Jesus. This has been our experience for which we give Him our thanks.

The Rev. John Hadley, a Baptist minister, has found many of the same fruits from his own experience of tongues. After reading an article by Jean Stone, an Episcopal laywoman who has been active in the movement, he decided that he must receive this spiritual gift. He went to a Christian Life Advance meeting and there had hands laid upon him and spoke in tongues. The next Sunday, filled with a new conviction, he told his congregation of his experience in a sermon which lasted a full hour.

This conviction is especially strong among those Baptists in the South who have come to know the experience, often in different ways. The Rev. Marvin Crow, a Southern Baptist, has written of his first contact when he was a student pastor in a poor community in the South. He was looking for the experience which brings people salvation, but six uneventful months went by until one Saturday night. Praying desperately, he felt sure that something was about to happen. The next morning it did. During the song service a woman who had been singing with the congregation threw up her hands and began to talk in an unknown language. Just imagine, he says, in a Baptist church, a Southern Baptist church! The service halted, and she turned round and round expressing her wonderful feelings in English. The young pastor asked for the offering. And he prayed. Then he opened his Bible and preached on the second chapter of Acts. He goes on to tell of sixteen conversions and baptisms into the church in the next six weeks, and of his own later experience of tongues. This came through a former Baptist congregation in Houston; it came during a pre-ordination prayer meeting, in an experience which he has described as praise and worship and the pent-up woes of his soul being poured out to God all at once.

For one Baptist layman, the son of Virginia's Senator A. Willis Robertson, speaking in tongues came when he was alone with his wife praying at the bedside of their sick child.

He simply put the child in God's hands, and her temperature fell as he began to offer praise in a strange tongue. In other parts of the country there are also Baptist leaders who speak out strongly for the movement and its full effect in men's lives. Dr. Francis E. Whiting, a leader in Michigan, is one who has stated clearly his belief that the salvation of the world lies in just such charismatic gifts as the gift of tongues.

THE METHODISTS ARE NOT IMMUNE

Methodists have not been immune to the experience of tongue speaking. The Rev. Marvin Buck, minister of the Methodist Church in Beach, North Dakota, tells how he read of the moving of the Holy Spirit in *Christian Life* magazine and later was visited by friends who were bubbling over with a new joy after having had the experience of speaking in tongues. They told him of an Episcopal service in which this gift was given. He went with his wife and both of them received the laying on of hands and the gift of tongues. He returned to his church, where he then imparted this gift to the superintendent of the church school. His eight-year-old daughter and six-year-old son soon also received the gift. He has told that following this experience everything in his ministry came alive, and with it the desire that all Christians might have this gift.

From his Methodist church in Baton Rouge, Louisiana, the Rev. Roy Mouser has written of his first experience of speaking in tongues at a Full Gospel Business Men's Fellowship convention in Florida. His wife also received the laying on of hands and spoke in another tongue. When they returned to their own community, he simply announced that they had received the Holy Spirit in this way and that they would be glad to discuss this with any who were interested. Through the following summer the invitations to meet with small groups came fast, and within a few months over thirty members of his church, including several of the leaders, had found a similar experience.

Dr. Robert Frost, a Ph.D. and instructor in anatomy at Baylor University Medical School, has told specifically how he received the gift. He belonged to an independent Bible-centered church. After simply hearing about the gift of tongues he spoke in tongues as he was opening a can of soup for his children's lunch. He was filled with a great sense of God's love; finding that he did not have words to express his feelings, he allowed the spontaneous praise which was forming upon his lips to take place and spoke in tongues.

Almost every one of these accounts, written by men who are leaders of their own historic churches and also of a new movement within these churches, speaks of a new quality of faith which spreads to others, and of enthusiasm and vitality. One minister in the East remarks on how different his life is, saying that it has come alive with expectation and has become sheer adventure. Almost every account tells also of the healings which occur around those who have had the experience, and of gifts of knowledge through intuitions and visions. Dr. John L. Peters, the Methodist minister who has headed World Neighbors during most of that organization's program abroad, has expressed his own knowledge of this contact with the Spirit in these words: "This I do know: I now find a new and deeper intimacy in the quality of my relationship to my Lord, a new and deeper bond with those who know and love Him . . . And I look forward to the day when I shall return to those hungry millions—my brothers and sisters—who wait in the dust and darkness of the 'underprivileged areas.' Again I hope to go, offering them a way to food and shelter and healing and companionship . . . But men are hungry at more than one level. And this time, like Peter of old, I hope to be able to say, 'Such as I have I give unto you . . .' "[4]

4. *The Methodists and the Baptism of the Holy Spirit,* Los Angeles, Full Gospel Businessmen's Fellowship International, 1963, p. 33.

THE OPPOSITION

These experiences, however, represent only one side of the movement of tongue speaking into the major, traditional churches. As we have indicated in certain cases, the most recent history of glossolalia has also been the occasion of conflict and opposition. Among church leaders who have come into contact with the movement but have not had a personal experience of speaking in tongues, there have been almost as many different reactions as there are ways of learning about other people's experiences. Obviously, many of these instances can be discussed only in general terms.

In denominations where there has been an outbreak of tongues during a formal service of the church, reactions have varied from cases in which a small number who were displeased have left the congregation and gone elsewhere, to instances in which a minister has resigned or has left taking his tongue-speaking congregation with him to form a church of their own. The Rev. John H. Osteen, in Houston, Texas, left the Baptist church in the 1950s along with 190 members of his congregation. In Van Nuys, California, the Rev. Dennis Bennett, whose story has been told at length, resigned as rector of his Episcopal church. In the same area one minister of another denomination, who was known to speak in tongues, resigned from his church and returned to it later as a member of the congregation. A Free Evangelical church in Minneapolis was recently split over the issue of tongues, while the Free Methodist pastor in one well-known college town resigned rather than keep silent about his experience of tongues.

In other cases in which there has been no public demonstration of tongues, the reactions have been equally strong. Another Episcopal minister, a tongue speaker who had resigned from his church after tongue speaking became an open issue, was serving under the rector of another church in the same diocese. In prayer services he administered the laying on of hands for healing for a man who, a few days later, had the experience of speaking in tongues. He was immediately removed from his position, and it was several months before he found an opening, this time in a different diocese. When this summary action was protested by other clergy in the area, particularly on the basis of St. Paul's direction not to forbid tongues, a church spokesman replied, "Yes, but times have changed. St. Paul isn't the bishop here."

One Nazarene minister in Washington recently was removed from his church because he and his whole family spoke in tongues and taught about the practice. In 1957 a Southern Baptist field worker was given the choice of resigning her job with the church, or of giving up a prayer group held in her home in which tongues were spoken and spiritual healing and the baptism of the Holy Spirit were discussed. When she chose to continue in what she believed, thirty others were also relieved of all activities in the same church because of their association with the group.

At Lafayette, Indiana, when the First North American Reformed and Presbyterian Youth Assembly was recently held in the Purdue University auditorium, an incident involving the tongues movement occurred. A United Presbyterian minister, making his way to the stage to ask a young man to repent and receive the Holy Spirit in this way, was stopped by a church officer and then was escorted out of the meeting by a campus policeman.

Bishop Pike's pastoral letter on glossolalia, issued in May 1963, also contained advice and several strong directives to his clergy in the Episcopal Diocese of California (the churches in and around San Francisco), as well as certain suggestions about the meaning of the practice. He advised the clergy not to take any part in any services or meetings held for the purpose of expressing or promoting tongue speaking; although the devotional practice was specifically exempted, he asked those who do speak in tongues to examine the theological premises and the terminology of the movement in order to bring it into conformity with present doctrine, worship, and discipline.

His directives were even more specific. He asked that the clergy "exert no pressure in any form" to induce the experience in another person. Laying on of hands, he directed, should be administered only in the service of Unction of the Sick, and there should be no tongue speaking by clergy as the bishop lays on hands in Confirmation, nor should communicants be presented for reaffimation of their Confirmation vows. Further, in discussing glossolalia, he stated that "in more extreme forms it is associated with schizophrenia" and that we should not feel safe in such an expression without the benefit of psychiatric oversight. Finally, he termed the movement and the practice "heresy in embryo."

Where, then, does the practice of speaking in tongues occur in the ordinary Protestant church?

TONGUES IN THE SMALL PRAYER GROUP

The Holy Spirit Fellowship is the group in which most non-Pentecostal tongue speaking takes place. Often these meetings are little different from any informal prayer group except for occasional speaking in tongues, but the practices do vary. One group with which I am acquainted is a small one that meets in the home of an associate minister; this particular group has been in existence for nearly four years. In the beginning it had the guidance of several people who had been in the Pentecostal movement for many years and knew its dangers and pitfalls, as well as its values. This group, like many of the others, crosses denominational boundaries and has regular members from other churches. A good many of the people who attend regularly have had no experience of tongues and no desire for it, and yet they testify that the spirit and fellowship of this gathering have become one of the most valuable parts of their lives.

As the group arrives for an evening meeting, for half an

hour or so they move about chatting and drinking coffee together. These people have become close friends, with a real sense of concern for each other, a sense of belonging in the fellowship. At eight o'clock they settle down, somewhat in a circle and some sitting on the floor. There is a period of silence, and then singing. For fifteen minutes or more songs that have had some meaning for the members—a significance in church camp or at informal meetings, or even in church itself—are asked for and sung. Sometimes, instead, Bach or another favorite recording may be played, or at times one of the formal services is read. Then there is quiet again. Out of this time of quiet the leader begins to pray, joined one at a time by others with prayers of thanksgiving, of praise, of petition. And then, softly, the praise turns to tongues. The tongue is melodious, quieter than the normal voice, and there is an interpretation, often by the person who has spoken. Often it is a message of reassurance and confidence; others then offer their prayers of praise and thanksgiving and petition. Again someone speaks in tongues and tells the interpretation . . . for half an hour or longer each one speaks in his own way of the matters that come to him. One is not conscious of time, for it does not drag.

Then a chair is placed in the center of the room—a sturdy old piece of carved cherry which carries sentiment the members are not afraid to express—and anyone who wishes special prayer may sit in it so that others, as many of them as want to, may gather close enough to lay a hand on the person and pray with him for whatever is requested. During this time the people get up and move about, getting coffee cups refilled or taking part just as they feel. Generally they return to the circle then for more singing, before another time of intercessions with long periods of quiet and an occasional tongue. At ten o'clock they sing another hymn or two, and those who must leave say their good nights, while others remain, chatting and returning to quiet and to prayer as they are guided.

This, then, is what happens in one Holy Spirit fellowship

in which tongue speaking is practiced. It is a time of Christian fellowship which seems close to what the New Testament describes as worship in the early church. Paul's descriptions of what the service was to be like in Corinth (I Corinthians 14:26–33) is the model for both this group and the prayer group whose atmosphere is described next. Even the late hours recall Paul's preaching past midnight which was nearly Eutychus' undoing. (Acts 20:7–12)

Another description of the groups in which there is tongue speaking outside of Pentecostalism was written by the Rev. Dennis Bennett, who resigned from his Van Nuys church when it was split over the practice. Certain details from his description will add to a picture of these groups.

> The setting of the meeting is informal. The people who attend are the same people who take part in, and rejoice in the highly-structured and formal services of their Church at public worship on Sunday, and would be the first to object to any modification of it. This is a different kind of meeting . . . The spirit of the occasion is lighthearted and joyful . . .

He then describes practices very similar in order to the first group, except that these groups sometimes include a brief instruction or a time of study. He goes on:

> After the intercessions, there may be a period of silent prayer, and then, "out of the silence," may arise any one of a number of different offerings to praise or prayer. One person may speak in simple praise to God, quietly giving love and thanks to the Father. Another may be moved by the Holy Spirit to speak prophetically . . . in the Scriptural meaning of "thus saith the Lord," . . . [while] others may be quietly responding to what is being said.
>
> [After centering down again] . . . This time several may speak, testifying to what God has been doing in their lives during the past week. There may be discussions as to the best way to deal with a spiritual problem. At any point the

> group is open to the moving of the Spirit, and a member may be moved to speak from God in prophecy, or in an "unknown tongue." Without any emotional buildup or preliminary, and just as simply as he speaks in his own language to pray or praise God, a person will begin to speak in another language . . . The interpretation . . . often will be in a flowing and beautiful English, beyond the ordinary ability of the person speaking. So objective and real is this gift of interpretation that many times, after the first interpreter has spoken, one or two others will say, "I received essentially the same interpretation." Occasionally, another person will continue further with the same interpretation, in the same style and vein. Listening to the whole process, one finds it difficult to deny that its source is God the Holy Spirit.[5]

The Rev. James H. Brown in Parkesburg, Pennsylvania, has described what happened after the Spirit struck with the evidence of tongues in the small Saturday night group which met to pray for the Sunday service. He says that they began to see signs, wonders and miracles which have never ceased. From a group of nine, the attendance has increased to about one hundred in seven years, coming from many places and from many denominations to be prayed for, as well as to find fellowship with Spirit-filled Christians. In the group, he tells, many people have been saved, healed, and filled with the Spirit, and many have remained to become active church members in their United Presbyterian church.

In Christian Advance gatherings, whose one purpose is to tell the story of the meaning which men and women have found in the experience of tongues, tongue speaking itself takes place almost entirely in smaller groups. Ministers from several denominations often take part. There are both scheduled meetings held after the main sessions and informal,

5. "Pentecost: When Episcopalians Start Speaking in Tongues," by the Rev. Dennis J. Bennett, *The Living Church*, Vol. 142, No. 1, January 1, 1961, pp. 12 f.

spontaneous meetings. At the series of conferences held in Los Angeles during the latter part of November, 1963, two rooms were set aside as prayer rooms for use at the end of the evening. One group centered on prayer for healing, while the other room was filled with people earnestly praying in anticipation of the gift of tongues.

In this room most people were sitting on straight chairs arranged in rows to accommodate them all, and members of the Blessed Trinity Society moved among them, talking with some, praying and administering the laying on of hands with others. There was a certain tension which often seems to accompany first experiences of glossolalia. One woman kept leaning anxiously over her companion—who prayed fervently—sometimes in encouragement, sometimes as if she would have liked to halt the whole process. Out of the group one sad-looking old man jabbered as if possessed until others prayed quietly but strongly with him and he stopped. Tongue speaking was heard from different parts of the room softly, and two or three times in full strength. The atmosphere in this room was a mixture of concentration and informality, the feeling woven of quiet movement and speech, of restraint and expectation.

One unusual story has been told of a spontaneous Christian Advance prayer group a few months ago. A bishop of one of the larger Protestant denominations was taking part in the planned program, and his wife became interested personally in the experience of tongues. She talked with some of the women, and as the bishop's wife and two laywomen started down the hall, they were joined by a very presentable young man who asked if he might pray with them for the gift of the Spirit. There was something odd, one of the laywomen felt, but, then, not too odd, and it is difficult to say no to such a request. The four of them went into a quiet room and prayed together, and shortly the young man spoke in a flowing new tongue; the bishop's wife also spoke in tongues.

And then a story came out. The young man had embezzled

a sizable chunk of money from one of the armed services and was about to take to his heels rather than face court-martial. The laywomen were aghast at what they had done. It was almost impossible to think of the bishop's wife and the embezzler receiving in the same spirit. But several months later they saw the picture from another side. For they had received a letter from the young man telling that, because of his new faith in the Spirit, he had given himself up and was finding punishment not only tolerable but sometimes surprisingly hopeful. And certainly one small prayer group felt they had tasted the meaning of the Spirit.

THEORY AND PRACTICE OF TONGUE SPEAKING

Ministers within the historic Protestant churches speak in tongues. What, then, is their attitude towards this experience? The Rev. Larry Christenson, pastor of Trinity Lutheran Church in San Pedro, has had extensive experience of tongue speaking and has written clearly about the theory and practice of tongues in the traditional denominations; copies of his conclusions may be obtained from him.

Pastor Christenson's main point is that this is only one gift of the Spirit and is not necessary to salvation. Those who have not received it should not feel inferior, and yet they must not reject those who have spoken in tongues and found meaning in the experience. He suggests that persons who do speak in tongues use it primarily for their private devotions and to edify themselves, that they be modest and quiet about their experience and seek fellowship with others who understand and appreciate the experience they have had. For the congregation as a whole, the pastor's suggestions are very specific. Tongue speaking is not to be encouraged in his regular Sunday services, although it will occur occasionally, and with interpretation, in prayer groups. He asks that these groups meet in the church rather than in private homes.

His proposal to these prayer groups, specifically discouraging Pentecostal traditions and usages, is that they develop instead their own indigenous practices. He also states the basis, adopted by his church, upon which people seek the experience of tongues. "We do not pray for the 'gift of tongues,' as such," he writes, "but we pray for the Holy Spirit." Finally, he specifies that no emphasis should be brought into the church school at this time. In many ways Pastor Christenson's conclusions and suggestions for his own church restate the basic view shaped by Dr. A. B. Simpson in 1907 for the Christian and Missionary Alliance. His central conclusion for today is that this is a valuable experience, one that should not be forbidden, and he asks Christian love and understanding from those who have not had the experience.

The Rev. Tod Ewald, rector of the Episcopal church in Corte Madera, California, endorsed these views so completely that they were published in almost the same form under his name in the June 2, 1963, issue of the national Episcopal magazine, *The Living Church.* Indeed, the majority of the tongue speakers among the older Protestant denominations share Pastor Christenson's views on tongues and on experience of the Holy Spirit. Other tongue speakers in these denominations, those who do not agree with this point of view, accept the essential Pentecostal doctrine that tongues is *the* sign of the infilling of the Holy Spirit and is therefore a necessary experience. The latter are obviously more militant and so attract more attention.

Two other opinions of ministers belonging to major denominations are available in printed or mimeographed form from the authors. The first is a careful study by the Rev. Howard M. Ervin, Th.D., Pastor of Emmanuel Baptist Church in Atlantic Highlands, New Jersey. He demonstrates very clearly that the objections of many Biblical scholars to present-day tongue speaking are based on a lack of understanding of the Biblical texts involved. His manuscript began as a series of letters to a young friend who was troubled by the violent prejudice against baptism in the Holy Spirit which he had encountered. Dr. Ervin writes: "Because of an increasing awareness that others are also perplexed, even misled, by these un-Scriptural, and oft-times extravagant arguments against the baptism in the Holy Spirit—particularly against the Biblical phenomenon of 'tongues'—these letters are herewith shared with a larger audience." He presents many of the Biblical facts and also many of the conclusions about them which we have presented.

The second discussion is a serious theological attempt to discover what relationship exists between the Holy Spirit and the educational process. It is written by the Rev. F. Roderick Dail, minister of Memorial Methodist Church, White Plains, New York. He lays a theological foundation upon which Christian education can integrate experiences of the Holy Spirit such as tongues. He concludes that young people should be led by Christian educators "to the moment of personal rebirth when the inner structure of one's being is reorganized and spiritual values of God's Kingdom become central concerns of life." Education then becomes the process of preparing young and old for a decisive experience of the Holy Spirit rather than the mere imparting of knowledge. In such an experience tongues may well have a part.

In addition the movement has also begun to attract interest from outside the church. A thoroughgoing cultural and psychological survey of the religious practice of tongue speaking was begun in the spring of 1963. This is the project of Dr. Stanley C. Plog, assistant professor of psychology at the University of California at Los Angeles. From his position as associate director of the relatively new Division of Social and Community Psychiatry, Dr. Plog has a broad and continuing interest in religious phenomena; he is also a clinical psychologist. In this research he is working primarily with tongue speakers in the traditional Protestant churches, and he wants to know what it is that attracts people to the movement, what lack in their religious lives or what dissatisfaction moves them, and what they are finding. The areas of his study are also extensive, with questions ranging from the social, economic and political backgrounds of the tongue speaker to the religious impact of the experience on him, its effect on family and associates, and their reception of it. He projects an equally broad base of as many as 2000 general questionnaires, at least 200 detailed personal inquiries, and ten to twelve case studies by personal interview over a lengthy period of time.

In talking with Dr. Plog one is impressed by his effort to conduct an unbiased inquiry in a field of study where this is unusual. He is very interested in avoiding preconceptions about his research, both in himself and in the individuals he is studying, so that his conclusions may be determined by facts. About two years of basic research and statistical work on the data are expected before any conclusions can be reached. But Dr. Plog does discuss his general impressions of the movement. "One thing," he remarked to us, "has been shown; this movement includes a greater representation of all age, sex and class groupings than most other religious movements. It cuts across the usual cultural fences, and is a growing and very vibrant movement." He discussed the openness of non-Pentecostal tongue speakers and their willingness to co-operate in his research and help him in getting information. Certain Pentecostal groups had turned down his request to study their experience not long before he began the present research. He also remarked on the fact that he had yet to meet a schizophrenic tongue speaker in the new movement. Dr. Plog's work at the University keeps him in touch with community leaders in various fields as well as with the practicing psychiatrists who take advanced work in his division.

A TONGUE SPEAKER EVALUATES HIS EXPERIENCE

One tongue speaker within the traditional Protestant church has written a personal account of his experience which summarizes very well what this experience means to many others like him. He is a mature and dedicated Christian minister, who has had seven years of college and professional school, training in journalism, and a job as a reporter following his service in the Navy during the war. He has had extensive experience of psychotherapy and has overcome childhood traumas which would have defeated a lesser man.

> As a "sacramentalist" I believe firmly in the Sacramental principle that Spirit indwelling the material (either a person or a thing) provides a channel for God's grace and power. Therefore, I know that I received the Holy Spirit at Baptism. Through nurture in a Christian home (in which many problems and tragedies had to be met and overcome), the Spirit helped me come to know Jesus Christ as my personal Lord and Saviour. This is a living, vital relationship for which I daily give thanks. At Confirmation I was ready for an increase in Spirit, ready for the strengthening gifts. And I believe that the Bishop, who represented the Church, meant it when he laid hands on me and prayed for a daily increase in the Holy Spirit more and more. (Prayerbook, p. 297) And I believe that an increase began at that time as requested—"Ask and ye shall receive." There were and still are many things to overcome, there is still much to learn, there is still need for further growth, but this was a new beginning. The Christian way is hard and it takes time.
>
> It was, I'm sure, with the increased Spirit within that I was guided and directed through high school, a time in the armed services, college, and then a secular job. In the "sacramental way" our Lord used me in all of these places, too, as witness has verified. It was the Spirit within, I'm sure that guided me finally to seminary and the priesthood. Twice more I received the Sacramental Laying on of Hands for particular functions (deaconate and priesthood), and I'm sure an increase of Spirit came through these acts to meet these new situations in which I was placed. God calls and God meets the needs to fulfill the call. I believe this. In my Ordination to the priesthood the Bishop exhorted me ". . . ye ought, and have need to pray earnestly for His Holy Spirit." And again, ". . . ye will continually pray to God the Father,

by the mediation of our only Saviour Jesus Christ, for heavenly assistance of the Holy Ghost . . ." (Prayerbook, pp. 540–1) This, coupled with the Bishop's prayer for me at Confirmation, I have taken seriously, and still pray daily for an increase of the Holy Spirit and God's perfect will for me in every detail.

In the first days of my ministry, of particular gifts of the Holy Spirit, "listening" seemed to come first. This was the setting down in a record book of the things I seemed to get from our Lord during times of prayer and meditation. These were always personal and not for others—something I have long respected; I get suspicious of those who get "messages" for everyone but themselves! This listening was usually in connection with my own growth in the Spirit and my ministry.

When I was led to my present service, I know the Spirit had a hand. My life here has been a real challenge. The challenges and hard places certainly seem to beget the greatest growth, and certainly this has been true for me, although the real growing pains so often seem more like evil than welfare.

A new moving ahead came while participating in a healing mission lead by one well-known in the Church's healing ministry. I received the laying on of hands before administering the same to others in the congregation. The prayer on that occasion was that my ordination gifts be stirred up, strengthened and sharpened for our Lord's use through me. After that there were reported healings from the mid-week services which I conduct.

There also came a growing dissatisfaction with myself and my relationships with a few key friends and associates, so much so that I came definitely to that place of wanting to change in spite of the cost, the pain, the humiliation that might be involved. And I prayed more seriously for our Lord's will for me in every detail and especially in regard to these particular relationships. The work of the Spirit is to convict, convert and consecrate. . . . He was doing His duty and it hurt, but it was a good pain.

Soon after this, I attended a conference on healing and the

inner life. It was a tremendous experience and I found myself in a small prayer group of five people. Each night we prayed for the conference and its leaders, and we also prayed that we should increase in the Holy Spirit more and more (following the Bishop's prayer and exhortation). After one night's prayer time I asked our Lord to reveal to me anything that might be blocking my growth in Him. That night I had a dream. It was of a situation dating into my far past that had not been honestly accepted and faced. I offered it to our Lord that morning at Holy Communion. That did not take the situation away automatically, but it made it faceable and the offering of it somehow showed my real desire to be as open to God as possible. That night in prayer, when the rest were praying for me, I had a definite experience which to the best of my understanding can only be equated to what some people call the Second Baptism, the Baptism of the Holy Spirit or of Fire. I shall try to describe this experience, but before I do, I want to stress that *words are not the same as things*. Therefore the words I use will not be the same as the experience, but perhaps they can be "sacramental" and convey some of the feeling of the experience.

I was kneeling as the four others prayed for me. They put their hands on my head and on my shoulders. I in turn took hold of a cross; while I do not feel this was significant or necessary, I report the circumstances as they were. The prayer was simple—a request for a greater flow of Spirit within me. I was open and expectant. And then it happened! ("It" being the experience which still continues in various forms and must be what the Bible refers to as life in the Spirit.) It was like a baptism. I felt that I was going down, then coming up. Or, the feeling was like draining out, and refilling. It was all an inner thing—down and then up. As I "came up" I spoke in tongues (glossolalia) and interpreted.

Besides the tongue and interpretation, my hands felt full, as if there was much to pass through them—and on out. I was filled with a tremendous joy. Laughter came easily. It was tremendously exhilarating, and it was not easy to sleep that night! The next day was much the same. I felt different,

I was different. I did not know about tongues before and so sought explanation and read about it in the Bible. Passages of scripture I had read before and did not understand were opened in this and many other areas. It was the revealing of new things, as the promised Spirit was said to do. I knew then, as I continue to discover, that words are not the same as things. Experiences began to reveal the written words and speak deeply. All passages concerning the Holy Spirit began to open with new meaning and joy. Our Lord's words made sense, that "the world cannot receive him, because the world neither sees nor knows him; but you know him, because he dwells with you and is in you." (John 14:17)

The pattern of speaking and interpreting persisted. I have found that once received the "gift of tongues" is mine. I can speak in tongues at any time. I am in control of the gift and its steward so to speak. I do not need to be in prayer or meditation. It is a tongue which is mine just like my command of the English language. The tongue, however, bypasses my rational mind. I do not know what it says; I only know that it is primarily praising God, and for me any praise opens me more and more to God.

I do not often ask for interpretation when my tongue is thus used in private devotions to praise God and open myself to Him. But I also use my tongue in a small prayer group which our Lord has called together. Those of us with this gift often use our tongue softly in the lifting time to "center in" on our Lord. Sometimes one feels moved to speak out in tongues, and at such times the speaker or another interprets. This is not translation but English words given to them, much like the listening gift I received earlier in my ministry. Again a feeling tells you when to speak up either in a tongue or interpretation. We seek the verification of others as to the correctness of an interpretation. Tongues also plays a part in prayers for others, when the Spirit prays for the deeper thing or unconscious needs not perceived in the conscious mind. Again you can tell when the tongue is speaking to a deeper place and need not be interpreted. The tongue is but part of the greater experience and should not in my opinion be too highly exalted!! For me, it is important and I'm glad I have this gift, but it must always be kept in its proper perspective.

But now, with the first experience, there was so much I had not understood before which began to unfold, and this persists too; the reading of scripture from that time on has been exciting. I knew what it was to be accused of being drunk at 9:00 A.M. without so much as a drop! The world seemed brighter—it was like having small screen vision suddenly replaced by a large screen. I am sure that I had the Holy Spirit before, but never like this. I can't explain, but it was an experience I would never trade.

Then after the initial joy came the "wilderness period" and some mighty tough times! More than my tongue had been released!! I have long since come to understand that for me one of the greatest works of the Spirit in me is to reveal the hidden things of darkness, and also to put into motion the power to deal with these things and transform them. This would be the process of sanctification in theological terms, I suppose, or to be perfected or to become whole, or to restore the image of God within. I realize for myself the long way yet to go, but I rejoice in each new victory and each new place. When I returned home from the conference, it was interesting to see how our Lord gathered a fellowship. First one, then another name appeared on the guest register. In making these parish calls, I was led to share my experience with this one or that one. It was soon no surprise to find that they too had had such an experience, either years before or recently. Our Lord blessed me with many "old-timers in the Spirit" who knew many of the pitfalls and problems. I have valued their sage wisdom and advice. "Seek the Giver and not the Gift" is one strong and oft repeated warning. As our core group came together, so the fellowship expanded to this friend or that.

One cannot express the value of this shared fellowship. At our informal prayer group sessions the gifts of the Spirit are in evidence "decently and in order" relative to our own group, but obviously different from the tradition of our formal worship, which we have no intention of changing. And still, when the Spirit is flowing, the formal liturgy of the church is far from "stylized words from a book." It is interesting to note that of our Holy Spirit Fellowship, almost all are actively involved in the adult education program at Church and all serve the Church in some particular and valuable way. About half of us are using the avenues and truths of clinical psychology as a part of our growth process, and we see this as part of the whole picture, as a religious experience in which the Spirit brings the hidden things of darkness into light and is also the one to deal with these things. The counselor (who is a psychologist) is like the Confessor of old—one who is also traveling the way, adding his insight and wisdom, standing with us, growing with us.

The joy is constant, even in the "tribulation" of self discovery, because it all figures into the growth process and the becoming. The earthen vessel wants to be as open as possible for the daily increase, not for self gains, but for the spread of God's kingdom and the honor and glory of his holy name. The needs of men are so great and only God's power can help them. He needs dedicated and open workers daring enough to let him work through them. We need to be stripped and pruned and refined. When we say in the creed, "he shall come to judge," one wants to shout out, "Oh yes Lord, come and judge me. I want to change and be what you want me to be." The exhilaration lasts, returns and changes.

Other gifts of the Spirit are now manifest, and the fruits of the Spirit are ripening. Others see it, I can feel it. I know I have changed and am changing. One could, in this "razor's edge way" become very inflated and feel self important and thus stifle the Spirit's work and present a very distasteful witness. Or one can become sensitive to the very deep work of the Spirit and know how insignificant he is, and still discover that, even though he is a material thing of no spiritual worth by himself (like water or bread or wine) he can be indwelt by Spirit and used in a "sacramental" way to convey the grace and power of God. One is still imperfect, in process. Failures come, but when the Spirit is at work and perceived by the fruits, it must be likened to what Peter said when the mighty acts of God were seen through the disciples: "Exalted thus with God's right hand, he received the Holy Spirit from the Father, as was promised, and all that you now see and hear flows from him." (Acts 2:33)

For the moment we are up to date. So let us summarize quickly. Speaking in tongues is Biblical in background, but it has had a spasmodic history from the third century until our time. Now it is an essential part of the widespread and vigorous Pentecostal movement. This movement has broken over these bounds and spread into the old-line Protestant churches. Ministers and lay people of these churches speak of the value of the experience. Some have found this experience through their contacts with Pentecostal ministers. Some have found it through the Full Gospel Business Men's Fellowship. Some have found it within the spiritual healing movement. Some have found it through non-Pentecostal groups which have gathered together for fellowship while remaining loyal to their own churches. And finally, at least one group has found it in a Christian fellowship in the rational atmosphere of an Ivy League college campus.

These are the facts. The church through the ages has given a variety of interpretations to these facts. Let us now look at these various ways in which the church has explained and understood the experience.

Chapter VI

WHAT CAN THIS MEAN?

The people who first witnessed speaking in tongues were amazed and confused. Some in Jerusalem at Pentecost simply thought that the Christians had soaked up too much new wine, others were deeply impressed, while most of them, I am sure, did not know what to think. These have been the basic reactions of people throughout history, and they are still current today. And so the first question we come to is a basic one:

What have people thought about this speech and its interpretation? What explanations have been offered for the experiences of tongues which are scattered through the New Testament, the history of Christianity, and the churches today? There are four different explanations of glossolalia which give us answers, four different answers. The first is probably the most widely held, the thinking that tongues has little value or meaning, because it simply results from an upthrust of primitive mentality, or from psychological abnormality, or as some people see it, from demon possession. The second line of reasoning finds meaning in the events which occurred so long ago but feels that they were never interpreted quite correctly, and so it must have been a different experience from the one which seemed to be described. A third view is held by still other Christians, who think of tongues as an experience which was useful in the establishment of the church but is no longer of any value. And then, finally, there are those who believe that the experience is a valuable religious experience in which the Holy Spirit gives the ability to speak a language other than one's own.

No one of these explanations is easy to accept. If, however, there is something to be gained from the obscure and the strange in man's experience, let us have a go at delving into them to see what meaning there is in tongues.

THE MOST COMMON EXPLANATION

The most common method of explaining tongues is to relate the phenomenon to certain other ecstatic experiences known in the ancient world, and recurring in modern times. It is held to be comparable to the ecstatic frenzy common among primitive peoples, more or less like a Bacchic or Corybantic revel in modified Christian garb. In these primitive expressions there is ecstatic speech, moaning, groaning, dancing, wailing, which release pent-up frustration. This is the kind of frenzy our sophisticated modern age expresses in war and cocktail parties, where feelings of which men are not aware force them into violent action. Speaking in tongues, it is reasoned, was like this primitive frenzy and was overvalued by the authors of the New Testament, who did not know the world well enough to have any basis for comparing and understanding what was actually happening to them. Modern experiences of tongues are explained in the same way, usually by comparison with modern frenzied states, or with one form or another of emotional abnormality, or with demon possession, and so there is nothing of particular religious value in the Christian experience of tongues.

This explanation is well illustrated in the following quotation, which simply associates tongue-speech with frenzied forgetfulness of self.

> Speaking with tongues is rapid, ecstatic speech, usually unintelligible even to the speaker, but sometimes explained by one who has another Pentecostal gift, that of interpretation. Evidence of the descent of the Holy Spirit is seen by

> Pentecostalists in the bodily rhythmic or spasmodic movements common at country revivals and camp-meetings . . . Prophesying is preaching, but preaching is not prophesying unless it be very fervent and full of familiar Bible quotations, accompanied by many gestures.[1]

The Interpreter's Bible offers the same basic explanation in the first exposition which is given on the passages about tongues in I Corinthians. John Short writes that "students of the psychology of religion have noted [glossolalia], and describe it in terms of the release of strong emotion which cannot find satisfying expression in more normal ways . . . [It is] an innocuous way of letting off superfluous spiritual steam."[2] Later on the same basic explanation is offered in the exegesis by Clarence Craig. After he has restated Paul's meaning clearly, that tongues is speech directed towards God and caused by the Spirit, he goes on: "Words and sounds which are without connection and meaning to men are uttered in ecstasy. The phenomenon is well known to students of the psychology of primitive and emotional types of religion. Such outbursts were known in the Hellenistic mystical religions of the time, and some parallels are also to be found in Judaism. The magical papyri show formulas which contained a jumble of incoherent ejaculations. There have also been secular forms of tongues." These two statements represent one very widely held view of the experience of tongues.

Johannes Weiss, the eminent historian of the early church, essentially ignores the subject of tongues because he believes that it is a vestigial remnant of primitive religion which the church soon overcame. In his authoritative eight-hundred-page history of the first hundred years of the nascent church's life, he makes only one reference to the subject, in which he says: "Thus alongside the one Spirit which permeates all

1. Charles Francis Potter, *The Faiths Men Live By,* New York, Prentice-Hall Co., 1954, pp. 301 f.

2. *The Interpreter's Bible,* New York, Abingdon Press, 1951–55, Vol. X, p. 155.

Christians there are the separate 'spirits of the prophets' (I Cor. 14:14,32). The latter is an age-old *animistic* view . . . which Paul has essentially overcome. . . ."[3] The same essential meaning is found in E. Andrews' article in the recently published four-volume work, *The Interpreter's Dictionary of the Bible.*

A similar parallel is often drawn between tongues and the somewhat more subtle phenomenon of the oracle at Delphi where the Pythia spoke out of a trance. This speech, however, was quite different from that referred to by Paul, for the Pythia's words could be understood; it was their meaning which was obscure. There is no record that the language of the Pythia or Sybil needed translation like the interpretation of tongues to make it intelligible to her hearers. Still another comparison is made to the Greek experience of "belly-talking" mentioned by Aristophanes and Plato. In this speech a second voice seemed to come through the speaker, a voice different from his usual one. E. R. Dodds in *The Greeks and the Irrational* has demonstrated that these passages refer to the condition of the trance medium, which is far more comparable to the spirit of divination Paul cast out from the slave girl at Philippi (Acts 16:16) than to tongues.

Other attempts have been made to find similarities between Old Testament phenomena and tongues. On the one side are the Pentecostals who are trying to show that tongues was at least foretold in the Jewish scripture. The passages which are quoted, however, refer to prophecy and other gifts, but never clearly to tongues, nor do any of them clearly foretell the debut of tongues. In Genesis and Exodus, where it is mentioned that God has breathed his spirit into man, a reference to tongues is seen (Genesis 1:2, 2:7; Exodus 31:2,3) and also in the several passages in Psalms and Job in which the spirit or breath of God—the words "spirit" and "breath" are

3. Johannes Weiss, *The History of Primitive Christianity,* New York, Wilson-Erickson, 1937, p. 626.

interchangeable in Hebrew—move in the world or in man. (Job 26:13, 33:4; Psalms 33:6, 104:4,30) The burning coal placed on his tongue in Isaiah 6, Ezekiel's being caught up between heaven and earth and having the spirit of God poured into him (8:1–3, 36:25–29), and Joel's foretelling that the spirit would be poured forth upon men (2:28) are all thought of as suggesting tongues. These references were all discussed by Myer Pearlman in his book *The Heavenly Gift*. On the other side we find Ira Jay Martin in his study on *Glossolalia in the Apostolic Church* suggesting that tongues is similar to the ecstatic and frenzied experiences of the Bible. The parallels he draws, however, show little relation to the experience of tongues as described by Paul, or Luke in the Book of Acts.

Actually there is nothing to be found in either Hebrew or Greek antecedents comparable to the experience described by Paul's letters and the Book of Acts as speaking in tongues. And if it is suggested that it could not be a new experience but must have been known and not described, we must consider how unlikely this would have been among people who valued such experiences so highly. Had anything so spontaneous and impressive as tongues occurred, it would have received the same treatment that was accorded visions and other aspects of irrational human experience. The peoples of the ancient world held these experiences of the unknown to be worth attention and reverence. We forget that even the Greeks were far more cordial to the irrational than our stress on their golden age of reason would make us believe. It almost takes a laboratory study of these elements, such as Dodds has put together, to make us realize how superstitious we often are about the rational Greeks.

Thus, if we look with a cold historical eye at the material as fact, there was no experience we know of in ancient times which is not clearly differentiated from speaking in tongues, and in several ways. First, tongue-speech is not a frenzy; it can usually be controlled, and in most cases it is, so that it can be turned off at any time. Second, loss of consciousness, or the state of trance, is not a necessary part of the experience. There may be individuals who, at one time or another, have lost consciousness in association with tongue-speech, but this is probably due to the presence of other factors, rather than directly to the experience itself. And, last, tongue speaking always requires interpretation, and the ability to interpret can be given. The ancient writers did not describe any experience comparable to this.

When we study facts, then, rather than suppositions about tongue speaking, we find only four parallels to it in ancient literature, and these are all considered post-Christian. Three are found in non-canonical writings, the Book of Enoch (71:11), the Apocalypse of Abraham (17), and the Ascension of Assiah (8:17); each describe an ecstasy in which the person is able to speak, sing, and understand the "language of the angels." Enoch, for instance, was taken into heaven where he heard and understood the four archangels. The fourth is found in the Testament of Job, in which the patriarch gives a magic girdle to his daughters which gives them the power to go into the greater world, to live in heaven. Each of the daughters as she puts it on receives a new heart and begins to speak in superhuman language. The first speaks in the tongue of an angel, the second in the tongue of principalities, and the third in the tongue of those on high, the cherubim. Let me be specific in regard to these four descriptions; they do not refer to history, quite obviously, but they do indicate an acquaintance with a current phenomenon. It is doubtful that such descriptions were conjured up out of whole cloth in the four authors' minds. Undoubtedly they represent some kind of touch with the experience of tongues itself.

Philo, the great Jewish mystic who plead for the Jews in Rome a few years after the crucifixion, wrote of knowing that the divine spirit can replace the human will. Describing how the Spirit of God spoke through the prophet, he still did not indicate anything like glossolalia, but only prophecy in the common language.[4]

It has also been suggested that something comparable to glossolalia was known among the Sufi of Islam. This sect arose in the ninth century, essentially as a protest against juridical formalism and worldliness, and their heritage did include elements from mystical Christianity. They continued a tradition of God's unintelligible speech, a tradition which had originated about the Prophet telling that he heard sounds and confused speech which he understood only after they had ceased, and that it was a great effort for him to pass to the "state of logical and intelligible speech." The later writers described such a speech,[5] and it is possible that these descriptions do relate to a practice comparable to tongues. They specify, however, hearing and translating a speech which is beyond comprehension, and they do not mention uttering such a speech in an unintelligible form.

Thus, in the light of serious studies about these various phenomena, the New Testament speaking in tongues cannot be put down as simply another occurrence of something that was going on all over the ancient world. The Christian experience was one which was quite different both in kind and in quality from other contemporary experiences to which it has been compared and this is the best knowledge we have, based on sound, scholarly work.

EMOTIONALISM IS NOT NECESSARY

The linking of tongues with violent religious emotionalism and trance states does persist, however, continuing to confound the actual meanings, and so it is essential to examine the sources of this identification in people's minds. The im-

4. Philo, *Quis Rerum Divinarum Heres,* Loeb Classical Library, New York, G. P. Putnam, 1932, Vol. IV, p. 258.

5. Emile Dermenghem, *Muhammad and the Islamic Tradition,* New York, Harper & Brothers, 1958, pp. 30, 142 and 167 f.

portant eleventh edition of the Britannica has been of no help to scholars in search of a head-on look at glossolalia. Conybeare's article, reprinted without substantial change in the most recent edition, simply assumes that the Greek phrase describing the phenomenon in the New Testament was borrowed from current use, and so refers to an utterance out of the same kind of madness which the Greeks, including even Plato, prized so highly. He assumes, apparently without any first-hand facts about tongues, that they are strictly comparable to "oracular possessions" among both savages and the cultured ancients.

> Virgil [he cites] draws a life-like picture of the ancient prophetess "speaking with tongues." He depicts her quick changes of colour, her dishevelled hair, her panting breast, her apparent increase in stature as the god draws nigh and fills her with his divine afflatus. Then her voice loses its mortal's ring: "nec mortale somans." The same morbid and abnormal trance utterances recur in Christian revivals in every age, e.g., among the mendicant friars of the 13th century, among the Jansenists, the early Quakers, the converts of Wesley and Whitefield, the persecuted protestants of the Cevennes, the Irvingites.[6]

Virgil may have been describing the state of the ancient seeress to a nicety, and the anthropologist cited probably was spelling out exactly what he had seen, but Conybeare apparently had no experience of tongues to draw on. And so he passed on to classical scholars an unquestioned assumption which he could not have held to if he had known the experience he was writing about. He has utterly confused the experience itself with the atmosphere which has sometimes been known to surround it.

This thinking is not found only in religious and classical works; it can crop up wherever tongue speaking is discussed. For instance, in 1956 the *American Anthropologist* carried

6. *The Encyclopaedia Britannica,* eleventh edition, New York, 1911, Vol. 27, pp. 9 f.

an article surveying glossolalia in non-Christian religions. The writer carefully criticized his own scientific sources of fact, terming the descriptions of the ethnographers infrequent, brief, and vague. Yet his conclusions rest on the inference that the utterances described, both the ecstatic speech of the shaman and the speech of his people during hysterical frenzy, are essentially comparable to Christian tongues. One wonders from what source the author obtained his impressions of Christian glossolalia.

Tongues *can* occur in a highly charged atmosphere, *but it can also occur in quiet surroundings, and the unleashing of emotionalism is simply not a necessary part of speaking in tongues.* For example, just before leaving California three years ago, the Rev. Dennis Bennett spoke in tongues, without any frenzy, before television cameras. Father Bennett's tongue speaking had contributed to a controversy which had split one of the largest Episcopal churches in the Southwest. During his discussion on the Paul Coates news program on KTTV, Los Angeles, Father Bennett demonstrated that one does not have to turn an emotional hair in order to speak in tongues.

We have shown that tongue speaking free of emotionalism can be observed in modern Pentecostal churches, and this is stressed in the main Pentecostal position today. Yet this prejudice, which obscures the real meaning of the experience, is hard to dislodge. I was recently permitted by a small devotional group to record the tongue-speech of three members so that it could be heard by a study group with whom I was discussing the subject. "Why! that has meaning . . . it's not an outburst . . . not even excited . . . and it's beautiful," were typical responses to hearing the tape. This ten-minute recording did more to bring an understanding of the nature of tongues than anything else I did in five evenings of discussion.

Ronald Knox, whose major work covers the history of such movements as tongue speaking, shows very clearly what difficulties one is led into by identifying tongues with either primitive or modern frenzy. While he is not enthusiastic about the enthusiasm his book describes, he is very careful about his facts; he also concludes that enthusiasm (as he defines it) and tongues are essentially separable phenomena. "If you consult the works of reference," he says, "you will find a long litany, copied from one encyclopaedia into another, purporting to show that all the enthusiastic movements have in fact given rise to glossolaly." Thus, he continues, Conybeare in the Britannica seems credible when he speaks of the morbid and abnormal trance utterances in Christian revivals, until his early evidence for tongues is examined "and in each case you find that there is a reference to ecstatic prophecy, but no mention of strange languages. It is the old, discredited Frazer technique of piling up parallels which are not parallels at all."[7] Indeed, it is just such sources, taken in conjunction with such facts as revivals, which have made this comparison into an iron-bound prejudice.

Another of these explanations of tongues links the experience with unbalanced mental states. Tongue speaking is understood simply as the result of a psychological disturbance, and it has little or no value other than as an evidence of a pathological or abnormal psychological process. Thus, tongues has been interpreted as the result of group-suggestion or autosuggestion, something stirred up by the mind in its plastic substratum. Or it is linked to schizophrenia, hysteria, catalepsy, or an abnormal trance state. These are significant evaluations, for if tongues is reduced essentially to these phenomena, then it has but little religious value. We shall delay our detailed analysis of this criticism until we have examined the psychological points of view current in our world and so have a basis upon which to study this interpretation.

Finally, tongues has been linked to the spiritualistic trance in which some other spirit speaks through the individual.

7. Knox, op. cit., p. 550.

Two psychologists, Theodore Flournoy and William James, have written of such spiritualistic phenomena in which something comparable to tongues was a part of the experience. We have already referred to several examples of tongues in which the ability to speak in other languages was allegedly given by demonic forces rather than by the Holy Spirit. Leon Christiani, a Roman Catholic priest whose work we have already cited, gives two detailed and documented examples, from our own century, of demon possession in which there was speaking in strange tongues. One of them, from the 1920s, occurred in the village of Piacenza in Italy, and the other during the 1950s in a town in France. This is the official Roman Catholic explanation of most tongue speaking and is still seriously maintained in many Christian quarters today. Among them are a number of missionaries who report cases of demonic possession from their experience in the Orient. One particularly interesting study of such phenomena together with the mention of experiences similar to tongues is found in Hugh White's *Demonism Verified,* published first in 1922, and recently made available by University Microfilms in Ann Arbor, Michigan.

Another very clear and interesting identification of tongue-speech with demonic agency is found in Alma White's book, *Demons and Tongues*. Mrs. White, a leader of the Pillar of Fire Holiness Church, had good reason for her view. Her husband ran off and left her in his pursuit of the experience of tongues. She sees the experience exhibited in most Pentecostal assemblies as evil and demonic in inspiration. Its fruits are bad. The basic theory here is that the willed desire to set aside the individual ego and the individual consciousness opens the personality to an intrusion of spiritual powers beyond itself, and that it is evil rather than divine powers which are ready to step in and take over.

There are several basic difficulties with this explanation. If modern tongues are caused by demons, further explanations must be offered to explain the difference between the

Biblical phenomenon and the modern one. Furthermore, this interpretation puts a sinister judgment on modern Pentecostals, all two million of them. It does not throw any cold water on the speaker's being in the grip of a real experience, but infers that the reality contacted is essentially evil. The explanation overlooks the most significant criterion for deciding whether glossolalia is of demonic or divine etiology, the result of the experience. If we see that which builds up and transforms for good as the result of divine agency, and that which destroys and divides as coming from some other agency, then it would take at least several impartial, objective studies to support the identification of tongue speaking with totally evil results, and this has not been done.

In addition, the demonic tongue-speech which is described by most authors is associated with trance states, violence, and parapsychological phenomena which do not occur in most Pentecostal cases of tongue-speech. If one wishes to discover a clear example of demonic tongue-speech, he really has to hunt for it and may, after years of search, still be empty-handed, while he can find glossolalia which purports to be of the Holy Spirit in any Assembly of God church any Sunday morning. The question as to whether this interpretation can be taken seriously must be delayed until after our theological and psychological study.

A CASE AGAINST THE DEMONIC THEORY

The following story, however, gives evidence against the demonic explanation of tongues. It tells the quiet devotional quality which surrounded this experience for at least one tongue speaker. This young man has recently graduated from college *cum laude*. He received a degree in Religion and worked for the chairman of that department as a reader. He has had extensive experience in psychotherapy to help resolve some of his problems, and a complete battery of tests reveals a basically sound personality. He is also a happily married man.

This experience became a part of my devotional life during the summer of 1960. About a week before the actual "first experience" I began to feel an active feeling inside that was different from a feeling of excitement in quality. Something within me was new, and that newness wanted to express its presence.

The actual first experience came one evening as two friends and I were praying in the church. It was late and we were praying for a friend's doubts as a culmination to a discussion. At first, before there was fluency, there were mutterings and a great feeling of satisfied expression. Many times after that I felt a great inner joy when I would use this gift at prayer groups or in private devotions. I might mention at the same time my ability to freely express the totality of my personality.

When I went to the university to finish my education, I encountered people who felt that this was an invalid manifestation of inner turmoil. These people, along with the general atmosphere of the "rational" centered academic community set my mind to questioning not only this phenomenon, but the totality of my Christian faith. I was at this time still speaking in tongues in my private devotional life. And I began to be aware that this practice was no longer accompanied with "a great deal" of emotional feeling. This practice did not seem to be dependent upon a feeling of happiness, but was still satisfactory and fulfilling even when I was quietly calm or even unhappy. I began to understand this phenomenon as a rather mysterious communicative experience between God and myself regardless of the emotional state in which I found myself. It is worth adding that the validity I felt inherent in this activity was not shaken by the attacks upon my religious position.

Intellectual and academic problems in the field of Religion had little bearing upon the existential experience (this is not to imply that the two areas within the field of Religion are separate and not capable of an interconnected relationship). I now find that I use this phenomenon almost entirely within my mind, that is to say that I hardly ever speak in tongues, but "think" the activity in the same way that I am now thinking in English as I type this information on the paper.

For me, I use it in this manner almost entirely in personal devotions. It is very easy for instance to pray in tongues after praying in English, all within the mind. I feel that the phenomenon is entirely within my control, and is, therefore, rational in the sense that my mind is able to control the frequency of the expression, and the syntax of this "speaking."

I feel that the value of this gift lies in the fact that I am able to communicate with God in a form other than English on the conscious level. At the same time it would be well to mention that I do not feel that this gift is necessary for salvation, but rather is, as St. Paul states, one of the lesser gifts of the Spirit.

AN ALTERED MIRACLE

The next, basically different explanation of tongues does accept the fact that there was a miracle at Pentecost, but maintains that it was one of miraculous hearing, not of miraculous speaking. It was the crowd who were empowered, each to *hear* in his own strange tongue what the Galileans voiced in their ordinary words. It is interesting that this treatment of the story, in the spirit of modern Biblical criticism, was suggested and rejected by Gregory of Nazianzen as early as 350 A.D. The stumbling block of tongues was being met even then. Alma White uses this explanation in the pamphlet we have mentioned to explain the absence of tongues in the Holiness movement of which she is a part. Her argument is based on sheer strength of numbers; it must have been a greater miracle for the multitude to hear. This is an explanation frequently used among fundamentalists who do not believe in the experience of tongues and yet must account for it in the New Testament.

The real objection to this theory is that it ignores the sense of fulfillment and release which is a part of the experience of speaking, and not of hearing, whether miraculous or not. Further, on the accepted facts, it is hard to see why the crowd should mock the disciples as being drunk with new wine if nothing more was being experienced than hearing a voice speak one's own language. Nor is this theory borne out today; modern congregations do not understand tongues without interpretation, except in very occasional instances, no matter what their linguistic backgrounds. Finally, this explanation leaves out several other passages in Acts and Paul's letters as if they had no relation to the accepted fact at Pentecost.

A USEFUL TOOL

Undoubtedly the most common theological explanation of tongues has been the theory that it was given as a useful instrument for converting the pagan world of the Mediterranean to Christianity. It was useful first in giving foreign languages which helped evangelize the foreign peoples, and then as a supernatural sign which helped to convert people in those first centuries after Christ. Actually these two explanations account mainly for the disappearance of the gift. Quite logically, as soon as the whole known world was more or less reached by Christianity and converted to it, there was no further reason for glossolalia and so it was withdrawn as a Christian ability.

This first suggestion, that tongues was merely a supernatural gift of foreign languages, has been held by many writers from Augustine on. It holds that the disciples themselves were given a permanent language at Pentecost, and that others received a similar gift when it was needed. This explanation thus accepts all the facts which are presented in Acts 2.

The difficulty with this view is that it overlooks a most important distinction. True, occasionally someone speaking in tongues does break out in a foreign language; this is one of the attested facts of glossolalia. But it is also true of tongues that the speaker does not exercise conscious control over either the language or the message. Some force beyond his conscious personality speaks through him. If, on the contrary, the speaker is given the ability to communicate with people whose language he has never before known, this would be a gift of knowledge, not of tongues. The gift of a new foreign language for a conscious purpose, either for spreading the gospel or for any other purpose, would be an extraordinary gift of a special knowledge, one ready to use selectively to get ideas across, rather than having words and thought come all in one fell swoop. Apparently there have been instances of such a gift, but very few authenticated ones. It is said that St. Pachomius, St. Vincent Ferrer, St. Francis Xavier, and St. Louis Bertrand all had such an ability, although careful historical study suggests caution in claiming the gift for them.

As we have indicated, however, there is no doubt that now and then those gripped by the experience of tongue speaking have broken forth in language other than their own, and the tradition about these saints may well have started with such an experience. The stories of uneducated persons who suddenly spoke Latin or Greek, or the cultured form of their own tongue, are also probably instances of glossolalia. These people, however, do not have conscious control of the language spoken, nor can they be sure when they speak in tongues that any particular language or any particular message will be forthcoming.

SHE SPOKE A REAL FOREIGN LANGUAGE

An interesting example of speaking in words which later turned out to be a foreign language is the account of a friend of mine whose integrity is beyond reproach, one who has spent the past twenty years in attempting to become as mature as she could, using every possible tool from devotional reading to Jungian analysis. She is a woman of middle age who has been a Christian all her life. She had been converted as a young girl and had had several religious experiences of real significance; in one of them she came close to what she later experienced as tongues. A teacher with an excellent education at the time her account begins, she had taken on the Christian responsibility of teaching a class of over fifty business and professional women. This task seemed monumental to her and she was led to Bethel Temple in Los Angeles, where the Rev. and Mrs. Turnbull were in charge of the services, to receive spiritual sustenance for the religious task which she was trying to fulfill. From this point we shall let her tell her story in her own words:

> I knew they held meetings on every Friday for those who were seeking the Infilling of the Spirit. I finally in desperation decided I would go and seek also. I said to myself, "I must either have more of God dwelling within me and instructing me directly, or I shall have to give up the class." So I went on Wednesday night to their Prayer Meeting and spoke to the woman in charge of the Friday meeting. She told me, "You go home, eat as little as possible, pray much, read the Book of Acts, and come on Friday and God will fill you with His Holy Spirit."
>
> When this day, August 17, 1932, came, I went to Bethel Temple in a sense with a great eagerness and expectation, but there was one great dread in my mind. I did NOT want to speak in tongues. And I knew these people thought one must do so in order to have an authentic baptism in the Spirit. I sat and listened with a few others to the reading of the account of Paul going to Ephesus in Acts 19. Then after a short and simple prayer, those of us who had come for help were told to go up on the platform and begin to seek in prayer. I decided I would go to a chair off by myself in the circle, as people praying aloud had always been very distracting to me in praying. I knelt in front of a chair and began the business of seeking my heart's desire from God, and entered into it as if it were real work to be accomplished, knowing that so much that was close to my heart was at stake. I soon found myself saying in a low voice to God, "Do what you will with me. Baptize me as you will. You know, Lord, these people think you have to

speak in tongues. If You want me to do so it is all right with me."

Almost immediately, out of my mouth began to pour sentence after sentence in a strange language. I spoke more fluently than I could ever have done in English and with a beautiful cadence. It seemed to come from down in the Center, and not from my mind. With it at first was such indescribable joy, such a sense of power from beyond, and such an unquestioning assurance that this was God doing His work. After a time the emotional overtone changed from one of joy to cries of grief which wrenched my entire physical being. I did not know what any of the individual words meant but I did sense that the first speaking was praise and that the latter was the cries of grief of our Lord for the whole world, for its suffering. Tears streamed down my cheeks and my dress was soaking wet where the tears fell for, I suppose, something over an hour. But the Voice which used my lips was so different from my own. It was so gentle, full of kindness and compassion and love.

After a time the speaking gradually ceased. I became aware that there were a number of people around me, all praising God for His goodness to me and one man kept thanking God for "the gift of such a *beautiful* language." For a number of years I remembered a number of the words. When my husband and I were post World War II rehabilitation missionaries in the Philippines in 1947–48, I learned from some Moro students in one of my Bible classes in Silliman University that the words which I could recall were Moro.

During my first semester at Silliman University, I taught a Bible class (a requirement in every student's curriculum) to one group of pre-law students and also to another group of pre-medical students. The course for this first semester was The Life of Christ. In the pre-law group, there were two young men, probably about thirty years of age, who were Moros from the Island of Mindanao. One, named Lagume Uka, married and the father of several children, had been teaching in the public schools among his people for about ten years. He was tall, slender and had a wonderful smile besides being highly intelligent. He was there to study law in order that he might defend his people in their community from unscrupulous outside men who were forever trying to rob them of their meager landholdings. The other, short and stockily built, Mr. Abdulah, had come for the same reason and the two were fast friends.

Moro is the name used to designate a Philippine Mohammedan. But they do not look like the other Philippinos, their ancestors having come up to Mindanao by way of the many stepping-stone islands between Mindanao and Borneo, and earlier still from India.

These two young men used to stay after class just to talk with me and to learn more of that wonderful America; any small thing was of interest to them. They would come up to our house on Sunday mornings after our early church service (they did not attend our Christian service, of course) and they would spend a couple of hours in our sala looking at *Life, National Geographic, The Post* and anything else which we might have with colored pictures of people and places in the States. They did not want to be entertained with conversation at such times. Often they would not speak a word to each other for a long time, so engrossed were they in the magazines. We became very good friends and after class when they would stay to ask me about Christianity and its beliefs, I, taking a leaf from Dr. Frank Laubach's notebook, asked them to tell me about their Koran and its teaching.

When the second semester began, these two friends brought to the University four other Moros from the island of Jolo, through their persuasion and their accounts of "the red-haired woman from the States who taught a Bible class and also had become their good friend." This time the course was the Book of Acts. When we reached the second and succeeding chapters, the question period became very lively. "Did this experience ever happen to anyone else?" "Had I ever really known anyone who had spoken in an unknown tongue?" I could do no other than be true to what God had given me to know and experience of His Blessed Holy Spirit. I did not enlarge upon it, merely made the statement that I, myself, had been so baptized and that I knew a number of other people who had also received.

The group staying after class to ask more questions was large those late afternoons. They were so eager to know! They would not be put off. They simply had to know the facts and in detail. Finally the evening came when Lagume and his close friend were the only ones to stay. They began to ask me the same questions all over again. It seemed as if they believed that I would never let *them* down by any slight misrepresentation and so they had to ask the questions themselves and hear the answers for themselves alone. I soon noted on this late afternoon that the four Jolo Moros had returned and had joined us. One of the boys asked me what the language which I spoke that August day sounded like. I explained that while I didn't understand the meaning of the individual words, I was given a sense of the meaning as a whole, but that the words were very different from English words both in their structure and in their cadence. Then all of a sudden it occurred to me to say something like this: "For all these years I have remembered some of the words which were repeated over and over again as I spoke this heavenly language that day. One of the words was ——— another was ————." I noted as I said these two words and one other that there was an electrifying energy which seemed to have stricken them all. They were terribly solemn, startled, and their bodily posture was tense and as if ready to spring into action. There was a look of urgent eagerness to *know,* to understand the unknown, when Lagume, their recognized leader, cried out to me, "Mum, do you know what these words are? The first word is our Moro word for praying or prayer and the second word means grief, sorrow, suffering." I do not remember the meaning he gave of the third word, but it was also Moro.

I had never once heard these Moros speak their language among themselves. They always spoke English except when alone in their quarters. And I have never been able to recall those three words since.

It was not long after this that one afternoon in class, Lagume stood up to speak to a point in the class discussion period, and he prefaced his comment with the following phrase: "If Jesus Christ is the Son of God, and I believe He is, then. . . ." Thus my new found friend of the Spirit felt impelled from within to make his public confession of faith.

Another example of speaking in foreign tongues which led to evangelization has been told by William Caldwell, a Pentecostal evangelist, in the booklet *Pentecostal Baptism.* During a revival crusade he conducted in southern California a few years ago, the pastor of the local church spoke in tongues when a rabbinical student who had worked on a co-operative farm in Israel was present. The young Jew immediately identified the speech as fluent Hebrew, which he understood clearly, but which the pastor had never learned, and the young man was himself convinced by the power of this evidence.

This occasional occurrence, however, is not the only meaning of tongues as some have suggested. The total complex phenomenon also includes unintelligible speech and, most important, the speaker's sense of joy and release. The belief that glossolalia is only speech in a foreign language gives little or no consideration to Paul's long dissertation on tongues in I Corinthians 14. The Greek text simply does not support this meaning as the only one; when the writers referred to foreign tongues and meant specific ones, they said so quite clearly. In fact, even the most enthusiastic Pentecostals have abandoned this as a prime explanation. Experience, sometimes sad experience, has taught them much about both tongues and foreign evangelization.

The other of these explanations which view tongues as a useful but outmoded religious expression accepts all of the New Testament facts about speaking in tongues; namely, that the gift of tongues was an ecstatic gift; that a real and unknown tongue may be spoken by the one who has the gift; and that it does have a supernatural origin. The theory then maintains, however, that the gift was given only to get the church established. It was a supernatural sign which induced non-believers to give credence to the church, and which was gradually replaced with understanding and reasoning. This view does have the support of early historical evidence on its side, since glossolalia did, for all practical purposes, die out after the time of Tertullian.

This is essentially the point of view proposed by Hastings' *Dictionary of the Bible;* first published in 1909 and reprinted many times since, it is the source of a great deal of popular thinking on Biblical subjects. Glossolalia, as described in the article on the gift of tongues, is an "ecstatic utterance of praise, not only in poetic and symbolic speech, but also in languages or dialects not ordinarily spoken." The author of the discussion then goes on to state that the gift was given only for the critical period of the church's life and was not meant to be a permanent gift for the church.

A committee of the Episcopal Diocese of Los Angeles expressed this idea with even greater clarity in its report to the bishop in 1960 on modern glossolalia and the church. The report concludes: "The abnormal physical and psychological phenomena, which attracted so much attention on the day of Pentecost, tended to disappear within the Body of Christ, and at the last seem to have died out. The Whitsunday phenomena could be compared to a scaffolding surrounding a new edifice. Once the edifice (the Church) has been completed, the scaffolding became unnecessary and was discarded. 'When I was a child, I spake as a child . . . but when I became a man, I put away childish things.' (I Corinthians 13:11) The glossolalia occurred in the infancy of the Church. With her growth and maturity the Church wisely discarded the marks of infancy." Support has also been given this point of view by a suggestion elsewhere that the usual interpretation of tongues is "jejune and puerile."

This explanation, too, has its difficulties. On the basis of I Corinthians 13, both knowledge and prophecy would also have to be classified as childish if this understanding of Paul is accepted, for tongues is linked with them in that chapter. In addition, even in the next chapter where Paul does suggest that tongues be played down, he still maintains an emphasis on tongue speaking as a valuable personal religious experience.

There were reasons for the disappearance of tongues in the early church, several of them. The church grew up in a world which valued the irrational far more than ours does. There was not the need to keep these aspects of experience before the eyes of men; undoubtedly their need was more for restraint, a leash on their conscious irrationality. And of course, the fact is that the church did misuse this gift. One particular heretical group, the Montanists, for whom tongue-speech held central significance, split off and so the church threw the baby out with the bath water. There is always tension between those who stand for individual experience and those who stand for ecclesiastical authority. Because the church at that time had to have authority to survive, Montanism with its characteristic experience was thrust outside the Catholic church. This same tension accounts for much of the modern rejection of tongues. It is also true that the enthusiasm which often goes along with tongue speaking became an embarrassment and a source of difficulty as the church solidified its position. Tongue-speech was discouraged, and it seems to require some encouragement to persist; like a plant that is not watered, it died untended.

One evaluation of the report to the Los Angeles diocese, by a man who is neither tongue speaker nor clergy, is worth quoting: "To an unlearned layman . . . it is presumed that what is meant is that in early days glossolalia was needed as a crutch to the Church, but now the Church is strong and no longer needs the crutch. Therefore, whether glossolalia is authentic or not is not at issue. The entire controversy boils down to the fact that some authorities feel the Church has so matured as to be able to discard such manifestations of the

Holy Spirit . . . Truly it is difficult to imagine anyone, be he theologian, priest, bishop, or a mere layman, who could possibly consider that in matters involving God and religion we, as mortals, are anything other than infants or cripples."[8] To borrow the image of scaffolding, perhaps the edifice of the church could use some rebuilding.

AN EXPERIENCE OF THE HOLY SPIRIT

There is one further explanation of glossolalia, the view which accepts the interpretation of the New Testament writers, and this is the point of view of modern Pentecostalism, as well as of the entire movement in the Protestant churches. To understand this explanation we must know what is said in the original Greek, and this necessitates a short analysis.

The plain sense of the Greek is that those who speak in tongues are speaking in another language, a language which can be translated. The word "glosso-lalia" comes from two Greek words: tongues (γλώσσαις) and to speak (λαλεῖν). The following variations of the phrase were used:

in Acts 2:4, to speak in other tongues (λαλεῖν ἑτέραις γλώσσαις)

in Mark 16:17, to speak in new tongues (γλώσσαις λαλεῖν καιναῖς)

in Paul's reference to kinds of tongues (γένη γλωσσῶν)

The word "glossa" or tongue has several clearly differentiated meanings. It means a tongue, the actual physical organ. It also means an antiquated or obsolete expression which needs explaining. It signifies a language or dialect. These were meanings in common Greek usage, and there is little or no doubt from the context what the authors of the Greek text implied: speaking in tongues was speaking a language, a different, a new, or a foreign language.

What zeros us in on Paul's belief, however, is his use of

8. D. D. Stone, "The Speaking in Tongues and the Episcopal Church," *Trinity*, Vol. 1, No. 3, Eastertide, 1962, p. 10.

the word we read as "interpret" in most English versions of the Bible. Paul believed that it was fine to speak in tongues in private for one's own edification, but in public it must *be interpreted,* or it would carry no more meaning than its sound—than so much gibberish. He believed that speaking in tongues was essentially meaningful in itself and could be "interpreted" or, as he put it in Greek, "translated," in the same sense that a court interpreter or the United Nations interpreters render the sense of a message on the spot.

The word Paul used (ἑρμηνεύαιν or its variants) is found twenty-one times in the New Testament and the Greek version of the Old Testament. In eighteen of these twenty-one passages the word clearly means "to translate." As J. G. Davies has developed in his article on "Pentecost and Glossolalia" in the *Journal of Theological Studies,* Paul used this word "to translate," meaning to reproduce the message of an unintelligible utterance in tongues into ordinary, understandable language. Thus, when we read in Paul that a tongue can be interpreted, we know that he means translated, although not by conscious thought, it is true. The translation comes through the unconscious, the Spirit, as does the tongue-speech.

If we read the Greek sense and listen to Paul, we find he believed that those who spoke in tongues spoke a new, an angelic, or a foreign language, which was capable of being translated into ordinary speech by one moved in the Spirit. And Paul was an authority on speaking in tongues. Paul talking about tongues was a different matter from Paul talking on the subject, say, of women and hats. He spoke in tongues more than all the others—and he made this quite clear by the way he lit into the subject with the Corinthians.

The New Testament Greek also indicates quite clearly that Paul and the other New Testament writers believed that when the Holy Spirit was given to an individual, he was endowed with certain supernatural gifts. They believed that God gave these more than human abilities, or charismata, to a man as the divine spirit indwelt him. Paul listed nine of these gifts: gifts of knowledge, wisdom, faith, healing, miraculous powers, discernment of spirits, prophecy, tongues, and the interpretation of tongues. These gifts consisted of special knowledge or power which was conveyed directly through spiritual intuitions, visions, dreams, and automatic speech. According to the New Testament these things are all of one piece. Tongues is but another example of a divine gift in which the Spirit possesses the vocal chords rather than the visual screen or the individual consciousness. If tongues is seen in this context, and it is realized how much a part of the New Testament world view these charismata are, then it becomes easier to understand the New Testament view of glossolalia as a more than human gift, a spontaneous gift from beyond the human personality.

In at least one place in the New Testament, in Acts 2, the experience of tongues was that of foreign languages which were understood directly by those who were present. In addition the descriptions in Paul's letters and Acts indicate that a religious experience usually accompanied the occurrence of tongues. In most of the accounts of Acts speaking in tongues was an outer manifestation of a deeply significant conversion experience. It was an outer sign of the entrance of the individual into new life.

All of these qualities recur in modern tongue-speech. Once one realizes that there are verifiable instances of foreign languages spoken spontaneously in tongue speaking, then it is relatively easy to accept Paul's idea that tongues which are not understandable may be non-human or angelic—or even demonic—speech. Two more short examples bear out this point.

The eminent and psychologically well-versed author, Anton Boisen, gives a present-day example of glossolalia involving a foreign language in his work *Religion in Crisis and Custom:*

> On one occasion an ignorant colored woman (as the world counts wisdom) addressed the meeting and under the power of the Holy Ghost she broke forth with the marvel of an unknown tongue, a tongue that the intelligent observer could

> easily perceive was classic. Although I could not understand the utterance, I detected at once its Latin origin. When this demonstration ceased, the sister said, "Now you all know that wasn't me. I can't speak my own language right, much less a foreign one. That wasn't me. That was the Holy Ghost." The leader then called for an interpreter. A sister rose and said, "I am not an interpreter but I can speak the Spanish language and the sister spoke in that tongue. I didn't get it all, but the last phrase was, Glory to the precious name of Jesus."[9]

A second instance is known personally to me. A few years ago a close friend of mine was in a group in which she was moved to speak in tongues. One of the men present happened to be a seminary professor. When she had finished, he informed her that he was a Hebrew scholar and that she had given a reasonably good talk in Hebrew, of which she had no knowledge.

The spontaneous or gift-like quality of tongues, its complete givenness, is most strikingly seen when it occurs in the private devotional life of a person who has not identified it with a particular form of worship or a Biblical pattern of experience. I first learned that this could happen several years ago when a friend, out of curiosity, attended a group in which there was tongue speaking. She was surprised to find that this was the practice which she had been using for some time in private prayer, independently of any direct suggestion from outside. For her tongues had "just happened," and she had fallen into the New Testament pattern without questioning it. Another instance is that of the young Baptist minister who recently told me of his first experience of tongues when he was a boy of twelve, at prayer alone in his room. It had happened to him, also, without preparation or warning, and since it was meaningful to him, he continued to speak in tongues without discussing it outside the family.

9. Anton J. Boisen, *Religion in Crisis and Custom: A Sociological and Psychological Study*, New York, Harper & Brothers, 1955, p. 80.

THE POWER OF TONGUE SPEAKING

The religious power of an experience of tongue speaking can only be told by the person himself. The following account was written by a young man who had had severe emotional problems and for over a year had required counseling. The real step forward religiously, as well as psychologically did not come until he had the experience of speaking in tongues which he describes. He is now a happily married and stable young man, the father of a child. His own words speak for him.

> There were several people in the room that night, one a girl whom I was to marry later, but did not know at the moment. What were we doing there? In the first place the room was just an average living room belonging to the associate priest of our church. It was nothing fancy, like you would see in "Better Homes and Gardens" or some other magazine. It was plain and homey with a nice fireplace, a clock that ticked louder than usual, a couch and enough chairs for all to sit on, though some chose to sit on the floor.
>
> It was not my first time to be in this room with most of these same people. I had been there a time or two before. I guess I came because of the people and the atmosphere created about them. They were not unusual people, no great scholars or movie stars, just plain, every-day, run of the mill, hard working people. But why did we gather there every Tuesday night? It was simple. We were waiting for and wanting something; only two or three of the group really had any conception of what to expect. Least of all did I know what was to happen this night.
>
> My being there goes back before this time; about two years. I was a new number in the Church of Christ and especially this church. It was different from other churches I had been to. Why? I don't know. Many of its members tried to explain and have come up with wonderful answers, but I always felt they were for them, not for me. Somehow my attraction and

being led to this church was different from theirs, though I am sure they were there for similar reasons.

As a youth I had attended many churches in my search for the Christ, but none of them ever affected me as strangely as this one . . .

Both my parents worked hard to provide nice material things in life; a fine home; a car for me; money when I needed it. I was quite active in high school society. I even ran for President of the school. I didn't win the election, but was appointed to a high position in the winner's cabinet; a little coalition we two had worked out together before the election!

The junior college life was pretty much the same routine, only in a different setting and atmosphere. I was Associated Men Students' President and yell leader of the school, and somehow through all of this I managed a good grade point average. Life for me at that time was certainly on the surface wonderful, aspiring, and going places, or so I thought.

But why was I led to this church? Why did I like it there? The answer, I know now; but at that time it was just a mystery. It seems that this well rounded, educated, and socially acceptable person of my youth had a hidden life he was leading and was so clever at hiding it from every one. So well hidden was it that it hadn't really made any kind of an impression on my conscious being as to where it was actually leading me. I can only say that in the end the results would have been disastrous. Because of its psychological intensity and because this paper is not intended as a résumé of my psychological development step by step, but instead of my spiritual development, I will leave this second life as it was in its problems. The important thing to note here is that I am sure now that the Lord led me to this church and its psychological guidance by its Rector. I am firmly convinced that the Lord led me to this church because I couldn't hide my other life from Him as cleverly as I hid it from others and myself.

From my first day at this church I felt the Lord's pulling power and my need for a more spiritual, as well as psychological, understanding of myself. As it was, the Lord knew I was only half the whole me on the surface, and fortunately I recognized my need to discover the whole me, the whole inner realm of my life which lay dormant until I entered this church.

My development was not easy. There was much hardship to endure through the next two years. A complete twist in my life was taking place. The real me was coming alive. As I developed, it grew worse. The temptation was ever-present. Several times it overtook me, but always the outcome seemed to be one step further in my new self-realization. The real me was becoming something other than the prideful, but naive self which I was living. The pace, I realize now, was very fast for a person in my psychological and spiritual void. I grew and grew at a very fast pace. The awareness was not evident to me then, but the change was being recognized.

Part of this development, I am sure now was being a member of this Tuesday night prayer group. It wasn't a new group; it had been around for a long time. There was, however, something new about the group. A new movement was being started within. Only a few knew about it. Those few, I felt at the time, were keeping it to themselves. I can't say that I was not aware of this new movement; I had heard Father mention it several times. As I sat there this night, I found it hard to pray during the intercessions for the needy in prayer. Something was troubling me that night. After several of the others had gone home, I stayed for a while longer. As we talked, we mentioned this movement. Later, as I recall, we were in prayer again, but praying was still hard. Somehow I knew if I was to receive any help with this problem I needed the laying on of hands as an assistance. This sacrament was usually done at the prayer group with the recipient sitting in a chair provided for its administration in the center of the living room. Because I was one of the unusual ones who found it more comfortable to sit on the floor, I decided this night not to sit in the chair, but instead placed my hands on it. The following episode that took place was the highlight of my growth and development in my becoming a whole man in Christ. Because of this fact I choose to relate the following from the record book I generally keep:

"The uplifting I received was complete. As I knelt there in front of the chair, with my hands flat on it, Father and his wife placed their hands on my head and shoulders. As they prayed for me to receive the gift of the Holy Spirit . . . I was filled . . . every part of me, every bone, tissue, and muscle. So complete was Its electrifying presence that my hands became heavy and felt as though they were bursting with electricity. Then both hands began to rise and Father placed his hand on them and his other hand on my cheek and I burst out in an unknown tongue. My spirit, the inner man was completely in the control of the Holy Spirit. So beautiful and so wonderful was this giving of my spirit to Christ. My whole body tingled and was filled with his warmth. Praise God. Praise God."

Why was this moment so important to me in my development? Because from this night onward I knew, first, there really was a God, a God who controls and directs his children because He knows their needs. Secondly from this night onward my whole life and my awareness of it seemed to quicken. The fire of the Lord was now open and given complete freedom to express and burn itself within me. It seemed, now, as if all the torture of my second life was behind me. I realize, of course, I will never completely be rid of this life's temptation, but because of this outpouring of the Holy Spirit, this one experience, I knew there was hope. This completeness in my union with Christ hastened the awareness which I now have in my relationship to myself, my fellow men, and my God. It so quickened my pace in development that I was able in a relatively short time to be released from my counseling. I was set free a new man. I was able to face objectively my second self and realize that only as I endeavor in the Christ and seek His guidance, will this new life be stable.

A few months after this release, I married the girl whom I mentioned earlier. Today life is very happy, and we have a new completeness in our lives. We have a son. Together, now, we both realize and praise God for the impact of that night. The outpouring of God's Spirit in our lives has made a union everlasting and wonderful.

If speaking in tongues is accepted as a Christian phenomenon, in the way the writers of the New Testament saw and described it, the experience is seen as far more complex than many people believe. It is a supernatural gift of a foreign or non-human language given at the time of the breakthrough of the Holy Spirit into an individual life. The speaker, as many have expressed it, has the sense of being filled with a reality beyond himself which speaks through him. Once this experience has been known, one can enter into it at will, and he finds an immediate way of relating to God and the Holy Spirit. This language can be interpreted either by the individual or by another person possessed by the Spirit. It indicates that something beyond the human ego is in possession of the human life.

There are difficulties to this interpretation also. It runs counter to the world we live in. Few people even consider seriously the idea that divine powers actually do possess human beings. The rationalistic materialism of our age which is certainly the dominant philosophy of our time can find no place for such an experience. This world which has been so successful in creating antibiotics and atom bombs finds its credulity taxed by the experience of a strange, foreign tongue which purports (for no seeming good purpose) to be given by a divine spirit as a sign of its indwelling. This is simply incomprehensible to many modern men.

The conclusion as to which of these explanations is more plausible depends upon something more than the evidence we have presented. What one can make of this experience will be determined by the world view from which he regards it. Whether tongues is viewed as a psychological anomaly or a religious experience of real worth will depend not so much upon the facts as upon the way we look at the world in which we live, whether our world view has a place for such experiences or not. It is now our task to sketch two Christian world views current in our world today to provide a backdrop against which we can evaluate the experience of tongues.

Chapter VII

UNDERSTANDING TONGUES

There are two fundamentally different ideas about the way man comes to know God. Both have had wide currency in the Christian tradition. One of them has been accepted by Western Christianity, both Catholic and Protestant, for the past five centuries and it has supplied the groundwork for our unique Western civilization. But it has little place for a direct experience of God and, so, little place for tongues. If we are to find value in this recurring experience of tongues, we must turn to the other world view about how man knows God, and this is a world view, we find, which is scarcely known at all among us who are Western Christians. Although it was the view of the Christian church for well over a thousand years, today it is one we have to picture for ourselves, and we must describe it in relation to our own culture if we are to come to a sympathetic understanding of tongues.

The basic view of the Western world is that man gets his knowledge of all reality, God included, through his sense experience and his reason making inferences upon it. According to this belief man has no direct contact with the spiritual reality which lies behind the material world. If it is only across this threshold that God and reality reach man, through his sense experience and thus his reason, then man has no transcendental knowledge. This is essentially the view of Aristotle. Thus limited to this world, man has made the most of it and developed our science and technology which have transformed this world around us.

The other view about how man knows God has not only

been part of the Christian tradition; it is the view of most cultures not touched by the thinking of Western Europe. This was essentially the view of Plato. It maintains that man has knowledge of the world in which he lives not only through sense experience and reason, but also through direct experience of the non-physical world. This view adds another dimension to experience and introduces a greater complexity to human experience.

This point of view sees man as standing between two worlds, an outer one of material reality with endless potentiality, and an inner one of spiritual reality, equally potent and inexhaustible. The only way he has to know anything about the inner world is to know it within himself, to live it, touch it, examine it as he does the outer, physical world. He can know it best by experiences—through his dreams, his visions and fantasies, his spiritual intuitions, his experiences of tongues, and other contacts—and then by examining and assessing them all as carefully as possible. His subjective experiences are just as real and important as his experience of the outer world; they take just as much effort to discover and live out, and they have an equally determining effect on the experiences he does have in the outer world.

In this point of view the experience of tongues is a piece of data, important, interesting, and valuable, as important as any other. It is a fact which keeps recurring, a subjective experience which has something to tell us about men and their contact with spiritual reality. From this point of view there is nothing absurd about it. Of course it arouses prejudice; it is personal, subjective, often occurring in strange surroundings, but it gives us an actual contact with this inner world.

Once we look at tongues from this world view, we can look at the evidence for it, taking examples from both the simplest surroundings and the most sophisticated, using the ability to reason and analyze. We can look at the histories of those who have had the experience, comparing the different circumstances from which they come to it, really listening to what they have to say. We may be able to observe the change in their inner religious lives because of the experience, as well as the difference in their outer lives. We can talk with them and try to enter into their experience sympathetically. Only then is it possible to decide about the theological value and significance of an experience such as speaking in tongues.

It may seem that tongues is an experience which does not fit, which seems inconsequential or even absurd, but it can change a man's way of looking at himself and his world, and so can change him and other men. Remember, it was not a well-laid blockbuster, but the absurd antics inside a very rare atom which changed the philosophy of modern science and the course of modern life. There seems to be something equally persistent and strange about speaking in tongues. This experience simply is; it must be assessed as fact.

It is difficult to understand sympathetically any world view other than our own. A world view becomes part of the very experiences we have of that world, and it is only with real effort that we can shake ourselves loose from the point of view we hold and look objectively upon it. Perhaps the best way to look at our own philosophy is to describe another belief held by people who are as intelligent and sincere as we. Then we are in a position to decide which frame of reference we wish to have as our way of looking at the world. If we of the Western world are to try seriously to assess the place of tongues, we must try to understand this other world view, for the experience makes no sense in our own.

The belief that man has direct contact with more than physical reality has a long and illustrious history. It has been held by some of the greatest philosophers and theologians among men, and so we shall sketch its history. In recent years this world view has received interesting confirmation from one of the empirical sciences. Two medical psychologists, Freud and Jung, in their attempt to help sick people get well, found that man is influenced by far more than his physical environment and the people around him. They discovered that they could not help these people recover without understanding a vast area of psychic reality of which man is not conscious—hence it is termed the unconscious—which has a direct effect on his emotions, his body, and his actions. The school of psychology which has followed the lead of Dr. Jung has described in detail this realm of non-physical or psychic reality and the "entities" in it. This offshoot of the physical sciences has offered the most recent confirmation of a non-physical realm with which man is in direct contact. In the thinking of these men and their followers there is nothing absurd about either direct contact with non-physical reality or the experience of glossolalia.

THE WORLD OF THE NON-PHYSICAL

Among most peoples, primitive and culturally advanced, there is a belief that man is not only in contact with the material world, but with a non-material one as well. Thinkers in Western Europe, however, have come to consider it superstitious to believe in the non-material world, and as they came to this conclusion, they looked for confirmation of their point of view in some other culture. They came to believe that the Greeks of the magnificent golden age in the fifth and fourth centuries before Christ had viewed the world much as they were coming to see it. This has been a very persuasive thought, for the Greeks did start man upon his quest for a rational understanding of the world in which we live. But they were not as rational or as sensible as we sometimes like to believe.

While the Greeks did bring an appreciation of human reason, they did not in any way reject as unreasonable those experiences which could not be explained as resulting from sense experience. As a people they believed in two worlds, in two kinds of experience. The Greeks still valued the irrational experiences of life—the dream, the Pythian oracle, the Dionysian revel, the poetic ecstasy, the erotic possession of madness. They believed that through these experiences man made contact with a non-physical, more than human reality. This fact has been demonstrated in a thoroughly documented study by the Regius Professor of Greek at Oxford, E. R. Dodds.

One of the greatest thinkers of all times was the incomparable Plato, who expressed the rational side of Greek genius as well as any man. Again, there has been more romantic thinking about him than objective analysis of what he said. We tend to recognize him, along with his master Socrates, only as the father of rational human thought, who developed dialectic and shaped the canons of rational thinking. But few people realize that he accepted without question the value of religious experience, of what the Greeks called "divine madness." "Our greatest blessings come to us by way of madness; provided the madness is given us by divine gift," Plato wrote. (Or, in another translation: ". . . we owe our greatest blessings to madness; if only it be granted by Heaven's bounty." Phaedrus, 244.) And he went on at some length to describe and show his deep appreciation for four kinds of irrational experience, the divine madness of love, prophecy, Dionysian ecstasy, and poetic intuition. Plato did not believe, as moderns do, that we get all of our knowledge and feeling through sense experience and reason. He believed that men had contact with a realm of non-physical reality.

When Plato came to write the *Republic* and the *Laws*, he recognized the danger of everyone having experiences of God. Society would simply disintegrate, and so these experiences were to be confined to licensed prophets or to the oracle at Delphi. Throughout the *Republic* Plato was writing from the belief that men are reasonable enough to follow these directions, and so he did not spend much time on sanctions to enforce them. Writing the *Laws* in his old age, after having seen the society of the "rational" Greeks crumble and dissolve before his eyes, Plato concluded that religious uniformity must be enforced by law.

Even though Plato perceived all the dangers in his belief that there were two worlds, it never occurred to him to alter this idea in order to avoid the dangers. He believed that ordinary men had contact with two worlds, and this was a dangerous truth, but still a description of the nature of reality, a fact that had to be dealt with. For centuries the ancient world accepted his view of reality as nearly axiomatic, and thinkers of all ages have turned back to read the insights of this great man. Clearly the man who paid such reverence to the oracle at Delphi would have seen nothing inherently absurd in tongues.

THE WORLD VIEW OF JESUS

While Jesus of Nazareth was not a philosopher in the ordinary sense, his importance is obvious even to those who do not accept him as the son of God. Even they realize that he was a man of deep religious experience, and so they may be interested in the world view which his words and actions imply. Jesus of Nazareth did not state an explicit theory of knowledge, but he had an implicit one, one implied in what he did, which was very much like the theory Plato worked out so carefully. It is for this reason that the early church found it so easy to fit the teachings and practice of Jesus into the philosophy of Plato to give the world the first real theology it had known. Since the implicit theory of knowledge of Jesus was so similar to that of Plato, it seldom occurred to ancient theologians to examine Jesus' view of reality. It is a good exercise for us who have been brought up in another world view to see how sharply the essential world view of Jesus conflicts with that of our time.

Jesus believed in the reality of our contact with a non-physical world. He believed in communion with God. He also believed that he had to thrash it out with the devil before he could be clear about his own destiny. He also believed, according to the gospel accounts, in a variety of spiritual beings which had a direct effect upon men and could be directly experienced by one with sufficient perception. He called these beings angels, unclean spirits, evil spirits (there is a list of colorful names for them). He believed in both angels and demons. Indeed, the gospel narrative is shot through with them. There are 196 such references, scattered through every part of each of the Four Gospels, and for the most part the words and actions of Jesus make very little sense unless these realities are taken into account. The list of passages in which they occur is included in Appendix A.

One recognition of the world view of Jesus among orthodox churchmen has come from a scholarly Dominican priest with a knowledge of depth psychology. Writing from Oxford in 1952, Victor White said to the theological world:

> In the pages of the New Testament, Satan and the devils may be said to be fairly ubiquitous from the beginning to the end. The polite efforts of nineteenth-century Liberal criticism to exorcise the demons from the New Testament, to explain away its more "devilish" passages as a later and superstitious adulteration of the pure ethical milk of the Gospel, or at least to apologize for them as an unimportant concession to contemporary illusions, have proved a dismal failure. Even the most radical criticism of *Formgeschichte* holds that these passages belong to the most primitive strata, the essential core, of the evangelical tradition. Especially since Schweitzer and Otto, it has become difficult to read the Gospels at all otherwise than as an account of the struggle between the *de jure* Reign of God and the *de facto* Reign of Satan—the actual "prince" or "god" of this world over human hearts, minds and affairs. "The devil," Tertullian will say, with customary exaggeration and insight, "is fully known only to Christians." . . . Not only the words and actions of Christ as related in the Gospels, but also the Epistles, and

> still more obviously the Apocalypse, are largely unintelligible except on the supposition of the reality and activity of Satan and other malevolent spirits.[1]

And, we would add, of the Holy Spirit and its manifestations. It should be noted too, of course, that when Jesus and the other Biblical writers referred to demons and angels, they did not turn them into concrete absurdities, but viewed them as visionary experiences which were real and yet not material.

There are only a limited number of conclusions we can make regarding this neglected aspect of Jesus' belief about reality. Either Jesus knew what he was talking about and there are two worlds, a physical one and a spiritual one, or Jesus was wrong. If he was wrong, he was taken in by the world view of his time along with Plato, Athanasius, Augustine, and Chrysostom (all competent philosophers). In any case, serious consideration of Jesus of Nazareth demands a serious consideration of *his* world view and his theory of knowledge.

Most modern, educated Christians have been brought up to believe that Jesus' concern with the realm of the angelic and the demonic was determined simply by the naïve world view of his own century and by his being caught in it. It was a contemporary illusion, and therefore we must just dismiss this aspect of his ministry. At a recent conference of clergymen, when I proposed to discuss the subject of the angelic realm, exactly this objection was raised, and then suddenly the objector said: "Yes, I see. I have simply assumed that my world view was the correct one, and that of Jesus was incorrect—really without ever critically examining one against the other."

According to the gospel record neither Jesus nor those around him spoke in tongues during his earthly ministry, but Jesus did discourse with the demons who possessed those

1. Victor White, *God and the Unconscious,* New York, The World Publishing Company (Meridian Books), 1961, pp. 192 f.

whom he healed. If it is possible for a demon, a non-physical reality, to possess the voice of a man and to speak a known language, does it not follow that some angelic or demonic force, or even the Holy Spirit might equally well possess a human voice to speak an unknown language? The world view of Jesus opens wide the door to the actuality of tongues.

And Paul, according to his own words, did speak with tongues; we have seen that he had this gift more than any of the others. Since he believed in a spiritual world which was very close to men, with which they were in real contact, and which had a very real effect upon human lives, it was easy for him to value his experiences of tongues. It was another breakthrough from the side of spiritual reality. It is nearly impossible to understand Paul's message if one excises from it the belief in the spiritual world and its interaction with men. Paul's message of salvation is based on this belief and can only be understood in terms of it. His message is really quite simple.

He saw that men are beset by beings from a spiritual realm which has elements of both good and evil in it. If man is to escape being overcome by the evil elements, the forces abroad in the world which seek his destruction, he must take real religion seriously, enlisting the help of the Holy Spirit, the church, and positive spiritual forces. Salvation then is not just a matter of moral perfectionism. Salvation is the result of a battle in which we are rescued by the Holy Spirit from the evil in the world, and that evil is very real; it is evil in the form of malignant spiritual entities.

About this Paul is very clear. He writes in Galatians 4:8, "Formerly, when you did not acknowledge God, you were the slaves of beings which in their nature are no gods. But now that you do acknowledge God—or rather, now that he has acknowledged you—how can you turn back to the mean and beggarly spirits of the elements?" His magnificent thanksgiving for salvation in Romans 8 ends with the words, "For I am convinced that there is nothing in death or life, in the realm of spirits or superhuman powers [angels and archons in the Greek text], in the world as it is or the world as it shall be, in the forces of the universe, in heights or depths—nothing in all creation that can separate us from the love of God in Christ Jesus our Lord." This is not just nice poetry; it is spiritual realism. In Colossians 2:15 he states that Christ "discarded the cosmic powers and authorities like a garment; he made a public spectacle of them and led them as captives in his triumphal procession." Paul had many names for spiritual reality and he used them frequently; the complete list of these references is found in Appendix A.

To one who viewed reality as Paul did, who believed that man has direct experience of the non-physical, spiritual world, the experience of tongues did not raise the questions that it does with so many today. Paul had just one problem with tongues. He had the same problem Plato had with his prophets. Tongue speakers sometimes developed a God complex and would not listen to anyone else. Bedlam reigned, and yet it never occurred to Paul simply to suggest to the Corinthians that they were having a meaningless experience.

What he did point out to the Corinthians were the things they had to take into account if this experience were to be a fruitful one. The trouble with most people is that they cannot stand the tension between sense experience on the one side and these direct religious experiences on the other, and so they end up siding with one and avoiding the other completely. They reject the validity of the religious experience—the direct, experienced confrontation with non-physical reality as a part of the lives of ordinary men—or else they give themselves over to direct religious experience and reject the authority of sense experience and reason in connection with it. Indeed there is good reason why Paul's words have some authority for Christians.

The rest of the New Testament writers had the same world view as Paul; this is most clearly seen in the references to angels and demons which we find scattered through the pages they wrote. In Acts, for instance, we cannot ignore the fact that the story hinges on these realities which spring from the spiritual world. The references, which will also be found listed in Appendix A, show the same concern for this other world. None of these writers would have found anything absurd in tongues and in none of them do we find any criticism of a practice which, according to Acts, was very much in evidence. The world view of the New Testament had a place for tongues, and tongues seems to have raised the question of whether we have any place for the world view of the New Testament.

Although some people argue that the authors of the New Testament were not sufficiently educated to appreciate the difficulties of their beliefs in the spiritual realm, the same argument simply does not hold water for the early fathers of the church. Most of them were men schooled in Greek philosophy and learning, some, like Origen, acknowledged as the greatest minds of their time. These fathers, who shaped the very foundations of the Christian faith, were as aware and reflective as the best minds today. The neglect these men receive today may be due to the embarrassment which is caused as we read of their belief in the direct action of the spiritual world upon the lives of men.

We might say that these beings are almost as thick in the pages of the ante-Nicene fathers as in the pages of the New Testament. This was the climate of thought in which these men thought and lived and moved. They believed in a spiritual world of spiritual entities which had important consequences for human lives, and they also believed that some of these beings were malignant and some good. Origen, for one, taught that angels do exist, although he did not believe he could explain what they are or why they exist. But he wrote many pages describing the various kinds and their heavenly tasks. They devote themselves to God; knowing which men are worthy of divine approval, they co-operate with these men, bearing the human supplications to heavenly places and returning to confer the benefits of God. They also dispose of the hostility of demons, and just because some angels, persuaded by that principal apostate the devil, have fallen away, this does not change their basic nature as servants in accomplishing the salvation of men. Clement of Rome, Barnabas, and Ignatius included similar discussions in their works.

Justin Martyr, Methodius, and Lactantius all discuss the transgression of the angels and their fall at some length and in a way not nearly so metaphysical as the ideas in Revelation. Originally, they tell, God committed the care of men and all things under heaven to angels, but they went astray. Thus fallen they subdued the human race through magical writings, fears and punishments, taught men to offer sacrifices, sowed murders, wars, adulteries, and all wickedness. Instead of protecting men, they are now busy bedeviling the very creatures they were sent to care for.[2]

There was the same concern among the later fathers; for instance, Augustine's *City of God,* his *Confessions,* and his other works keep the reality of angel and demon powers constantly before the reader. They form an essential part of his thinking about salvation. He asks, after all, what is man to be saved from? It is the demonic world, and one of the great agencies committed to this work is the very positive host of heaven.

We have already noted the references to tongue-speech which occur in the writings of the fathers. The idea of tongues was a credible one from their view of the world, for they believed that men have direct access to spiritual reality;

2. *The Ante-Nicene Fathers,* op. cit.
Origen, *De Principiis,* Pref. 6–10; I, V, 1–5; I, VIII, 1–4.
The Recognitions of Clement, II, XLII ff.
Epistle of Barnabas, XVIII.
Ignatius, *Epistle to the Trallians,* V; *to the Philippians,* IV–XI.
Justin Martyr, *First Apology,* LVI–LVIII; *Second Apology,* V.
Methodius, *The Discourse on the Resurrection,* III, 1.
Lactantius, *The Divine Institutes,* II, XV–XVIII, *Epitome of the Divine Institutes,* XXVII–XXVIII.

as we have seen, the idea of tongues was never rejected or turned into an absurdity. The practice continued for several centuries, and it died out when it was overdone by one group, the Montanists. For practical reasons rather than theoretical ones, speaking in tongues was ignored; it was an embarrassment in a world that wanted to pin something perverse onto Christians, and an embarrassment to a church that was beginning to assert its authority over men, at best none too easy to control. And so tongues were not heard for many centuries in the West.

We have already described one branch of Christendom, however, which has continued in the tradition of the fathers of the church and of Plato. In the Eastern Orthodox tradition the contact of the individual with the spiritual world is still a concrete possibility. No wonder my Russian priest friend had so much difficulty understanding the furor about tongues, and so little trouble discussing the subject with openness and warmth. He did not have to be defensive. He stands within a philosophical tradition in which it is possible for tongues to be meaningful.

RETURN TO PLATO

This Platonic point of view has not gained much favor in Western theology for reasons we are about to demonstrate. And yet this tradition in Christianity has never been lost entirely in the West. Both deeply thoughtful men and enthusiastic religious movements have returned to it, among them for instance, the Cambridge Platonists in the seventeenth century. This brilliant and attractive group, notably Henry More, Ralph Cudworth, John Norris, and Whichcote, revived a Christian interest in Plato in opposition to the doctrines of John Calvin on the one side and the philosophy of Hobbes on the other. Like More—whose thinking was influenced by the spiritual experiences of an early Quaker, Lady Ann Conway—all of these men were deeply interested in spiritual phenomena.

While, at the time they wrote, they seemed to be swimming against a current far too great for them, their work had a strong influence in English theology and thought.

In recent years several top-flight Western thinkers have returned to the Platonic point of view in an attempt to develop a comprehensive view of reality. The outstanding English Platonic scholar, A. E. Taylor, for one, has written extensively in the field of Christian theology, incorporating a basic Platonism into his Christian view. His Gifford Lectures, published as *The Faith of a Moralist,* comprise one of the most sophisticated apologies for Christianity in the last century.

The profound and deeply mystical Baron von Hügel has also written from an essentially Platonic point of view. He studied the mystical experience of an exceptional woman, St. Catherine of Genoa, and of the group which gathered around her.[3] In her life it is obvious that the power of God broke through in the same way in which it shows through the pages of the New Testament. Von Hügel's approach was to study these lives in which the power of spiritual reality was alive. Thus, he attempted to develop a theology based on actual experience which was similar to what once happened in the life of Jesus and the early church, and to relate it to the outer facts and thinking of the world in which he was living. He very nearly came to condemnation by the Catholic church for his efforts, but because of his risk there were people like Evelyn Underhill who came to know a fuller life than they had thought possible.

The renowned mathematician and philosopher, Alfred North Whitehead, clearly acknowledged the Platonic inspiration for his thinking. Among the fertile ideas of Plato which

3. Baron Friedrich von Hügel, *The Mystical Element of Religion as Studied in Saint Catherine of Genoa and Her Friends,* Vol. I, Introduction and Biographies; Vol. II, Critical Studies, London, J. M. Dent & Sons, 1927. Von Hügel composed his thoroughly German phrases in English and, apparently with pride, listed his honorary degrees from St. Andrew's and Oxford on his title pages.

he used, the *Timaeus* was a particular source upon which he built his philosophical system. He, too, believed that man has contact with more than material reality.

All of the religious movements from the Lollards through the Anabaptists, the Camisards, the Jansenists, the Methodists, down to the modern Pentecostals are living witnesses to the idea that men still have direct contact with spiritual reality. The Pentecostals are the most recent and most clamorous witnesses to the idea that original religious experience is available to all who truly desire it. In our materialistic world it had to be expressed concretely (materialistically) in an outer manifestation or it would not have been heard at all. The present movement is a cry of protest against the materialism and formalism of Western Christianity.

There are practical difficulties to this point of view which we can observe throughout the history of Platonism. Plato could conceive of no way to control man's intuitions of the spiritual other than through law. Paul's letter to the Corinthians is an eloquent testimony to his problem. The history of Eastern Orthodoxy is constantly marred with spiritual excesses of the monks. The fanaticism of the Anabaptists, the Camisards, the early Methodists, and the Pentecostals are well known. Undeniably, there is a problem and a human one. Where man believes that he has direct access to spiritual reality, he can become inflated by his spiritual experience and he is then no longer a docile member of the social group. This does not make for either a tidy church or a tidy social organization.

THE OPPOSITE POINT OF VIEW

There is another fundamental philosophical point of view about the world we live in and how we come to know it, which was first clearly formulated by Plato's great pupil, Aristotle. This viewpoint does provide a more stable foundation for organized society, and while its significance was not appreciated in the ancient world, it has become the cornerstone of Western civilization. Aristotle believed that we have knowledge only through sense experience, what we know through our five senses, and through inferences which reason can make upon the data of these senses. Since this truth is applied to knowledge of God as well as anything else, therefore man's knowledge of God must also be inferred from sense experience. And this belief, then, casts doubts upon most direct religious experience of a non-physical realm.

Aristotle's thinking had not been very popular among the philosophers of the ancient world, and since his works were not preserved intact, as were the works of Plato, we must trace the way by which Aristotelian ideas came to a Christian formulation. They came first into the hands of the Arabs after centuries of obscurity. During the Arab renaissance of the ninth century Aristotle's thinking was elaborated by the leaders of the new Islamic rationalism. Gradually these works were imported across the Mediterranean into western Europe and, providing a basis for medical, mathematical, and other scientific thinking, they soon became the intellectual rage. Aristotle's resurrected works provided the philosophical basis for a new way of life, a life which stressed the importance of sense experience and the things of this world. Whether his philosophy mothered or was only wet nurse for the reaction to medieval otherworldliness we cannot be certain; Aristotle did provide a ready-made line of reasoning for gradually legitimizing sense experience alongside of authority. And this took the work of another great genius.

By the middle of the thirteenth century Thomas Aquinas was facing the fact that Christian thinking based on Plato, even as Augustine and Gregory of Rome had interpreted Plato, could not be sold to a world that was being swept by the new thought. Aquinas set himself to the task of reconciling the experience of the church with this new kind of thinking, the philosophy of Aristotle, and spent the rest of his life in the attempt. It could not have been done without his genius, for there is a deep cleavage between the world view of apostolic Christianity and that of Aristotle.

Aquinas kept one part of Aristotle's thought without expansion, his basic theory of knowledge: Man comes to know the world around him only through sense experience and through the almost infallible human reason working upon it. Together the senses and our reason not only bring all our knowledge to us; they make *absolute* knowledge available to us. The direct contact with God—either as a two-way line between man and God, or as a line back and forth between spiritual reality and man—does not exist at all except as mediated through matter, and thus through sense experience. Angels, which are very immaterial, can make contact with a human being only as they stir up the liver or the bile which then brings images before the conscious mind in visions and dreams. They cannot make any direct contact with man's consciousness. The only other way spiritual reality can be known is by rational inference based on just such sense experience.

And then, after spending his whole life demonstrating how man has no direct contact with immaterial reality, Aquinas, shortly before his death, had such an overwhelming direct experience of God that he wrote no more. Urged by a friend to complete his great work, the *Summa Theologica,* he answered, "I can do no more; such things have been revealed to me that all I have written seems as straw, and I now await the end of my life."

It is clearly difficult to integrate direct contact with spiritual reality into the point of view of Aristotle and Aquinas. Thus, there is little emphasis in Aquinas upon direct experience of the Holy Spirit, on revelation through dreams and visions and spiritual intuitions, on angels and demons, or on speaking in tongues.

Aquinas' influence comes close to being determinative. At first his thinking had to fight it out with contending philosophies, but one by one they went down, and by the time of the Reformation it had become the dominant Catholic world view. Aquinas was confirmed as *the* theologian of the Catholic church through the encyclical letter of Pope Leo XIII, *Aeterni Patris,* in 1879, and in this way Aristotle's basic thought became the foundation of all modern Catholicism. This is one reason why there is little glossolalia in the Catholic church.

Protestant theology simply broke up a train on the same track and got up a new head of steam, using for fuel the revolt against authoritarian limits on experience. But the track was still the basic rationalism and empiricism of Aristotle and Aquinas, which *was* helpful in freeing the physical sciences to take a look at their material. Virtually all conservative Protestant theology, and this comprises the great bulk of Protestant thought which attempts to deal with the actual experiences of the New Testament, follows the track of the basic rationalism of Aristotle and Aquinas, and so has little place for any direct experience of the spiritual, tongues included.

It is seldom realized how close the rationalism of the modern Protestant is to the scholasticism of the Catholic church. Two recent theological works comment on this, both of them in discussing the psychological approach to knowledge of God. Geddes MacGregor points out the persistence of the Aristotelian scholastic tradition in Protestant theology, and then remarks, "For various complex historical reasons, logic and theology had been developed in the Middle Ages together, so that it was difficult to extricate the one from the other. The Reformation produced a theology that was as closely allied in many ways with medieval logic as the pre-Reformation theology had been."[4] Dewar comments on the same matter in a little different way. "It is, indeed," he says, "a strange

4. Geddes MacGregor, *Introduction to Religious Philosophy,* Boston, Houghton Mifflin Company, 1959, p. 173. Henry P. Van Dusen's *Spirit, Son and Father* (New York, Charles Scribner's Sons, 1958, pp. 80 f.) makes the same point in laying the groundwork for theological discussion of the Holy Spirit.

fact that Calvin nowhere in his *Institutes* comes to grips with the question of what constitutes inspiration."[5]

The best and most sophisticated modern Protestant theology continues the basic theory of knowledge of Aristotle and Aquinas. F. R. Tennant's major work on the subject continues this same tradition. He states clearly that religious knowledge, apart from psychology (which he dismisses), depends entirely on sense experience and reason. "Such immediate *rapport* between God and the human soul as theism asserts, cannot be discerned with (ps) immediacy . . . nor can any transcendent faculty, mediating such contact, be empirically traced."[6] It is clear from his discussion of mysticism that visionary experiences, dreams, or tongues would none of them be meaningful within his theology.

Samuel Miller at Harvard has carried this thinking out logically in the following passage from his new book, based on his Beecher lectures:

> The world today is stripped down, absolved of all supernatural alliances, scrubbed clean of special events divinely arranged, deprived of the *deus ex machina,* the undeniable proof, the outright arrogance of miracle. Yet it is God's creation; He made it. The fact that we are no longer children or adolescents, propped up and sustained in our credulity by such assertions of direct invasion, or of immediate and implacably authoritative acts of the divine, means that we have entered a new stage of religion. Our faith now must be in a God not seen directly; a God whose acts are not separable from existence itself; a God in whom we must have faith, not because we have been overwhelmed by direct epiphanies, but because His glory pervades the common structure of things.[7]

5. Lindsay Dewar, *The Holy Spirit and Modern Thought,* New York, Harper & Brothers, 1959, p. 191.

6. F. R. Tennant, *Philosophical Theology,* Cambridge, England, The Cambridge University Press, 1956, pp. 324 f.; also pp. 311 f.

7. Samuel H. Miller, *The Dilemma of Modern Belief,* New York, Harper & Row 1963, pp. 16 f.

It is no wonder that Protestant theology has as much difficulty in giving serious consideration to tongues as does Roman Catholicism, particularly in view of the excesses and fanaticism to which it has been able to point as a part of this religious expression. Tongue speaking makes room for the direct contact of man with the spiritual realm, and this is a possibility which modern theology does not allow.[8] Instead, the controversy rages around books like Bishop Robinson's *Honest to God* and the recent *Objections to Christian Belief*, while the world of spirit, with its gifts of faith and knowledge and wisdom, its intimations of a world beyond, is largely forgotten.

FREUD AND JUNG

We have sketched two different world views, one of which has a place for tongues. Confirmation for this view, that man is in contact with non-physical reality as well as with material reality, comes to us from a somewhat unexpected quarter. It comes from the writing and practice of the great psychiatrist, Carl G. Jung. His works show that the realm of the non-physical can be treated empirically and with respect by a scientific-minded man of today, and the psychological point of view

8. There is another strand of this story which we have not touched on. It is the contribution of René Descartes to modern philosophy and theology. Both Aristotle and Aquinas believed that man's mind was greater than his consciousness, and that strange and mysterious intuitions did come to men. From the time of Descartes (and due to his influence), however, man's knowing capacity became understood as strictly limited to his conscious reason. Sense experience and reason were even more sharply split from spiritual intuition, which usually springs out of the "unconscious," and thus theological thinking was alienated even more from most experiences of direct contact with God. Discussion of this subject is beyond the scope of this volume. For those who would understand the basic, very complex problem, we suggest L. L. Whyte's *The Unconscious Before Freud* (New York, Basic Books, Inc., 1960), particularly pp. 26 f. and 31 f. A more complete study of modern theology would require consideration at length of the influence of Descartes.

which Jung expressed is not only the result of his own work, but of a whole school of thought. Without the monumental discoveries of Freud the thought of Jung would hardly have been possible. Philosophy had been theorizing about the non-physical aspect of reality and had even called it the unconscious, but from Schopenhauer and Nietzsche to Carus and Von Hartmann, the interest in this realm had been undisciplined, though intense. While much of the intellectual preparation had been made for the acceptance of Freud's discoveries, as L. L. Whyte has shown in *The Unconscious Before Freud*, yet it was Freud, with an excellent medical discipline, who turned the unconscious into empirical fact.

He had worked with Josef Breuer on the famous "Anna" who talked about the unpleasant things in her father's last illness whenever she was hypnotized, and one by one dropped her fascinating symptoms by the way. Now in his own practice, bit by bit, layer upon mysterious layer, Freud turned up parts of the total psyche which had been buried so deep that they could not be remembered just by conscious effort. First by hypnosis, then by analyzing their associations, studying slips of the tongue, playing word games, and then with the limitless material of dreams, he kept his patients dredging up memories, talking about them, and finding their clinical symptoms vanish into thin air. Nothing more than dealing with unconscious ideas changed the physical health of his patients, as well as their mental attitudes.

Freud presented his observations, together with a theory to explain them, in *The Interpretation of Dreams*. For the first time in centuries a scientific man, carefully using the empirical method, sought to show that there were non-physical forces which influenced human life. *The Interpretation of Dreams* is more than a landmark in psychology; it is one of the most important religious books of the twentieth century, for it opened the door to a serious study of the realm of the unconscious, the non-physical, which religion calls the world of the spirit. Freud, however, never investigated the religious implications of his own discoveries. His conclusions about the unconscious reached their final stage in *Moses and Monotheism*. There Freud concluded that there were fragments of racial memories in the unconscious which had a powerful effect on human behavior.[9]

Jung's work carried a step further. With forty more years of experience and thought behind him, he came to believe that the unconscious contains more than just repressed memories, personal or racial. The culmination of his thought is expressed in *Psychology and Alchemy* and *Aion*. Jung described the path by which he came to his conclusions in his posthumously published autobiography, *Memories, Dreams and Reflections.*

Jung saw elements in the unconscious which lead man forward, elements which are *superior* to human consciousness. From his work with his patients and out of studies of mythology and medieval alchemy, he came to believe that the human psyche is in direct touch with forces which not only guide consciousness to new levels, but are usually hidden more deeply than the primitive elements; they are forces of which man is even less conscious. He wrote:

> The assumption that the human psyche possesses layers that lie *below* consciousness is not likely to arouse serious opposition. But that there could just as well be layers lying *above* consciousness seems to be a surmise which borders on a *crimen laesae majestatis humanae*. In my experience the conscious mind can only claim a relatively central position and must put up with the fact that the unconscious psyche transcends and as it were surrounds it on all sides. Unconscious contents connect it *backwards* with physiological states

9. Although Freud is usually viewed as having a negative attitude towards religion, there is more religion in Freud than meets the eye. Interesting evidence of this has been gathered by David Bakan in *Sigmund Freud and the Jewish Mystical Tradition*, Princeton, D. Van Nostrand Co., Inc., 1958.

> on the one hand and archetypal data on the other. But it is extended *forward* by intuitions which are conditioned partly by archetypes and partly by subliminal perceptions depending on the relativity of time and space in the unconscious.[10]

Jung has spoken of these elements as archetypes, those earliest human "thought-forms" which lead their own independent life in the unconscious psyche, very much like part-souls. They pop up in dreams, in myths and visions in very objectified form, looking like some familiar person or thing, but representing how the unconscious—the collective, universal side of man—unknown to him, feels about such an object.

Dr. Jung has met and described this vast realm of being both in himself and his patients, which he calls the objective psyche or the collective unconscious. His own words are better than mine.

> The spontaneous utterances of the unconscious do after all reveal a psyche which is not identical with consciousness and which is, at times, greatly at variance with it. These utterances occur as a natural psychic activity that can neither be learnt nor controlled by the will. The manifestation of the unconscious is therefore a revelation of the unknown in man. We have only to disregard the dependence of dream language on environment and substitute "eagle" for "aeroplane," "dragon" for "automobile" or "train," "snake-bite" for "injection," and so forth, in order to arrive at the more universal and more fundamental language of mythology. This gives us access to the primordial images that underlie all thinking and have a considerable influence even on our scientific ideas. In these archetypal forms, something, presumably, is expressing itself that must in some way be connected with the mysterious operation of a natural psyche—in other words, with a cosmic factor of the first order.[11]

10. C. G. Jung, *Collected Works,* Vol. 12, New York, Pantheon Books, Inc. (Bollingen Foundation), 1953, p. 132.

11. This quotation and the next two are found in the *Collected Works,* Vol. 11, pp. 289, 486, and 320.

He has frequently, and in connection with all kinds of experiences, expressed the fact that men are in contact with a realm of being which is not material, but which is just as real and important as the material world. In the same book he remarked, with a bit of tongue in cheek: "Quite apart from merely personal prejudices, the psyche assimilates external facts in its own way . . . the laws or patterns of apperception . . . do not change, although different ages or different parts of the world call them by different names. On a primitive level people are afraid of witches; on the modern level we are apprehensively aware of microbes. There everybody believes in ghosts, here everybody believes in vitamins. Once upon a time men were possessed by devils, now they are not less obsessed by ideas . . ." And again, according to Jung, "The tremendous power of the 'objective psychic' has been named 'demon' or 'God' in all epochs with the sole exception of the recent present. We have become so bashful in matters of religion that we correctly say 'unconscious,' because God has in fact become unconscious to us." (And, we may add, the devil, as well.) But as everyone who enters this realm discovers, the distinguishable realities, the entities—almost personalities—do exist, even when we see them only abstracted as ideas or obsessions. Jung has described them as complexes and archetypes; the church as angels and demons. The rose by any other name . . .

A LETTER FROM JUNG

Jung stated this more clearly than in anything else I have read in a letter he wrote to me on May 3, 1958, in which he said, "The real nature of the objects of human experience is still shrouded in darkness. The scientists cannot concede a higher intelligence to Theology than to any other branch of human cognition. We know as little of a Supreme Being as of Matter. But there is as little doubt of the existence of a Supreme Being as of Matter. The world beyond is a reality, an experiential fact. We only don't understand it."[12] Or, as many others have put it, we *know* God. Our sense experience tells us what it can of the external world, and we refine and sift it through reason. Dreams, visions, intuitions, even fortuitous mistakes, and the storytelling imagination bring us knowledge of the non-physical world, and we refine and sift it though reason. Both are avenues to reality.

These conclusions were based on empirical data carefully and painstakingly gathered. Jung sometimes became discouraged and impatient with people who refused to see the basis of experience which determined his conclusions, indeed the very broad medical experience with psychic facts produced by minds in all stages of sickness and creative adjustment to life. In one of his last major works he remarked, "Unfortunately I cannot pass on this experience to my public. I have tried in a number of publications, with the help of case material, to present the nature of these experiences and also the method of obtaining them. Wherever my methods were really applied the facts I give have been confirmed. One could see

12. In his last published writing Jung carried this understanding farther. In this work, in which he stepped out of the role of medical scientist and spoke as an old man telling his story—a book which he directed was not to be published as a part of his collected works—he said, "I have, therefore, even hazarded the postulate that the phenomenon of achetypal configurations—which are psychic events *par excellence*—may be founded upon a *psychoid* base, that is, upon an only partially psychic and possibly altogether different form of being. For lack of empirical data I have neither knowledge nor understanding of such forms of being, which are commonly called spiritual. From the point of view of science, it is immaterial what I may *believe* on that score, and I must accept my ignorance. But insofar as the archetypes act upon me, they are real and actual to me, even though I do not know what their real nature is . . . Nevertheless, we have good reason to suppose that behind this veil there exists the uncomprehended absolute object which affects and influences us—and to suppose it even, or particularly, in the case of psychic phenomena about which no verifiable statements can be made." *Memories, Dreams and Reflections* by C. G. Jung, recorded and edited by Aniela Jaffe, New York, Random House, Inc., 1963, pp. 351 f.

the moons of Jupiter even in Galileo's day if one took the trouble to use his telescope."[13]

The psyche, then, which Jung saw in his patients and in himself, is in contact with a psychic world containing elements which are superior to human consciousness. The dump heap of inferior elements sits right in the way, no question; but deeper in the unconscious there is a force—which can be perceived—striving towards synthesizing the fragments. This spontaneous integrating force was observed also by patient after patient through the depths of their own psyches. These people found guidance through something working deep in their own psyches helping them overcome their conflicts and problems. Jung began to realize that it was not the psychiatrist who does the healing, but that he brings the patient into contact with a force within which heals and integrates. When the unconscious psyche can be seen mediating an integrative force in this way, it opens up once again the discussion of the reality of revelation and transformation by spiritual experience.

Jung found that no permanent health, maturity, or freedom were achieved in any of his patients until something new emerged from the collective unconscious. The "something new" was an experienced psychic reality which somehow fused together the antagonistic elements of the individual personality. He observed that these warring opposites within the total personality, conscious and unconscious, came to reconciliation and peace through a highly charged archetype which he called "the self." The psychiatrist may lead the way, help to remove roadblocks, but the solution to the ultimate conflict in human life is given autonomously from the psychic depths.

The person who loses touch with the unconscious and the powers which it mediates sooner or later falls into mental, physical, or moral illness. The ego and consciousness cannot

[13] Jung, *Collected Works,* Vol. 9, Part II, pp. 33 f.

exist cut off from the vast reservoir of psychic reality and power which the church calls the realm of the spirit, and the person who has lost his religious orientation is sick. He has lost touch with an indispensable half of reality. (It is not, as psychology once suggested, religiously oriented people who are sick.) Psychology inherits the job of bringing the individual into creative relationship with the essential core of psychic totality, Holy Spirit or "self," when the church fails in this function. When this contact is made, healing of mind and soul and body actually follow.

When religion is alive, it brings the individual to vital contact with the Holy Spirit, the creative center of spirituality, and the same results occur. Those who have participated in the Pentecostal movement remark on the healings in mind and body which occur along with tongues. From the earliest days of Pentecostal groups there has been as much interest in the physical, mental, and moral healings which have taken place as in the phenomenon of tongues itself. The stories start with "the notable miracle" when Mary Arthur recovered her vision in Eldorado Springs, Missouri, in 1903, and continue to the present with stories like that told by the Presbyterian minister, James H. Brown, in Parkesburg, Pennsylvania, of the disappearance of a young man's stuttering after he had spoken in tongues. And for many others, like the Episcopal vicar of Sidney, Montana, Edwin Stube, who was healed of his emotional difficulties with his experience of tongues, the spiritual reality which Jung has made explicit is an actuality which cannot be ignored.

This is not to say that tongues is of necessity a healing medicine for everyone. It is clearly an experience which is healing for some people; yet it may not be so for others. In any case, it is an experience which opens men to the actual effect of spiritual reality upon their lives.

THE WORK OF THEODORE FLOURNOY

Jung has done more than present a psychological world view in which tongues could be viewed as meaningful. He has also been interested in the phenomenon itself. While he never wrote widely on the subject, those close to him have spoken of his interest, and there are several tantalizing references to glossolalia in his books which betray his deep interest and knowledge of it. One would not, however, realize this from a casual perusal of his published works.

It is no wonder that Jung was conversant with glossolalia. About the time of his break with Freud he formed a close friendship with the Swiss psychologist, Theodore Flournoy, whom he greatly admired. Flournoy's most important work was a study of glossolalia, among other related phenomena. In the German edition of Jung's autobiographical work, for some reason not translated in the English edition, is an appendix telling of his relationship to the Geneva professor. Jung writes: "I read his book 'Des Indes à la Planète Mars. Etude sur un Cas de Somnambulisme avec Glossolalie' [the discussion of glossolalia] which made a great impression on me. I wrote Flournoy that I would like to translate it into German. Only after half a year did I get an answer in which he excused himself for not writing sooner. To my regret he had already appointed another translator." Jung goes on to tell how greatly Flournoy helped him in developing an objective point of view; Jung's first great study, *The Psychology of the Unconscious,* which is now published as *Symbols of Transformation,* was based on one of his cases. It is interesting that he calls attention to Flournoy's relationship to William James, who had studied religious phenomena objectively. Jung visited Flournoy, *the* authority on tongue speaking in the psychological world, and even induced him to come, in 1912, to the Psycho-analytic Congress in Munich at which he split with Freud.

Jung's interest in the subject of tongues was more than passing. A personal letter to a clinical psychologist who teaches at Fresno State College speaks specifically about tongues in answer to a question which Dr. Tenney had asked. It was written from Küsnacht-Zürich, February 23, 1955. The paragraph about tongues is a very cautious and careful statement. It reads:

> Speaking with tongues (glossolalia) is observed in cases of ekstasis (=*abaissement du niveau mental,* predominance of the unconscious). It is probable that the strangeness of the unconscious contents not yet integrated in consciousness demands an equally strange language. As it does demand strange pictures of an unheard of character, it is also a traditional expectation that the spiritual demonic inspiration manifests itself either in hieratic or otherwise incomprehensible language. That is also the reason why primitives and civilized people still use archaic forms of language at ritual occasions (Sanskrit in India, old Coptic in the Coptic church, old Slavonic in the Greek-Orthodox church, Latin in the Catholic church and the mediaeval German or English in the Protestant church). There are case-reports about mediums that spoke foreign languages which were unknown to them in their waking state. Theodore Flournoy in Geneva has reported about such a case in which he showed that it was [a] matter of a cryptomnestic Sanskrit the medium had picked up in a Sanskrit grammar whose existence nobody was aware of. It is exceedingly difficult to establish the authenticity of these cases on account of cryptomnesia.

Jung's first reference to glossolalia occurs in his first published work, the dissertation for his medical degree, "On the Psychology and Pathology of So-Called Occult Phenomena." This work, which shows clearly the influence of Flournoy's thought, was printed in 1902. Jung describes here his one observation of the phenomenon of tongues in the principal case he is discussing. He classifies the phenomenon as a kind of somnambulism, or multiple personality in which some center other than the ego possesses the motor centers of the personality. Jung contends that somnambulism is not necessarily pathological or detrimental to the personality, and this conclusion applies to all of the phenomena discussed, including glossolalia. Indeed he writes: "In view of the difficulties that oppose the future character, the somnambulisms sometimes have an eminently teleological significance, in that they give the individual, who would otherwise inevitably succumb, the means of victory."[14] Likewise he believes that there are "teleological hallucinations" which have not been subjected to scientific study, although at this time he does put forward an explanation of glossolalia on the basis of cryptomnesia, or memory heightened by unconscious processes.

He concludes this study, however, with a careful statement that there are parallels to the materials of his patients among the gnostic systems which cannot be accounted for, and that the material produced by his cases was truly extraordinary. Since Jung at that time had not formulated a theory of the collective unconscious, he did not have the tools to do more than describe the experience of glossolalia which he encountered in his early years; yet this early work, as one editor suggests, foreshadows much of his later work.

In an article concerning the archetypes, published in 1936, Jung tells that he learned "to understand the nature of psychic disturbances within the setting of the human psyche as a whole" from two thinkers, Flournoy and William James.[15] So important was Flournoy's work on glossolalia and similar experiences that it helped shape Jung's methodological point of view. In 1948 Jung wrote "A Psychological Approach to the Trinity." In this work he quoted the section on tongues from the Roman Ritual as a footnote to support the following statement: "But the more the unconscious is split off, the more

14. *Collected Works,* Vol. 1, p. 79.
15. *Collected Works,* Vol. 9, Part I, p. 55.

formidable the shape in which it appears to the conscious mind—if not in divine form, then in the more unfavourable form of obsessions and outbursts of affect."[16] Thus the more inhibited and out of touch with the unconscious, the more likely a person is to be a candidate for tongues, which is undoubtedly preferable to most neurotic forms of behavior as a resolution to tension and inhibitions.

The most tantalizing of Jung's references to tongues is a casual one in the footnotes to his paper, "Transformation Symbolism in the Mass," written in 1940. He is describing how the invasion of the unconscious contents, with accompanying disorders, commonly occurs prior to integration of the personality. This, he said, was frequently found among early Christians. At this point the footnote refers to "'speaking with tongues' and glossolalia" as an example of this kind of invasion. It would seem from this reference that Jung believed that tongues could be a positive preparation for integration of personality.

Most of Jung's followers have sustained the same view of tongues as a genuine invasion into consciousness of contents from the deepest levels of the collective unconscious. Those with whom I have talked have evinced an interest in the experience. Three of them have each commented that one or more patients had had experiences of tongues which had led them to seek to integrate their lives. Without this experience they believed that these people would never have been able to come to psychological maturity. The experience of speaking in tongues opened them up to the unconscious and to fuller, though more difficult, life. Another commented that speaking in tongues was no doubt genuine, but that it was strong medicine and should be used sparingly and carefully.

16. This and the following reference are found in the *Collected Works,* Vol. 11, pp. 163 and 284.

A MEETING OF PSYCHIATRISTS

At a meeting of psychiatrists, analysts, and clergy at St. Thomas' church in New York City in 1962, the subject of tongues was discussed at length. There was great interest on the part of the psychologists in the recurrence of the experience in churches, since it demonstrates that the church is once again dealing with the unconscious depth of the individual. All twelve psychiatrists and psychologists present were in agreement that tongue-speech is a genuine manifestation of the collective psyche. A number of the group cast doubts upon its value because they did not see how an experience which is not always understood can be assimilated and have a positive effect upon the conscious development of the individual. This was countered, however, by the suggestion of one psychologist that the experience may well have the same effect as a dream which is not understood in all of its implications but still makes an impact upon the personality. How many things transform life without being understood. Another psychiatrist called attention to a case in which the total psyche of the patient seemed to call for an experience of tongues and to be affected positively by it in spite of the doubts and reservations of the psychiatrist working with him.

Still another psychiatrist, not of a Jungian background, has called my attention to a most interesting discussion of tongues from the *Proceedings of the Royal Society of Medicine*. The paper by Sargant,[17] one of the great men of British psychiatry, points out the similarity between group religious experiences and a variety of psychological healing methods. After a visit to the United States where he observed the phenomenon of revivalism, snake-handling services, and tongues, he came

17. "Some Cultural Group Abreactive Techniques and their Relation to Modern Treatments," by William Sargant, F.R.C.P., *Proceedings of the Royal Society of Medicine,* London, Longmans, Green & Co., 1949, pp. 367 ff.

to the conclusion that these experiences had much the same effect upon people as electro-shock therapy. Both in tongues and in shock therapy there is a cortical inhibition which breaks up prior conditioning of the individual and frees him to develop new patterns. This might explain the sense of freedom which so often occurs in the experience of tongues and also the change which so often occurs in the lives of the subjects.

Dr. Sargant refers to the observation of Pavlov in describing the reaction of some of his dogs to being nearly drowned in the Leningrad flood of 1924. After this traumatic experience some of the dogs fell into stupor. When they awakened it was discovered that the conditioned responses which had been developed in the dogs had been destroyed by the stupor. "By mounting psychologically induced nervous excitement to a stage which produced temporary cortical inhibition Pavlov had accidentally stumbled on a quick way of breaking up conditioned patterns of behaviour previously implanted by months of patient work." Sargant suggests that sleep may have somewhat the same effect.

Concluding his article, Dr. Sargant makes a plea for open-mindedness both in regard to these religious practices and about psychiatric therapy. He admits that shock therapy may appear as irrational to some medical men as tongues and similar experiences to the more orthodox churches. "But in psychiatry and religion we must examine facts before condemning on theory. In 1743, when England was in an uproar about Wesley's preaching methods, a certain Mr. Thomas Butts recorded this comment: 'As to persons crying out and being in fits, I shall not pretend to account exactly for that but only make this observation: it is well known that most of them who have been so exercised . . . have peace and joy in believing and are more holy and happy than ever they were before. And if this is so, no matter what remarks are made on their fits.' The same might be said today about some of our modern abreactive techniques and shock treatment in therapy." Or about tongues.

REPORTS IN MEDICAL LITERATURE

Actually there has been only one study of the religious practice of glossolalia reported in the medical literature, and this was written in 1912.[18] The distinction must be clearly understood between the study of glossolalia occurring within a religious group and study of a similar phenomenon occurring apart from any apparent religious connection, either among normal individuals or among the mentally ill. Work dealing with glossolalia in the mentally ill is almost equally scant, and is limited to a speech which neither originated nor was nurtured as an accepted religious practice. I know of only three such published works in the medical and psychological literature. Alphonse Maeder, who worked under Jung, has written of a case of paranoid schizophrenia in which the patient's private language was the form in which he handled the images arising from his mental condition. A psychiatrist in Oslo, Harald K. Schjelderup, has reported on a neurotic patient who began to speak in tongues during psychoanalysis. A Belgian, Jean Bobon, has written a long and interesting account of three psychotic patients in Liége, each of whom

18. A search has been made for me through the Library of the Los Angeles County Medical Association with the assistance of the extensive research facilities of the University of California at Los Angeles. Aside from William Sargant's article which we have just discussed, the following reports (discussed in the next paragraphs) are the only work related to tongues which could be found:

Harald K. Schjelderup (Oslo), "Psychologische Analyse eines Falles von Zungenreden," *Zeitschrift für Psychologie,* 1 Bd. 122, Heft 1 u. 2, 1931, pp. 1 ff. Jean Bobon, "Les Pseudo-Glossolalies Ludiques et Magiques," *Journal Belge de Neurologie et de Psychiatrie,* Vol. 47, April, 1947, pp. 219 ff., June, 1947, pp. 327 ff. Oskar Pfister, "Die psychologische Enträtselung der Religiösen Glossolalie und der automatischen Kryptographie," *Jahrbuch für psychoanalytische und psychopathologische Forschungen,* III Bd., 1912, pp. 427 ff., 730 ff.

In addition, Alphonse Maeder, "La Langue d'un Aliéné: Analyse d'un Cas de Glossolalie," *Archives de Psychologie,* March, 1910, pp. 208 ff.

spoke a private language based on fanciful elaborations of ordinary French.

In these three reports of "non-religious" glossolalia, representing a total of five patients requiring treatment, there are interesting conclusions about the spiritual nature of the individuals' problems and the meaning of the speech to them; there are fascinating conclusions about the psychic activity from which language arises; but they do not touch on the religious phenomenon of glossolalia. Even the speech itself, as described by careful observers, differed greatly in most of these cases from the tongue-speech heard in religious groups today. The speaking of the woman in Oslo was the one exception; a highly intelligent person suffering from neurosis, she was reviving a practice of her childhood which did resemble the religious tongue-speech she remembered having heard on one occasion. In the other four cases, who were all schizophrenic patients, the languages studied were not actually unintelligible, but on the contrary were made up of words with quite definite, objective meanings in the minds of the speakers. Although I have found no study comparing the forms of irrational speech in schizophrenia with Christian glossolalia, one psychologist who is familiar with both has pointed out to me that there is little outward similarity between them. And he went on to say that it is suprising how seldom one meets up with schizophrenic individuals who have experienced religious tongues.

It is also remarkable, considering that mental illness can copy any aspect of normal life, to realize how few cases of "non-religious" glossolalia are reported. In comparison, there are some two million tongue speakers in this country alone, apparently as healthy as the rest of us, who maintain that speaking in tongues is an invaluable religious experience which gave them entrance into a new and transformed life.

One study of their experience from a psychological viewpoint has been reported; this was the work published in 1912 by Oskar Pfister, the Swiss Evangelical pastor who was the friend and associate of Freud. His paper described his analysis of the tongue-speech of a young man in Zürich who had first spoken in tongues after his confirmation seven years before. Pfister's interest, however, was to understand the young man and his not uncommon problems from the point of view of psychoanalysis, rather than to understand the effect of his tongue speaking upon his life. This article was one of a number of contributions Pfister made to the publications of the psychoanalytic movement.

Besides this there have been two psychological studies of the experience of glossolalia in normal individuals outside of a specifically religious context. There is Théodore Flournoy's fascinating account of the trance medium and her private languages, written at the University of Geneva in 1900. About the same time the Society for Psychical Research, at the request of William James, published the personal record of a tongue speaker's experiences. This account was written, under the pseudonym of Albert Le Baron, by a literary man who had become deeply involved in spiritualism; the introduction and psychological discussion were written by James and F. W. H. Myers. And this represents the published work of psychologists dealing with the experience of glossolalia, religious or secular.

There is, however, an unpublished thesis on religious glossolalia, written for the psychiatry department of the university in Johannesburg, South Africa, which we have been able to secure on microfilm. This work, done by Dr. L. M. Van Eetveldt Vivier for his degree in medicine, consisted of psychological testing of a group of tongue speakers and of two control groups. The primary purpose of the thesis was to determine whether a basic weakness in the personality of the tongue speaker accounts for glossolalia as, therefore, a sign of psychopathology, or if the experience may be due instead to the impact of a religious dynamism. Dr. Vivier bases his conclusions on thoughtful selection of the groups tested and of the test materials and situations, and on careful statistical evaluation of the results.

His findings indicate clearly the normal personalities of the tongue speaking group, and the fact that some factor other than a pathological one must be found to explain the dissociation which occurs in the experience of glossolalia. This was found to be true in spite of the fact that disturbed home environments had subjected the tongue speaking group to significantly greater pressure and insecurity than either of the control groups. In general he found the test group more sensitive and yet with a greater ability to renounce immediate satisfactions for long-term goals.

In discussing the possibilities of a dynamic factor which accounts for the experience of tongue-speech, Dr. Vivier leans heavily on Jungian theory. He suggests that an understanding of the collective unconscious, as depicted by Dr. Jung, is a basis which cannot be ignored if religious glossolalia is to be understood and defined. His study includes a comprehensive survey of the historical occurrences, as well as extensive inquiries into the personal histories and religious attitudes of the groups studied. He also discusses basic theology and psychological theory, particularly in relation to the test materials. He does not attempt, however, to develop a psychological theory to interpret the experience; since he was not trying to integrate the basic Freudian approach with the Jungian ideas he presents, Dr. Vivier sees his final conclusion in the light of the work of others. Glossolalia, he concludes, can be understood psychologically on the basis of the strong convictions of the tongue speaking group and the strong association of thought and language. Accepting Jung's view of the collective unconscious, it can be understood as an experience of the Holy Spirit, and, finally, the results which have shown up in his study of tongue speakers suggest indirectly that glossolalia is prime evidence of the reality of religious experience.

Yet almost the oddest thing about glossolalia today is the psychological discussion which goes on about it. Although this discussion is a damaging and persistent psychological criticism of tongue speakers and tongue speaking, it is the theologians, not psychologists, who find that glossolalia needs to be discussed psychologically. Since in the common viewpoint of modern Protestantism it is no longer a theological or religious fact, the only way that it can be discussed is as a psychological phenomenon. Bishop Pike, in linking tongue speaking "in more extreme forms" with schizophrenia, and asking for psychiatric oversight of practices in connection with tongue speaking, is but the latest to suggest that tongue speaking is either a possible sign of psychological instability or abnormality or, at the least, nothing more than a meaningless psychological mechanism.

ARE TONGUE SPEAKERS SCHIZOPHRENIC?

The pervasiveness of this point of view was demonstrated in a group of clergy recently. Several bishops and a dozen clergymen, all from large churches, were together at a party where one of them told an anecdote about an English bishop. The story went that he had been asked what he knew about glossolalia and had replied with typical British firmness, "Well, we don't have much of that sort of thing in my diocese, but if anyone started it, I would send him to the nearest psychiatrist." And at this a ripple of approving laughter went through the group.

There are five essentially separate psychological criticisms of tongue speaking which are discussed. The most serious of them is the identification with ordinary schizophrenia, one form of psychosis. The schizophrenic is one whose ego has disintegrated and who is flooded by contents from the unconscious; he is unable to differentiate between the real outer world and his dream world. The criticism is made that since the tongue speaker allows such contents to possess him when he speaks in tongues, he is falling into the schizophrenic pattern. Or unfortunate examples are cited of individuals who have spoken in tongues and have been so overwhelmed by the experience that they never again regained psychological equilibrium.

In order to deal adequately with this criticism we must differentiate clearly between "normality," neurosis, and psychosis. In neurosis the ego (a man's conscious attitudes and morality) is bombarded from the unconscious. So threatened, the ego throws up defenses and compensations, suffers anxiety and depressions. It may even be flooded by unconscious contents, but it is able to distinguish itself from these contents. The ego is still intact and struggling. In "normality" the ego is able to adjust to all the stresses of the inner and outer world without either putting up defenses or falling into unbearable psychic pain. In psychosis, however, the ego is fragmented and cannot resist the invasion of the unconscious. Since the ego no longer exists as the organizing center of personality, the unconscious, with its wild, chaotic fecundity, takes over, and the individual has little relationship with the outer world. He becomes a pawn for unconscious forces. This state might be described as "living out one's dream life."

In comparison, in the experience of tongues, one content from the unconscious possesses the personality, while the ego still retains its contact with outer reality, and indeed often improves its relationship to the outer world. A weak ego can, of course, be inundated by an upthrust of the collective unconscious such as occurs in tongues and in several rather common psychic occurrences. If this is the case, and the ego loses its power to differentiate and control the dynamic energy of the unconscious, collective and personal, the result can be a break with reality and a psychotic state.

This is a fact which must be understood in relation to tongues, but understood also in relation to other facts about tongue speaking. One of these is the number of persons who tell of being healed, both of physical illness and of emotional or psychological difficulties, along with the experience of glossolalia. Tongue speaking may well be an unconscious resolution to neurosis. In glossolalia, to use another image, the individual whose ego is intact is submerged in the unconscious and emerges cleansed and restored from the dip.

I have known a few tongue speakers who were schizophrenic, but statistically very few, and there was little reason in any of these cases to correlate their schizophrenia with their tongue speaking. This conclusion was substantiated by the psychiatrist who knew two of these people. In each of these cases there was a weak ego which was responsible for the break with reality; speaking in tongues was only an incidental experience during their illness. This psychiatrist also told me of the case of a young man under his care who had suffered a psychotic break. When he called the father to report what had happened, the older man, a member of a conservative church, said immediately, "It was that tongue speaking he was involved in which caused this." The psychiatrist had a different idea and questioned the father as to when the experience of tongues had happened; he was told that it had been at least six or seven years before. The doctor then suggested that this was somewhat remote to be a cause of the present breakdown and pointed to the young man's constant attendance at a rationalistic revival just prior to his breakdown as an immediate cause. Talking with me, he commented that the rationalistic revival techniques which emphasized guilt and sin and conscious conversion were more likely to have such an effect than the liberating experience of tongues.

Tongue speaking is a powerful invasion of the unconscious. It can be dangerous for the weak ego and should never be forced on anyone. It occasionally does occur along with serious mental illness, but there does not appear to be a causal connection or, in fact, any but a casual relation between them. No study has been made of the relative number of religious tongue speakers in the psychotic population, and there has been no particular medical interest in making one. Apparently there has been little evidence to suggest a correlation between the two phenomena. Indeed if any large number of the two million Pentecostals in this country who have spoken in tongues were schizophrenic, one would hear from them in public, because lack of control is one characteristic of this disease.

THE LINK WITH HYSTERIA

A second criticism of tongue speaking finds it a neurotic manifestation, associated particularly with hysteria. In hysteria people are often able to remember things which they could not ordinarily recall and are in possession of other powers they do not have in ordinary circumstances. Probably, in the light of our deeper understanding today of both neurosis and psychosis, this is a very reasonable symptomatic classification. The trouble is that a description like this, again, leaves an impression that cause and result must both be identical. Hysteria and tongue speaking both unquestionably arise in the area of man's psyche known as the unconscious. But hysteria is a sickness which puts the mind and often the body, as well, out of commission, while tongue speaking is a religious experience which, from the evidence we have, seems to lead to a greater ability to function in the world.

I have observed one man whose neurosis seemed to be related to tongue-speech. He had had the experience as a young man and had identified it with the moral rigidity of the group in which it occurred. This was so crippling that he was not able as an adult to deal with his own inner darkness, and it took nearly a year of counseling to release him from this bondage so that he could lead a normal life. It must be stressed that the damage arose from the moral rigidity of his Pentecostalism, rather than from his experience of tongues. Also, in a case such as this, one does not know what might have happened if he had not had the experience of tongues in the first place. I have observed no case in which the individual was more neurotic after the experience of tongues, nor have I had any medical or psychological reports suggesting this.

One way the discussions of tongues have dismissed the experience is by valuing it solely in terms of one psychological mechanism. The simplest is a theory of exalted memory based on the standard repression theory. The actual experience of speaking in foreign tongues and phrases is dismissed on the basis that people living in a polyglot world have heard and retained far more of what they have heard of foreign languages than they consciously realize. During the experience of speaking in tongues the unconscious coughs up these undigested remnants of memory. No mechanism for exalting the memory, such as hysteria or hypnosis, is suggested. There is no reason offered to explain why the repressed memories of foreign languages contain such vocabularies for the praise of God and Jesus Christ. Nor is there any attempt to explain the numinous and healing qualities of the religious experience which occurs along with these "exalted memories." This theory is more of a description, and a fragmentary one, than an explanation.

Another mechanism theorized to explain tongue speaking is suggestion, either group or hypnotic. The idea of a person's being led to the experience under the powerful control of mass suggestion, or like the patient whose ego comes under the control of the hypnotist, appears on the surface to have a specific relation to glossolalia. In the hypnotic state the patient, again, has powers of memory he did not know about, and may even perform feats normally impossible; there is also a similar contact with the unconscious in both tongue-speech and states of suggestion. But I have yet to hear of anyone in the hypnotic state speaking forth in tongues. The fact is that in tongue speaking there is no rapport with others, while rapport is the essential characteristic of contact with the unconscious in states of suggestion. Hypnotism can open an individual to the unconscious; tongues appears to do the same. With this their similarity ceases.

One last psychological label fits tongues into modern thought as being merely autosuggestion. While undoubtedly it is possible to suggest certain ideas to one's unconscious so that changes take place in the personality, a person can hardly suggest what was not known in the first place, nor can one autosuggest one's self into a transforming religious experience. In any case, I am rather dubious about the essential meaning of autosuggestion or self-hypnosis, since the chief mark of suggestion is rapport and unless personality is seen as multiple in nature, there is nothing to have rapport with. What is usually called autosuggestion is in reality an opening of the conscious mind to control by some element of the unconscious, and this is anything but autosuggestion. It is possession by an unconscious content which the ego permits. Tongues may well belong to this latter category, but this has nothing to do with conscious suggestion, autosuggestion.

SIMILARITY TO DREAMS

None of the psychological mechanisms we have discussed gives an adequate parallel to tongues. There is, however, one common psychological state very similar to tongue speaking; this is the dream. In dreams there is a giving up, yielding oneself first to sleep. With conscious control given up in sleep, one is presented with visual images, and sometimes with auditory or tactile or olfactory impressions. There are even dream states of somnambulism and talking in one's sleep in which the content of the dream is expressed in a motor response rather than in images. The person who dreams knows that these images and responses do not refer to the ordinary outer world, and yet he has no more control over them than he does of the experiences which come to him from the physical world.

No one assumes that because consciousness has been so reduced in sleep as to let a dream appear that the dreamer's conscious mind is going to give up control when he awakens.

The intact personality can go from waking to sleep and back to waking with no difficulty, and no one is called schizophrenic or psychotic because he dreams. One is only psychotic when he can no longer distinguish dream from reality. According to Freud, dreams express the regressive images of the unconscious. According to Jung, they express symbolically the total meaning and purpose of the personal and collective unconscious and the spiritual realm which lies behind the unconscious psyche. Dreams are therefore of the greatest significance and may sometimes express the numinous quality of a religious experience.

Speaking in tongues is similar to the dream in all of these characteristics. In order to have the experience of glossolalia one must empty himself and give up conscious control, yielding himself to the experience. As in sleep the individual does not give up control to another person as he does in hypnosis or suggestion, but to something unknown which he seems to contact through the depth of himself. The experience of tongues is automatic, and one has no more conscious control of the words that come to his lips than the dreamer does of the images which come to him. The tongue speaker recognizes that the control of his body is not being exerted by any known outer, physical force, but by an inner, spiritual one. As in the dream, the tongue speaker can usually return to consciousness from his experience with no ill effects from it. In tongues one portion of the conscious mind, as it were, goes to sleep and permits unconscious contents to flow through the physical apparatus which is normally subject to consciousness. In a moment the mind returns to its previous relationship, with an added memory of words which have been spoken and possibly of their interpretation. It is a kind of somnambulism while awake, a sleepwalking with one's vocal chords while still conscious. Most tongue speakers testify to the numinous quality of their experience and they believe that this experience expresses some aspect of the spiritual realm in the same way that the dream, as Jung suggests, expresses the reality of the collective unconscious.

If tongue speaking is essentially comparable to dreams, then it will share in the significance of the dream. Not only has Jung attributed great significance to the dream, but he has pointed out the religious interest in the dream which is found in the Bible and the early church, as well as in most other religions. In most religions it is believed that through dreams men are brought into meaningful contact with spiritual reality, that God contacts men through dreams. The evidence for the Christian appreciation of the dream is voluminous. The reader will have to take my word for it since there is no book available which presents this evidence from its many, many sources, and a further discussion is out of place at this time.[19]

Once the dream is re-established as a medium of communication from the collective unconscious or the spiritual realm, then there is a present, continuous influence of non-personal, non-physical reality upon the lives of men, and the possibility of direct religious experience is reaffirmed. The implications for our subject are wide; if God (or some archetypal element of the collective unconscious) speaks through dreams, why not through the similar experience of tongues? The same significance can be attributed to tongues as is attributed to the dream. A religion which values the dream can equally well value tongue-speech. And a psychology which sees the dream as a meaningful contact with the realm of the unknown will see tongue-speech in the same light.

There is interesting evidence supporting an association of tongues with sleep and dreams in a pamphlet which describes the experiences of Hanneh Elias Aghaby, beginning on the

19. The author is preparing a study of the place of the dream in Christian tradition, which logically should precede the present work. Once the religious and Christian significance of the dream is understood, then it is far easier to understand all the other charismata, tongues included.

night of January 3, 1933, in Amman, the capital of Jordan. While she was sound asleep Mme. Aghaby spoke and sang messages of a deeply religious character in Hebrew, German, French, Greek, and Italian, languages she did not know, and then interpreted, sometimes sentence by sentence, into Arabic. For two months there were frequent occurrences of this speech, and members of the foreign colony as well as Arabs came to the home to listen. The speaker had no memory of what happened, however, except for a dream the night before her speaking began, in which she saw herself in a green place with others who were praying in a Germanic tongue.[20]

The Rev. Larry Christenson, whose story has already been given, had his first experience of tongues in sleep. A related experience is that of a retired minister whose dreams had directed him to seek a deeper spiritual life, and who was then led to a group in which he spoke, in tongues, a message of thanks for having found such a life.[21] Still another person of my acquaintance has told me of speaking in tongues in a dream, while he has never done it when conscious.

One other interesting correlation of dreams and sleep has come to me from a friend whose roommate acted in an unusual manner whenever they had surprise fire-drills in the middle of the night. "She would bolt out of bed, as we all did, when the alarm went off . . . but she would stand in the middle of the floor talking very intensely in words or language that I thought *very* weird. I knew she wasn't talking in her sleep, because her eyes were *widely* open. And she didn't mumble half-understandable words. . . . They were completely unfamiliar to me. I would try to get her to 'come to' so we could follow the fire-drill procedure. Eventually, she'd

20. *Signs and Wonders in Rabbath-Ammon,* Milwaukee, Word and Witness Publishing Co., 1934.

21. The Rev. William T. Sherwood, "The Lord Called Me Out of Retirement," *Trinity,* Whitsuntide, 1962, Vol. I, No. 4, pp. 32 ff.

become just a sleepy girl staggering out with the rest of us. She had less memory than any of us the next morning regarding the drill during the night, and never commented on her unusual speech. I can't remember what religion she was. . . . It wasn't important to us. But the fire-drill wasn't half as unnerving as her behavior! The first time I heard someone speak in tongues, I remembered my roommate and the fire-drills."

THE RELATION TO VISIONS

If there is reason to connect tongue-speech with dreams, it is even closer to the vision. Far more common than is ordinarily realized, the true vision is like tongue-speech in that it appears to an individual who is perfectly conscious, knows that something beyond his ego is invading his field of consciousness, and is able in most cases by averting his attention, to dismiss the experience or continue it. In the vision one dreams while awake; in tongue-speech he speaks from the unconscious while awake. Either tongue-speech or visions may be cultivated to recur, once they have been experienced, without losing the spontaneity of content. The importance of visions psychologically is suggested by the fact that Jung has developed ways of cultivating spontaneous fantasies so that one may have more contact with the unconscious than sleep provides. Through either one, tongues or visions, contact with the inner world is given when there is need and asking for it.

This is also a connection which is supported by experience. One evidence comes from the life of a young man, now the associate pastor of one of the major denominational churches, whose experience at the age of twelve I have already mentioned. He was alone and praying when the vision of a terrifying, clawlike hand appeared, reaching towards him. He tried to speak but no words came, and a moment later the hand was transformed into a vision of the hand of God, beckoning to him; it was shortly after this that he first spoke in the unknown tongue which he has since come to know well in his private devotional life. Another is the story of Demos Shakarian, already told in detail, about the vision which rose from within him as his wife was speaking an interpretation of tongues.

One further experience of this kind, which took place in a small prayer group in which there is tongue speaking, was told me by the man to whom it happened. While another member of the group was speaking in tongues, this young man suddenly saw himself in a vision, climbing a flight of stairs that appeared like the side of a pyramid and in perspective, but with steps that obviously grew bigger towards the top instead of diminishing into the distance. When the speaker stopped, the minister's wife began to interpret, saying that we must follow and are given stairs to use; but they gradually become harder to climb and narrower. My friend realized that he had received the same message in a different form.

If it is questioned that dreams and visions may be seen plainly while tongue-speech cannot be understood, this is hardly an issue. Most people are just about as much at a loss in interpreting their dreams and visions as they are in understanding tongue speaking. An uninterpreted dream usually makes no more sense than tongue speaking without interpretation. Both are primary data which make necessary the postulating of the collective unconscious and its unlimited supply of images—the images which are saying something we have *not* understood fully. Both are raw material of the human psyche, actual happenings and not someone's rational idea of what should happen based on a limited personal knowledge. These experiences cannot be judged and thrown out if they fail to meet our specifications and preconceptions, since they are among the prime data on which a psychology—our understanding of ourselves—can be based.

If the Jungian idea of the collective unconscious is accepted, speaking in tongues makes real sense, as a breakthrough into consciousness of a deep level of the collective unconscious similar to the dream. Linguistic patterns belonging to the past, to some other part of the present, or to some other level of being take possession of the individual and are expressed by him. Accepting this, of course, in no way prejudices an ultimate judgment about whether it is an inferior or a superior level of being which is seeking expression in this way. Only the actual moral and psychological results which occur in the personality *after* it has had the experience will enable us to judge the meaning of the experience. If it is further understood that psychologists have studied actual experiences of images, which have come before the minds of patients in dreams and visions, whose origin could only be explained as beyond the ordinary human psyche, and which had the numinous power to change lives, tongues again becomes more understandable as a significant psychological and religious phenomenon. It is equally possible that such expressions can take the form of glossolalia, and reach the individual consciousness as linguistic patterns which are accompanied by a similar numinous experience.

Chapter VIII

AN EVALUATION OF TONGUES

Dr. William Sargant, the distinguished British psychiatrist, has suggested that one can make up his mind about either psychotherapeutic techniques or strange religious practices only on the basis of facts and results. It is certainly true that the final decision on the validity and value of tongues has to come from the results of the experience. As rector of a church in which there is a group of tongue speakers and with which a psychological clinic is also associated, I have been able to observe the practical results of glossolalia in my own parish and to assess the psychological development of many of those who have had experience both in glossolalia and in psychotherapy. I have studied the case histories which have been published in *Trinity* magazine and have known a number of the people who tell their stories there.

A close association with many of the leaders of the tongues movement in the larger Protestant denominations has enabled me to meet people all over the country who have shared in this experience. We have talked at length and they have told me of their experiences and their attitudes towards tongue speaking in general. Since I am not a tongue speaker, many who are violently in opposition to tongues have shared their fears and concerns about the movement. In gathering all of this information together and surveying the history of glossolalia, one realizes clearly that there are both positive and negative aspects to the experience and the movement which it has produced. Let us delineate these opposing attitudes towards tongues and then evaluate the experience as best we can.

THE POSITIVE RESULTS

All who have written of their first experience of speaking in tongues call it one of the most valuable and transforming experiences of their lives. To many of them it was the most important event they had known. New doors opened into life, and with a new look at life as a whole, they came to have a real sense of personal value and destiny. They had been seeking, knocking, asking, and now they had found what they were looking for, and it was even more wonderful than they had hoped. Every one of them felt that his life had been changed, and that many fruits, both visible and invisible, came from the experience. Each one who told his story in writing made it clear that it was easier to have Christian love, to make the necessary sacrifices which life demands, and to get on with their Christian job of living. All of them found that, with religious convictions strengthened, their psychological problems were easier to handle. And, finally, in many cases a physical illness was healed at the time of the experience, or they experienced healing so soon after the occurrence of tongues that they could not help linking the two. These people claim that in the experience of tongues they found the religious meaning of life.

Psychologically this experience can be described as a reconnection with the deep unconscious, of which the glossolalia was a confirming manifestation. Of course, many people have been able to make this reconnection, or it has been made in them, without any experience of tongues. But for some speaking tongues has been at least an added impetus in this reconnection; whether it is more basically a prime mover or more likely a relatively unimportant side manifestation is difficult to determine.

In many of the cases which have been observed tongues appears to be associated with growth and integration of personality, with what Jung calls the constellation of the "self." We might say that this is wholeness, balance, perfection in motion; concurrently with the experience of tongues some of these people were able to handle their own problems and meet them in relation to life as a whole in a way they had not been able to do before. When the unconscious forces seeking integration break through, there may be an experience of tongue-speech, particularly if the person is open to it. And conversely, those who are seeking an experience of tongues may well be opening their lives for just such a spontaneous eruption of the archetype of the self. As the theologian would put it, the willingness or desire to receive tongues may itself open the person to an experience of the Holy Spirit.

There appears to be a close relationship between personality type and whether this resolution came with tongues or with some other religious (i.e., life) experience. This question involves Jung's best known psychological contribution, the description of introversion and extroversion, and also his basic conclusions about psychic function. By function he means the process which an individual, either introvert or extrovert, uses to the greatest extent in relating to reality—thinking, intuition, feeling, or sensation. For instance, the feeling introvert might be best at judging inner values and balancing people's needs with moral demands, while the feeling extrovert would know how to deal with people in politics and social groups. The thinking introvert can become the philosopher, while the thinking extrovert turns to applied science. It has been my experience that the extroverted person, the one most largely concerned with the outer world, in whom feeling or relating to differences in value is dominant, and who has been inhibited in the use of this function, is most likely to speak in tongues. The experience is also of great benefit to such a person, liberating him to use far more of this vital unconscious power. Tongues can be a breaking down of obsolete barriers and an entrance into a new life for such a person. This may at least help to explain why the experience comes to some and not to others.

Yet the experience is no respecter of persons and links together people of the most diverse backgrounds in a common religious experience. It comes to the unlettered and to those with the finest educational background and gives a common bond between them. It crosses denominational, cultural, and theological boundaries. It is a vital religious experience, depending on the desire of the individual to receive it, and is not dependent upon one's moral perfectionism or theological belief. Thus it brings Christians of the most diverse backgrounds together and enables them to communicate with one another.

Most of those who have had the experience testify to revitalization of the religious life which follows upon tongues. The church services and sacraments take on new meaning, the Bible comes to life, and prayer becomes alive and real. Through this experience, commitment to the formal religious way becomes easier and more meaningful. Many of them find tithing is no longer a problem. The whole realm of the supernatural, the spiritual, becomes more real to the one who has had this experience.

In addition to all this, tongue speakers make it clear that there is an emotional release. One finds that it is easier to express emotions and to give way to them in a creative way. There is also a sense of joy even in the midst of difficulties. Although subsequent experiences seldom equal the first one, the continued use of tongues provides a more adequate expression of praise than any similar conscious activity, and also brings a continuous sense of profound joy.

One psychologically sophisticated tongue speaker has written his summary of the values of the experience in these words:

If the Jungian approach to the collective unconscious is followed, it can be accepted that a numinous, supra-personal quality does enter the life of one who speaks in tongues. This phenomenon is not, therefore, pathological nor infantile. Instead, it can relate the conscious mind to the ground of its existence in the collective unconscious. It can free the conscious mind from its extreme rationalism. It can allow the emotional side of the psyche not only a means of expression but also a method of nurture. Speaking with tongues can be a most concrete means of expressing joy and praise to God. It is a genuine witness to the presence of the Holy Spirit in one's life. Speaking with tongues is one evidence of the Spirit of God working in the unconscious and bringing one to a new wholeness, a new integration of the total psyche, a process which the Church has traditionally called sanctification.

THE NEGATIVE ASPECTS

For the onlooker with no connection to the experience, glossolalia can be an unattractive, irrational, automatic, nonconscious phenomenon, even in its most devotional atmosphere. When it breaks out in the regular service of a church where it is not expected, it intrudes upon the devotions of those who are there and hinders them in their worship. When it breaks out uncontrolled in any group, it can result in utter bedlam and confusion. To one who does not understand or appreciate it the outburst of tongues appears to be utterly meaningless gibberish. It either makes no sense or else it testifies to possession of a rational human personality by some unknown psychic or cosmic force.

Man has struggled to come to his limited sensibleness. Tongue speaking seems to be a deliberate attempt to abandon one's self to the irrational, unknown forces which lie beyond consciousness. It strikes at the very center of our culture's rational meaning. It is an observable denial of the very genius which has rescued Western civilization from the chaos of the Dark Ages and unconsciousness. Tongues is a concrete example of giving one's self over to the unknown, the unconscious, and this to the modern rational mind is dangerous above all things. The more one fears this unknown, the more fearful he will be of tongues. It may well lead to God knows what new irrationality. No wonder the experience is viewed with such horror by most rational Christians.

It is easy to point to the conflict and division which have been caused by this irrational practice. The people who have this experience and value it will not be reasonable about it, and enmity develops within formerly peaceful church groups. The successor to Dennis Bennett (who resigned as rector when his Episcopal parish split over approval of his tongue speaking) has had reason for a recent statement in his weekly parish mailer to the people of St. Mark's Church, Van Nuys, California: "The practice of speaking in tongues (glossolalia) is divisive, often leading to overzealous claims for power." Bishop Pike also points out the same danger. The Christian and Missionary Alliance can testify to the same truth. Tongue speaking may well cause division among Christians. Indeed there have been times when I would have been just as happy if there were no such group in my own church.

Even more unattractive than tongue-speech are the actions of many tongue speakers. The experience is so meaningful to them that they assume it should be experienced by everyone else. They become inflated by the experience, proceeding to judge everyone else who has not spoken in tongues as religiously inferior and trying to force other people into the experience. This is spiritual disaster. It was against just this attitude that Paul wrote three chapters of his first letter to the Corinthians, 12, 13, and 14. In them Paul warned the Corinthians not to assume that each individual can be handed all the gifts of the Spirit.

Some persons who speak in tongues suddenly find themselves getting God by the tail and receiving messages that "God told me this about you . . ." or "God wants you to do this . . ." and these are usually the very people who receive messages for everyone but themselves. The same people will often use every emotional, social, and personal pressure to force other persons to have the experience of tongues. There is real danger here; under these circumstances tongues can be brought to one who has a weak ego, and may become a contribution to psychological illness. It is forced tongue speaking which accounts for most examples of the unfortunate results of tongue-speech. The practice of having children experience glossolalia (since they are close to the unconscious, it is easy for many of them) may also be dangerous. The danger may well lie in having the experience at any age before one is aware of his own conflicts, so that tongues becomes a way to suppress inner problems rather than resolving them.

Many tongue speakers overemphasize this gift in their own lives, and this may lead to a religious and psychological cul-de-sac. It is so easy for us human beings to have a tremendously meaningful religious experience and then to identify with the experience and to see ourselves as the only angels on earth—God's sole messengers from this realm. We become spiritual instead of relating to the spiritual realm. The less pleasant parts of the personality are then almost invariably rejected and pushed into the unconscious, where they build up until the pressure bursts out in some personal or social debacle. Isn't this just the case of the Sunday school superintendent—on weekdays a beloved husband and respected banker, speaking in tongues at the Wednesday evening prayer group—who one morning absconds with a choir girl and the bank reserves, and ends up blaming everyone else, even the girl? When we have identified only with the light and the positive, our own darkness is obscured, and how easily it can creep up on us and push us into some tragic corner. There are then demons instead of gifts of the Spirit.

This problem may be increased by the experience of tongues which is a liberating experience, freeing the unconscious to flood out into the individual. For the person who is already uninhibited and needs to keep a tight rein on what inhibitions he has, tongue speaking may allow too much freedom and too much breakdown of control. This accounts, at least in part, for the moral excesses of the early days of the Pentecostal movement so lamented by their more perceptive writers; some people were undoubtedly involved who were not suited for the experience and not prepared for it. Another valid criticism of tongue speaking is the emotionalism which often follows it. The experience may result in a starry-eyed burst of emotion which weakens the individual and makes him more unstable than before. Still another reaction to being faced with more in the unconscious than one is prepared to deal with is that of moral rigidity and perfectionism. It is equally valid to criticize tongue speakers who appear religious only from the outside, while at home their wives and children are tyrannized. I am reminded of Jung's remark that he made it a rule never to pass on the sanctity of a man until he had also met his wife.

Closely related to these reactions is the danger that tongue speaking can become a short cut to religious and psychological growth which stunts it instead of giving full measure. If the experience is seen as the center of Christian life, then Christ, in whom no one experience takes precedence, is displaced as the center, and Christian wholeness gets lost. Growing towards Christian maturity means continual shedding of skin, and when this experience is used as a substitute for this work, for the patience and suffering of growth, people get caught in tongue speaking and never go further. They then become "gift seekers" only, who want the gift, some of them only the "jag" or emotional experience, without paying the price or counting the cost of full religious commitment. These people are not difficult to find. The experience of tongues does not result in an experience of eternal bliss, but soon gives way to a period of dryness and testing. Many of the weaker people are simply not able to sustain this and fall back into a worse state than they were in before. Dealing with what has been opened up in them is more than they can handle.

Bishop Pike has intimated that tongue speaking may well be "heresy in embryo." Some tongue speakers certainly come close to this from an ecclesiastical point of view. They maintain that unless there is a conscious experience of contact with God, such as tongues, the sacraments and services of the church have no value or validity. One Pentecostal writer has stated that the ordinary sacraments which are supposed to offer Christian grace have about as much meaning as a marriage which has never been consummated. He writes:

> Thousands repeat the Apostles' Creed but have never known the apostolic experience. They "believe in the Holy Ghost" as a creedal statement but have never received the Holy Ghost as a personal experience. They may have participated in a ceremony in which hands were laid upon them and words pronounced over them but it may have been only a ceremony void of personal reality and life-changing power.
>
> Not that the ceremony is wrong. Did not the apostles lay their hands upon believers that they might receive the Holy Ghost? Assuredly so, as recorded in Acts 8 and chapters 9 and 19. The ceremony is not wrong. The wrong is in being satisfied with mere ceremony and rejecting the actual experience of receiving. The ceremony may be compared with a wedding. The marriage ceremony may be performed in all the solemnity and decorum of the church but the ceremony of marriage is not recognized by the law of the land unless it is consummated in experience. Without the consummation the wedding may be declared null and void—without effect—as though it never took place. So it is also in the ceremony of the imposition of hands. The ceremony is null and void—without effect—unless there is also the personal experience of receiving the Holy Ghost.[1]

1. George P. Tunks, "I Believe in the Holy Ghost," *The Pentecostal Evangel*, June 2, 1963, p. 7.

This is dogmatism on the other side. How can we possibly say about God that he acts *only* through our conscious experience of Him? There is also good evidence that the quiet, regular attendance at the church services, the patient and steady turning towards God in daily devotion, produce changes in lives, and this without any one startling experience of the divine. Maintaining that all religious experience must come in one way one can be led into pride and judging which soon turn to fanaticism.

"BUT ISN'T IT DANGEROUS?"

It would be difficult to find two more diverse attitudes than we find expressed towards the experience of tongues. On the one hand it is valued as the fountainhead of meaning and vitality, a direct contact with God. On the other, it is viewed as a dangerous experience giving the individual over to the unknown and hostile forces of reality, one which results in personal and social disaster.

There is no doubt that glossolalia is dangerous. In the words of one psychologist, it is strong medicine. It would be foolish to conclude that there are no dangers in tongue speaking. To say that glossolalia is a spiritual experience, a direct experience of God, does not mean that it is a safe, cushioned ride to the next playground. It does mean that it is an experience of the most basic and central reality of life, the realm of the spirit, of which so many people are unconscious and from which so many people are cut off. Much of the neurosis of our time derives from just this unconsciousness and separation.

There comes to mind an open-end discussion I recently had about the healing ministry. I was flying East to speak at a conference on spiritual healing and was talking about it with another clergyman on the plane. We paused, and suddenly he spoke softly: "But isn't it dangerous?" And the answer we couldn't help laughing over has become almost stock for me: "Yes, but isn't a dead church more dangerous than a dangerous one?" As the New Testament has tried to tell us, the real danger is in being half alive. When the dead is right in the center of things, inside oneself and society, its deadness can be disastrous. And so perhaps we are better off to live and face the dangers, those of tongues included.

Dealing with the living God *is* a dangerous adventure, as the Old Testament is constantly reminding us. Jesus and Paul believed that there was malignant spiritual reality, as well as good, and that it was dangerous. Man needed strong medicine to deal with it. For Jesus the cross was strong medicine. In apostolic times, as Acts tells, Ananias and Sapphira found dealing with God a deadly dangerous business. Spiritual reality has to be dealt with or it will deal with us, and tongues is one way, a strong medicine. It is like shock treatment, which makes no rational sense and should be used sparingly and carefully, but in some cases is the only thing that breaks up a pattern of mental illness so that healing can begin.

There are many sincere and intelligent Christians who believe that man does not have and does not need a direct, conscious experience of God. They believe that the individual obtains his relationship with God and the healing powers of the spiritual world through the church group, through belief and ritual, and that there is no particular value in a direct experience of God. To them the church is a transformer which reduces the current of a high-tension line to 110 volts standard. For those who find religious vitality through this means, it is the right way. Yet there are some people for whom the sacraments and beliefs of the traditional church transmit very little, or nothing at all, and these men and women clamor for life and some of them find it in the experience of tongues. There is real antagonism between these two groups and has been since the time of Plato.

Therefore, there are two basically different points of view about the dangers inherent in the direct experience of God and speaking in tongues. On one side is the view of Aristotle, Aquinas, and most of Western Christianity to the present, which theoretically denies its reality and value. On the other side is the attitude of Plato, the New Testament, the fathers, and Eastern Orthodoxy, and in our time of the Pentecostals, that such experience is extremely important if man is to know God. Since these are basically different, honestly held points of view, both with honorable lineage, a statement like that of Monsignor Knox is a little condescending: "Yet something may be written about enthusiasm by way of epilogue; if you will, of epitaph. . . . Basically it is the revolt of Platonism against the Aristotelian *mise en scène* of traditional Christianity. The issue hangs on the question whether the Divine Fact is something given, or something to be inferred."[2] This "enthusiasm," it may be well to remember, comes from the Greek, meaning to be "in God."

NOT A CLOSED CASE

The fact is that there is an issue here, not a closed case. There are two elements in Christianity, both of them very much alive. The theology of a direct contact with spiritual reality, which makes tongues a conceivable phenomenon, is not absurd. This has been borne out empirically by the psychology which demonstrates that individuals do have contact with the mysterious depths of the collective unconscious. On the other hand, a large part of Western thinking honestly believes that there is no choice between fanaticism and belief in the direct experience of the supersensible world. The final decision between Plato and Aristotle has not been made. Indeed the decision between them may well be made as much on the basis of temperament as of logic, as Dr. Jung suggests in *Psychological Types*. The important matter then is one of understanding and tolerance.

Granted, it is dangerous to believe in the direct experience of God and the world of the spirit. But life is dangerous. Belief in fissioning and fusing the atom is dangerous. But

2. Knox, op. cit., pp. 578 f.

it is also true. We do not consider it safe simply to say that we do not believe in the power of the atom. It is not any safer simply to close our eyes to the reality and power of spiritual experience, and we hide our heads while splitting ourselves when we deride anyone who accepts this fact. Tongues is one evidence of this fact which is occurring. If direct experience of a spiritual realm is possible and desirable, then those who will must face this primary danger, for tongues should be investigated.

Tongues undoubtedly causes conflict, but is conflict necessarily evil from a Christian point of view? Can there be any growth and development without conflict? I am not sure that Christianity is always meant to bring peace and harmony as a soothing salve, however much the ministers of the church (myself included) would like it to be so. How often we overlook the arrogance and enmity generated by the early Christians as they attempted to bring Jewish brethren and pagan friends to the light! They stirred up so much conflict that they were stoned and fed to wild beasts. Paul's life could scarcely be termed free of conflict. And I am reminded of the little quoted statement of Jesus from the Gospel of Luke: "I have come to set fire to the earth, and how I wish it were already kindled! I have a baptism to undergo, and how hampered I am until the ordeal is over! Do you suppose I came to establish peace on earth? No indeed, I have come to bring division." (12:49)

Our more conventional Christian attitudes are distressed by the display of emotion which is often a result of tongue speaking. Not long ago the experience of tongues broke forth among a group of teen-agers who became involved with deep emotion. There was weeping and a high pitch of feeling. Some of the leaders were understandably concerned until one of them suggested, "These youngsters get emotional over other things. My daughter cries about her hair-do and even the way I speak to her. And what about their football games?

Maybe we ought to stop and wonder if their religious life is simply having the same amount of real meaning for them." Adults too can get emotional over the stock market or integration. Perhaps they should get somewhat emotional about their religion as well.

The most unattractive aspect of the tongue speaking movement is the spiritual pride and arrogance which is found among many who practice it. This is not a unique problem of glossolalia, however. Men can become proud and arrogant over all sorts of things, secular and religious, and it must be admitted that most of the mature Pentecostal leaders emphasize this very point: tongues is not the end-all, far from it. From their point of view it is an entrance into a new life of great possibilities and vistas. Speaking in tongues is a *rite d'entrée* to the deeper levels of the psyche. It is an initiation rite in the deepest and truest meaning of that word. But since it gives no more than entrance, its values lie not so much in what it is, as in what it brings and what results follow it. Tongues can be a beginning of spiritual life, not the end, and for some people it may be the best, or even the only way of opening them to a religious experience. The essential unattractiveness of tongues is not so much a part of the phenomenon itself as it is the human and religious attitude with which it is often expressed.

Speaking in tongues, then, as one of the gifts of the Spirit, is a true Christian phenomenon. It is one entrance into the spiritual realm; by giving access to the unconscious, it is one contact with non-physical reality which allows God to speak directly to man. As a spiritual gift, it is given to some and not necessarily to others, is neither to be forced, nor most certainly to be rejected or ridiculed because it is not the most important or desirable gift. For one who has been caught up in a totally materialistic point of view, this experience gives a balance which only a religious experience can give, and it is certainly not an abnormal one psychologically. It must be remembered that this experience has been valued positively in historical times when the church has been alive and vital. It is also the central tenet of faith of a rapidly increasing body of Christians today, the Pentecostals, and is important to an unknown number of persons in the traditional Protestant denominations.

As a spiritual gift, it has value not only for the individual who speaks in tongues, but for the whole group. One of the greatest values of tongue speaking is that it forces us to consider the possibility of direct contact with non-physical or spiritual reality. It forces us to re-examine some of our basic Western theology, our presuppositions, indeed our certainty that there is nothing worth reaching for beyond the practical, sensory world. Any practice which encourages such re-evaluation is valuable. And like all spiritual endowments, when it is not seen in perspective, glossolalia becomes destructive and even demonic.

THE FINAL QUESTION

The final question, then, is: How can we permit this experience, which is vitally important for many people, without falling into the dangers and abuses which so often surround tongues? How can it be kept in perspective?

Glossolalia can be a regenerative influence with relatively few dangers when it occurs within a Christian community in which there is understanding of the mysterious spiritual levels of the human psyche and of the God which touches men at those levels. In such a group speaking in tongues would not be normative and so never forced. It would likewise never be forbidden. When it was spontaneous, it would be viewed with tolerance and understanding by those who did not experience it, and with humility and modesty by those who did. Tongue speakers would not separate out from those who find their religious fulfillment in other ways. Both would learn from one another and their different ways. They would try to understand their experiences in the best theological context which they are able to formulate, each taking into account the point of view of the one who differed from him.

The answer to the problem which speaking in tongues raises in the modern church was given by Paul nearly two millenniums ago. It is to be found in his first letter to the Corinthians when he was discussing this very subject. He makes it very clear that tongue-speech is one of the lesser gifts, and he counsels the tongue speakers to restrain themselves in public out of consideration for others. Since it apparently never occurred to anyone at the time that the experience would be totally rejected, he did not counsel tolerance on the other side, as he did in other matters. Paul did stress the importance of control, good taste, and humility on the part of tongue speakers, and orderliness and harmony in the church services. These could be achieved when Christians put genuine compassion, agape, love ahead of all other spiritual gifts and endowments. When Christians are striving to express this most difficult and mature embodiment of the Christian life, glossolalia is then allowed its place in the repertory of Christian gifts.

APPENDIX A

NON-PHYSICAL REALITIES IN THE GOSPELS

The subject of angels and demons is one that has not attracted much popular scholarship. In fact, Jesus' belief in the relationship of men to non-human spiritual (non-physical) reality has been almost completely ignored. Yet the following list of references is rather impressive.

In the New Testament three basic Greek words are used to describe non-material powers or beings: angels, spirit, and demons or to be demonized. All of these words can be used to describe either benevolent or malicious powers. Indeed, they have no reference to morality, but to ontology, to being; they refer to entities believed to exist. All of the realities described by these words affect human lives, exercising tremendous influence over men and directing human destiny for good and for ill. In addition we find several descriptions for the prince of the demons, Satan, the evil one, or the devil.

The references to these descriptions are listed for each of the Four Gospels:

Ἄγγελος—angel, as messenger or agent:

Matt.	Mark	Luke	John
1:20	1:13	1:11	1:51
1:24	8:38	1:13	5:4
2:13	12:25	1:18	12:29
2:19	13:27	1:19	20:12
4:6	13:32	1:26	
4:11		1:28	
13:39		1:30	
13:41		1:34	
13:49		1:35	
16:27		1:38	
18:10		2:9	
22:30		2:10	
24:31		2:13	
24:36		2:15	
25:31		2:21	
25:41		4:10	
26:53		9:26	
28:2		12:8	
28:5		12:9	
		15:10	
		16:22	
		20:36[a]	
		22:43	
		24:23	

[a] Ἰσάγγελος—equal to or like the angels.

Πνεῦμα ἀκάθαρτον—unclean spirit:

Matt.	10:1	Mark	1:23	Luke	4:36	John	
	12:43		1:26		6:18		
			1:27		8:29		
			3:11		9:39[a]		
			3:30		9:42		
			5:2		11:24		
			5:8				
			5:13				
			6:7				
			7:25				
			9:25				

[a] This spirit is described as "unclean" in verse 42.

Πνεῦμα—spirit, in various senses:

Matt.	8:16[b]	Mark	6:49[aa]	Luke	4:33[b]	John	
	12:45[c]		9:17[e]		7:21[c]		
	14:26[aa]		9:20[e]		8:2[c]		
			9:25[e]		10:20[bb]		
					11:26[c]		
					13:11[d]		
					24:37[a]		
					24:39[a]		

[a] Πνεῦμα (a spirit), or [aa] φάντασμα (an apparition).

[b] Πνεῦμα δαιμονίου ἀκαθαρτου (spirit of an unclean demon), πνεύματα (spirits of those) δαιμονιζομένους (possessed with demons), or [bb] referring to the "serpents . . . scorpions . . . enemy" (Luke 10:19).

[c] Πνευμάτων πονηρῶν, or πνεύματα πονηρότερα, (evil spirits, or more wicked spirits).

[d] Πνεῦμα ἀσθενείας (spirit causing infirmity).

[e] Πνεῦμα "αλαλον, or κωφόν (dumb, or deaf and dumb spirit).

Δαιμονίζομαι—to be demonized, possessed with a devil:

Matt.	4:24	Mark	1:32	Luke	8:36	John	10:21
	8:16		5:15				
	8:28		5:16				
	8:33		5:18				
	9:32						
	12:22						
	15:22						

Δαιμόνιον, δαίμων—god, inferior divinity, demon, shade, deified spirit:

Matt. 7:22	Mark 1:34	Luke 4:33	John 7:20
8:31	1:39	4:35	8:48
9:33	3:15	4:41	8:49
9:34	3:22	7:33	8:52
10:8	5:12	8:2	10:20
11:18	6:13	8:27	10:21
12:24	7:26	8:29	
12:27	7:29	8:30	
12:28	7:30	8:33	
17:18	9:38	8:35,38	
	16:9	9:1	
	16:17	9:42	
		9:49	
		10:17	
		11:14,15,18,19,20	
		13:32	

Σατᾶν, διάβολος—adversary, calumniator, false accuser, prince of demons, author of evil:

Matt. 4:1	Mark 1:13	Luke 4:2,3	John 8:44
4:5	3:23	4:5,6,8	13:2
4:8	3:26	4:13	13:27
4:10	4:15	8:12	
4:11		10:18	
12:26		11:18	
13:39		13:16	
25:41		22:3	
		22:31	

Βεελζεβούλ—prince of demons, probably another name for Satan:

Matt. 10:25	Mark 3:22	Luke 11:15
12:24		11:18
12:27		11:19

Ἀρχή (with *δαιμόνιον* or *κόσμος*)—prince of evil spirits, prince of this world:

Matt. 9:34	Mark 3:22	Luke 11:15	John 12:31
12:24			14:30
			16:11

Πονηρός or πονηροῦ—evil, the evil one, the devil:

Matt. 5:37	Luke 11:4 (RL)	John 17:15
6:13		
13:19		
13:38		

NON-PHYSICAL REALITIES IN PAUL'S LETTERS

Paul's belief in the existence of a spiritual or non-physical realm which was directly experienced is represented by the following list of the 79 references to it found in the Pauline corpus. All of the letters commonly attributed to Paul are included; in only two of them are there no such references:

	Figurative Names	Angels	Spirit	Demons	Evil one Devil Satan Archon
Romans		8:38			8:38
Spirit of Slavery			8:15		
Spirit of stupor			11:8		
Sin and death	5:12 ff. 6:9 ff. 8:10				
Servant and master	14:4				
"Neither death, nor life"	8:38				
I Corinthians		4:9	2:12	10:20	2:6
		6:3	14:32	10:21	5:5
		11:10			7:5
		13:1			
Idols, gods, lords	8:5				
Rule, authority, power	15:24				
Idols also 8:4, 8:7, 10:19 and 12:2					
II Corinthians		11:14	11:4		11:14
					12:7
					2:11
God of this age	4:4				4:4
Idols	6:16				
Galatians		1:8			
		3:19			
		4:14			
Evil age	1:4				
Elemental spirits	4:3				
—weak and beggarly	4:8 f.				

	Figurative Names	Angels	Spirit	Demons	Evil one Devil Satan Archon
Ephesians			2:2		4:27
					6:11
					6:16
All rule, authority	1:21				
Prince of the power of air	2:2				
Deceitful wiles	4:14				
Principalities & powers in heavenly places	3:10 6:12				
Philippians—(one wonders how exemplary a group they must have been).					
Colossians		2:18			
Dominion of darkness	1:13				
Thrones, dominions . . .	1:16				
All rule and authority	2:10				
Principalities & powers	2:15				
Elemental spirits	2:8,20				
Worship of idols	3:5				
I Thessalonians (archangel)		4:16			2:18
Idols	1:9				
Error, deceit, guile	2:3				
II Thessalonians		1:7	2:2		2:8
A god working error	2:11				2:9
I Timothy		3:16	4:1	4:1	3:6,7
		5:21			1:20
					5:15
II Timothy			1:7		2:26
Titus					
Rulers and authorities	3:1				
Slaves to passions & pleas	3:3				
Philemon—whom Paul called the obedient one, beyond even his requests.					

NON-PHYSICAL REALITIES IN ACTS AND THE LATER EPISTLES

The following references show that spiritual realities are mentioned just as frequently here as in Paul's writings and the Gospels:

	Figurative Names	Angels	Spirit	Demons	Evil one Devil Satan Archon
Acts		5:19	5:16	17:18	5:3
		6:15	8:7		10:38
		7:30	16:16		13:10
		7:35	16:18		26:18
		7:38	19:12		
		7:53	19:13		
		8:26	19:15		
		10:3	19:16		
		10:7	23:8		
		10:22	23:9		
		11:13			
		12:7			
		12:8			
		12:9			
		12:10			
		12:11			
		12:15			
		12:23			
		23:8			
		23:9			
		27:23			
Hebrews		1:4–7	1:7		2:14
		1:13	1:14		
		2:2	4:12		
		2:5	12:9		
		2:7,9			
		2:16			
		12:22			
		13:2			
Power of death	2:15				
Servants, flames of fire	1:7				
Our weakness or infirmities	4:15 5:2				
James				2:19	4:7
				3:15	

	Figurative Names	Angels	Spirit	Demons	Evil one Devil Satan Archon
I Peter					
		1:12	3:19		5:8
		3:22			
Authorities and powers	3:22				
Idolatry	4:3				
II Peter		2:4			
		2:11			
Error, guile	2:18				
Error of Lawless man	3:17				
Corruption in the world	1:4				
Creatures of instinct	2:12				
Elements which will be dissolved with fire	3:10 3:12				
I John			4:1,3		3:8,10
					2:13 f.
					3:12
					5:18 f.
Idols	5:21				
Spirit of error	4:6				
II John					
Deceivers, and antichrist	7				
III John					
Jude		14			9
		9			6
Archangel		6			
"Balaam's error"	11				

Spiritual realities are mentioned just as frequently throughout the writings of the church fathers, as well. This is good Christian evidence which should cause one to stop and think. In addition, it is impossible to take in this evidence without appreciating the evil aspects of the spiritual realm as well as the good. "Spiritual" which is equated with "good" is simply misunderstood. To anyone who insists on this definition I would suggest the magnificent novels of Tolkien or Charles Williams, not exactly to clear the air, but to be able to see the smog which is there. Once a man does confront the spiritual realm of being, his religious undertaking is no longer just a nice holiday outing. It is a vital necessity for the maintenance of decency and sanity. Religion is then imbued with utter urgency. It is forced on a man whether he finds it in the church or somewhere else. This is what Jung speaks of in telling of his encounter with the spiritual realm—the unconscious in today's psychological terminology—when the conventional church had failed to offer him any way of dealing with the spiritual reality life forced on him. (J. R. R. Tolkien's works are published by George Allen & Unwin, Ltd., London, and Charles Williams' by Faber and Faber, Ltd. Tolkien's *The Hobbit,* a light-hearted introduction which can be shared with children, is also published by Houghton Mifflin, and Williams' *All Hallows' Eve,* one of our favorites, has just been brought out in paperback by Noonday. We refer to Jung's *Memories, Dreams and Reflections,* previously cited.)

APPENDIX B

THE PENTECOSTAL CHURCHES

Established in			Number of Churches	Members
1919	Ala.	Apostolic Overcoming Holy Church of God	300	75,000
1914	U.S.	Assemblies of God	8273	514,317
1927	East	Christian Church of North America	148	17,500
		Churches of God		
1895	S., E., Midw.	Church of God in Christ	4000	411,466
1886	So.	Church of God	3338	179,651
1903	N.Y.	The Church of God	1852	71,606
1886	Tenn.	The (Original) Church of God	35	6,000
1903	Tenn.	The Church of God of Prophecy	1301	35,349
1919	N.Y.	Church of Our Lord Jesus Christ of Apostolic Faith	155	45,000
1921	So.	Congregational Holiness Church	147	4,664
1898	Ga.	Fire Baptized Holiness Church	53	988
1927	Calif.	Int'l Church of the Four-square Gospel	726	84,741
1921	Calif.	National David Spiritual Temple of Christ	66	40,815
1932[a]	Ia., W.	Open Bible Standard Churches	275	26,000
		Pentecostal Assemblies		
1931	Seattle	Calvary Pentecostal Church	22	8,000
1947	N.Y.	Elim Missionary Assemblies	75	4,000
1953	N.C.	Emmanuel Holiness Church	56	1,200
1921[a]	So., Midw.	International Pentecostal Assemblies	92	15,000
1914	So., Midw.	Pentecostal Assemblies of the World	550	45,000

[a] Established by a merger of existing church bodies.

Established in			Number of Churches	Members
1917	O., Ken.	Pentecostal Church of Christ	44	1,198
1919	Ill.	Pentecostal Church of God of America	1090	109,900
1960	Ore.	Pent'l Evangelical Ch. of God Nat'l & Int'l	4	229
1918	Ga.	Pentecostal Fire Baptized Holiness Church	41	573
1959	N.C.	Pentecostal Free Will Baptist Church	127	7,000
1900	So., Midw.	Pentecostal Holiness Church	1248	55,502
1945	So., Midw.	United Pentecostal Church	1900	175,000

COMPARATIVE MEMBERSHIP

Groups of Religious Bodies	*No. of Bodies*	*No. of Churches*	*Membership*
Baptist	28	91,840	21,396,223
Methodist	21	55,589	12,632,442
Lutheran	15	17,285	8,340,183
Presbyterian	10	14,656	4,327,261
Christian	2	26,468	4,047,466
Protestant Episcopal	1	7,155	3,269,325
Pentecostal	15	25,918	1,935,699
Latter Day Saints	5	4,580	1,758,518
Reformed	6	1,575	501,145

These figures come from the *Yearbook of American Churches.* New York, National Council of the Churches of Christ in the U.S.A., 1963. All the Pentecostal Churches listed by Klaude Kendrick in *The Promise Fulfilled* are included.

ACKNOWLEDGMENTS

There are several books which have been of help in writing this volume. The most important of these is the unpublished manuscript by the Rev. Adams Lovekin, *Glossolalia: A Critical Study of Alleged Origins, the New Testament and the Early Church.* His careful study of glossolalia in the ancient world and the early life of the church first gave me the conviction that the subject deserved serious consideration. I am deeply grateful to him for permission to draw upon this work.

Another invaluable aid in this study has been George Barton Cutten's *Speaking with Tongues: Historically and Psychologically Considered,* published by Yale University Press in 1927. This is the best and most objective historical study of the phenomenon of tongues and we draw upon it throughout our historical discussion. There is no other comparable historical discussion of the material.

Two books by Pentecostal writers offer an excellent picture of the movement in the twentieth century. Both are carefully documented and give an excellent base from which to view modern Pentecostalism. They are the works put out by the Gospel Publishing House in 1961 by Carl Brumback, *Suddenly . . . from Heaven,* and Klaude Kendrick, *The Promise Fulfilled.*

The Greeks and the Irrational by E. R. Dodds gives a clear picture of the irrationality of the Greek world in which Christianity developed and opens an understanding of the place which tongues had in the early church. This book is invaluable in breaking through the prejudices which so many people have about Greek thinking and life. Lancelot Law Whyte's *The Unconscious Before Freud* performs the same task for western Europe. This profound study of the development of ideas about the unconscious with its irrationality sets the stage for understanding the burst of interest in the irrational and the outbreak of tongues which came in the twentieth century.

We have quoted extensively from Carl G. Jung, but the understanding of Jung and his basic ideas was not derived from the books which we have quoted. Those who are intrigued by the ideas put forward by this man should read two basic and relatively simple books before going on to his more difficult works. *Modern Man in Search of a Soul* and *Two Essays on Analytical Psychology* present the basic introduction to his thinking. Jung's later works are based on the assumption that the reader has some knowledge of his thought, and unless the reader has this, he will soon be lost. It was Jung's thought which made a place for tongues in my own world view.

BIBLIOGRAPHY

A. WORKS RELATED TO TONGUES

Edward Deming Andrews, *The People Called Shakers*. New York, Oxford University Press, 1953.

Baptists and the Baptism of the Holy Spirit; The Methodists and the Baptism of the Holy Spirit; Presbyterians and the Baptism of the Holy Spirit. Los Angeles, Full Gospel Business Men's Fellowship International, 1963.

Maurice Barnett, *The Living Flame*. London, The Epworth Press, 1953.

Anton J. Boisen, *Religion in Crisis and Custom: A Sociological and Psychological Study*. New York, Harper & Brothers, 1955.

Frank M. Boyd, *The Holy Spirit: Teacher's Manual*. Springfield, Missouri, The Gospel Publishing House, no date.

Carl Brumback, *Suddenly . . . from Heaven: A History of the Assemblies of God*. Springfield, Missouri, The Gospel Publishing House, 1961.

———, *What Meaneth This? A Pentecostal Answer to a Pentecostal Question*. Springfield, Missouri, The Gospel Publishing House, 1947.

William Caldwell, *Pentecostal Baptism*. Tulsa, Oklahoma, Miracle Moments Evangelistic Association, Inc., 1963.

Leon Christiani, *Evidences of Satan in the Modern World*. New York, The Macmillan Company, 1962.

Elmer T. Clark, *The Small Sects in America*. New York, Abingdon-Cokesbury Press (rev. ed.), 1937.

George Barton Cutten, *Speaking with Tongues: Historically and Psychologically Considered*. New Haven, Yale University Press, 1927.

Robert Chandler Dalton, *Tongues Like As of Fire*. Springfield, Missouri, The Gospel Publishing House, 1945.

Lindsay Dewar, *The Holy Spirit and Modern Thought*. New York, Harper & Brothers, 1959.

David J. duPlessis, *The Spirit Bade Me Go*. Dallas, Texas, published by David J. duPlessis, 1961.

Frank J. Ewart, *The Phenomenon of Pentecost: A History of the Latter Rain*. St. Louis, Missouri, Pentecostal Publishing House, 1947.

Stanley H. Frodsham, *With Signs Following: The Story of the Pentecostal Revival in the Twentieth Century*. Springfield, Missouri, The Gospel Publishing House (rev. ed.), 1941.

Donald Gee, *Concerning Spiritual Gifts*. Springfield, Missouri, The Gospel Publishing House, no date.

Carter Eldredge Grant, *The Kingdom of God Restored*. Salt Lake City, Deseret Book Co., 2nd ed., 1955.

Harold Horton, *The Gifts of the Spirit*. London, Assemblies of God Publishing House, 1954.

Klaude Kendrick, *The Promise Fulfilled: A History of the Modern Pentecostal Movement*. Springfield, Missouri, The Gospel Publishing House, 1961.

Ronald A. Knox, *Enthusiasm: A Chapter in the History of Religion*. Oxford, The Clarendon Press, 1950.

Emile Lombard, *De la Glossolalie chez les Premiers Chrétiens et des Phénomènes Similaires*. Lausanne, Bridel, 1910.

Arthur Adams Lovekin, *Glossolalia: A Critical Study of Alleged Origins, the New Testament and the Early Church*. Unpublished master's thesis, Graduate School of Theology, University of the South, Sewanee, Tennessee, 1962.

Ira Jay Martin, *Glossolalia in the Apostolic Church*. Berea, Kentucky, Berea College Press, 1960.

Eddison Mosiman, *Das Zungenreden Geschichtlich und Psychologisch Untersucht*. Tübingen, Mohr, 1911.

Thomas R. Nickel, *The Amazing Shakarian Story*. Los Angeles, Full Gospel Business Men's Fellowship International, no date.

Myer Pearlman, *The Heavenly Gift*. Springfield, Missouri, The Gospel Publishing House, 1935.

Charles Francis Potter, *The Faiths Men Live By*. New York, Prentice-Hall Co., 1954.

J. R. Pridie, *The Spiritual Gifts*. London, Robert Scott, 1921.

C. W. Shumway, *A Critical History of Glossolalia*. Unpublished doctor's dissertation, Boston University, Boston, 1919.

Signs and Wonders in Rabbath-Ammon. Milwaukee, Word and Witness Publishing Co., 1934.

J. E. Stiles, *The Gift of the Holy Spirit*. Burbank, California, published by J. E. Stiles, no date.

Alma White, *Demons and Tongues*. Zarephath, New Jersey, Pillar of Fire, 1949.

Hugh White, *Demonism Verified*. Ann Arbor, Michigan, University Microfilms, 1963.

Periodicals

The Alliance Witness, May 1, 1963.
American Anthropologist, February, 1956.
The Banner, May 31, 1963.
Benedicite, Spring, 1963.
Christian Advocate, July 4, 1963.
Christian Life, July, 1963.
Christianity Today, September 13, 1963.
Dialog, Spring, 1963.
Eternity, July, 1963.
Full Gospel Business Men's *Voice.*
Journal of Theological Studies, October, 1952.
The Living Church, January 1, 1961, May 19, June 2, and September 22, 1963.
The Lutheran Standard, September 11, 1962.
Michigan Christian Advocate, April 4, 1963.
News Release: The Church of God.
The Pentecostal Evangel.
Presbyterian Life, September 1, 1963.
Trinity.
White Wing Messenger.

B. GENERAL RELIGIOUS WORKS

The Ante-Nicene Fathers, ed. Alexander Roberts and James Donaldson. Grand Rapids, Michigan, Wm. B. Eerdmans Company, 1950–51.

Thomas Aquinas, *Summa Theologica.* Great Books of the Western World, Vols. 19 and 20. Chicago, Encyclopaedia Britannica, Inc., 1952.

John Baillie, *The Idea of Revelation in Recent Thought.* New York, Columbia University Press, 1956.

———, *The Sense of the Presence of God.* London, Oxford University Press, 1962.

Ernst Benz, *The Eastern Orthodox Church: Its Thought and Life.* Garden City, New York, Doubleday Anchor, 1963.

Sergius Bulkagov, *The Orthodox Church.* London, The Centenary Press, no date.

Edwin A. Burtt, *Types of Religious Philosophy.* New York, Harper & Brothers, 1951.

B. F. Cate, *The Nine Gifts of the Spirit Are not in the Church Today.* Chicago, Regular Baptist Press, 1957.

The Catholic Encyclopedia. New York, The Universal Knowledge Foundation, Inc., 1907–13.

F. C. Copleston, *Aquinas*. Baltimore, Penguin Books, Inc., 1961.

Emile Dermenghem, *Muhammad and the Islamic Tradition*. New York, Harper & Brothers, 1958.

Anne Freemantle, ed., *A Treasury of Early Christianity*. New York, The New American Library of World Literature, Inc., 1960.

James Hastings, *Dictionary of the Bible*. New York, Charles Scribner's Sons, 1943.

Baron Friedrich von Hügel, *The Mystical Element of Religion as Studied in Saint Catherine of Genoa and Her Friends*. London, J. M. Dent & Sons, 1927.

The Interpreter's Bible. New York, Abingdon Press, 1951–55.

James H. McConkey, *The Three-Fold Secret of the Holy Spirit*. Pittsburgh, Pennsylvania, Silver Publishing Society, 1897.

Geddes MacGregor, *Introduction to Religious Philosophy*. Boston, Houghton Mifflin Company, 1959.

Douglas Clyde MacIntosh, *The Problem of Religious Knowledge*. New York, Harper & Brothers, 1940.

John McIntyre, "The Place of Imagination in Faith and Theology." *The Expository Times,* Edinburgh, October and November, 1962.

Samuel H. Miller, *The Dilemma of Modern Belief*. New York, Harper & Row, 1963.

The Nicene and Post-Nicene Fathers, First Series, ed. Philip Schaff; Second Series, ed. Philip Schaff and Henry Wace. Grand Rapids, Michigan, Wm. B. Eerdmans Co., 1952 and 1956.

Mrs. Penn-Lewis, *The Awakening in Wales* (*1904–5*). Leicester, England, Overcomer Book Room, 1922.

The Roman Ritual, the Rev. Philip T. Weller, trans. and ed. Milwaukee, The Bruce Publishing Company, 1952.

The Rudder (*Pedalion*), trans. D. Cummings. Chicago, The Orthodox Christian Educational Society, 1957.

Steven Runciman, *Byzantine Civilization*. New York, The World Publishing Company (Meridian Books), 1960.

Philip Schaff, *History of the Apostolic Church*. New York, Charles Scribner's Sons, 1893.

Phillip Sherrard, *Athos: The Mountain of Silence*. London, Oxford University Press, 1960.

A. E. Taylor, *The Faith of a Moralist*. London, The Macmillan Company, 1930.

F. R. Tennant, *Philosophical Theology*. Cambridge, England, The Cambridge University Press, 1956.

Joseph Henry Thayer, *Greek-English Lexicon of the New Testament.* New York, American Book Company, 1889.

Henry P. Van Dusen, *Spirit, Son and Father.* New York, Charles Scribner's Sons, 1958.

The Way of a Pilgrim, R. M. French, trans. London, S.P.C.K., 1963.

Johannes Weiss, *The History of Primitive Christianity.* New York, Wilson-Erickson, 1937.

Victor White, *God and the Unconscious.* New York, The World Publishing Company (Meridian Books), 1961.

Nicolas Zernov, *Eastern Christendom.* London, Weidenfeld & Nicolson, 1961.

Yearbook of American Churches, 31st annual edition, Benson Y. Landis, ed. New York, Office of Publication and Distribution, National Council of the Churches of Christ in the U.S.A., 1963.

C. PSYCHOLOGY

David Bakan, *Sigmund Freud and the Jewish Mystical Tradition.* Princeton, New Jersey, D. Van Nostrand Co., Inc., 1958.

Jean Bobon, "Les Pseudo-Glossolalies Ludiques et Magiques," *Journal Belge de Neurologie et de Psychiatrie,* Vol. 47, April and June, 1947.

Josef Breuer and Sigmund Freud, *Studies in Hysteria.* Boston, Beacon Press, 1958.

Théodore Flournoy, *Des Indes à la Planète Mars: Étude sur un Cas de Somnambulisme avec Glossolalie.* Genève, Ch. Eggimann & Cie., 1900.

Sigmund Freud, *Collected Papers.* New York, Basic Books, 1955.

———, *Interpretation of Dreams.* New York, Basic Books, 1955.

———, *Moses and Monotheism.* New York, Vintage Books, Inc., 1955.

———and Oskar Pfister, *Psychoanalysis and Faith: The Letters of Sigmund Freud and Oskar Pfister,* ed. Heinrich Menz and Ernst L. Freud. New York, Basic Books, 1963.

William James, *The Varieties of Religious Experience.* New York, Longmans, Green and Co., 1925.

C. G. Jung, *Collected Works.* New York, Pantheon Books, Inc., (Bollingen Foundation) esp.:
Vol. 1, *Psychiatric Studies.* 1957.
Vol. 5, *Symbols of Transformation.* 1956.
Vol. 7, *Two Essays on Analytical Psychology.* 1953.
Vol. 9, Part I, *Archetypes and the Collective Unconscious.* 1959.

Vol. 9, Part II, *Aion.* 1959.
Vol. 11, *Psychology and Religion: West and East.* 1958.
Vol. 12, *Psychology and Alchemy.* 1953.

———, *Memories, Dreams and Reflections.* New York, Pantheon Books, Inc., 1963.

———, *Modern Man in Search of a Soul.* New York, Harcourt, Brace and Company, 1933.

———, *Psychological Types.* London, Routledge & Kegan Paul, Ltd., 1953.

Albert Le Baron, "A Case of Psychic Automatism, Including 'Speaking with Tongues.'" *Proceedings of the Society for Psychical Research,* Vol. XII, 1896–97.

Alphonse Maeder, "La Langue d'un Aliéné: Analyse d'un Cas de Glossolalie," *Archives de Psychologie,* Tome IX, March, 1910.

Oskar Pfister, "Die psychologische Enträtselung der religiösen Glossolalie und der automatischen Kryptographie," *Jahrbuch für psychoanalytische und psychopathologische Forschungen,* III Bd., 1912.

William Sargant, "Some Cultural Group Abreactive Techniques and Their Relation to Modern Treatments," *Proceedings of the Royal Society of Medicine,* Vol. 42, May, 1949.

Harald K. Schjelderup (Oslo), "Psychologische Analyse eines Falles von Zungenreden," *Zeitschrift für Psychologie,* 1 Bd. 122, Heft 1 u. 2, 1931.

Lincoln Morse Van Eetveldt Vivier, *Glossolalia.* Unpublished doctor's thesis, Department of Psychiatry and Mental Hygiene, University of Witwatersrand, Johannesburg, South Africa, October, 1960. (Microfilm reprint by the Department of Photoduplication, University of Chicago Library, Chicago, Illinois.)

D. PHILOSOPHY AND LITERATURE

Francis Bacon, *Of the Proficience and Advancement of Learning Divine and Humane,* and the *New Atlantis.* Great Books of the Western World, Vol. 30. Chicago, Encyclopaedia Britannica, Inc., 1952.

M. W. Calkins, *The Persistent Problems of Philosophy.* New York, The Macmillan Company, 1936.

Dante Alighieri, *The Divine Comedy,* trans. Henry Francis Cary. New York, P. F. Collier, no date.

Raphael Demos, *The Philosophy of Plato.* New York, Charles Scribner's Sons, 1939.

E. R. Dodds, *The Greeks and the Irrational.* Boston, Beacon Press, 1957.

Philo, *Quis Rerum Divinarum Heres*. Loeb Classical Library. New York, G. P. Putnam, 1932.

Plato, *The Dialogues of Plato,* trans. B. Jowett. New York, Random House, 1937.

Plotinus, *The Six Enneads*. Great Books of the Western World, Vol. 17. Chicago, Encyclopaedia Britannica, Inc., 1952.

J. R. R. Tolkien, *The Lord of the Ring*. London, George Allen & Unwin, Ltd., 1954 and 1955.

Alfred North Whitehead, *Essays in Science and Philosophy*. New York, Philosophical Library, Inc., 1948.

Lancelot Law Whyte, *The Unconscious Before Freud*. New York, Basic Books, Inc., 1960.

Charles Williams, *All Hallows' Eve,* London, Faber & Faber Limited, 1945.

———, *War in Heaven*. London, Faber & Faber Limited, 1952.

E. REFERENCES TO THE FATHERS OF THE CHURCH

The Ante-Nicene Fathers:

Irenaeus Against Heresies, III, XII, 15; III, XVII, 2; II, XXXII, 4; V, VI, 1.

Epistle of Ignatius to the Philadelphians, V; *to the Trallians,* IV, V.

The Teaching of the Twelve Apostles (the Didache), XI, 7–11.

The Pastor of Hermas, I, 1, 1; I, 2, 1; III, 2, 11.

First Epistle of Clement to the Corinthians, II, VIII.

The Martyrdom of Polycarp, VII.

Dialogue of Justin, Philosopher and Martyr, with Trypho, a Jew, LXXXVII f.

Tertullian Against Marcion, V, VIII; *Against Praxeas,* I, II; *A Treatise on the Soul,* IX.

Origen Against Celsus, VII, VIII–XI; as to Paul's ability to communicate, see Origen's *Commentary on John* (Fragments), IV, 2.

The Nicene and Post-Nicene Fathers, First Series:

Chrysostom, *Homilies on the First Epistle of Paul to the Corinthians,* XXIX, 1.

Augustin, *Homilies on the First Epistle of John,* VI, 10.

Augustin, *On Baptism, Against the Donatists,* III, XVIII, 16.21.

The Nicene and Post-Nicene Fathers, Second Series:

The Ecclesiastical History of Salaminius Hermias Sozomenus, III, XIV.

Gennadius' Lives of Illustrious Men, VII.

Gregory Nazianzen, *Oration XLI,* "On Pentecost," XV, 15–18.

J2